Challenges in Volunteer Management

A volume in
Research in Public Management

Series Editors:
Lawrence R. Jones
and Nancy C. Roberts, *Naval Postgraduate*

Challenges in Volunteer Management

edited by

Matthew Liao-Troth
Western Washington University

Information Age Publishing, Inc.
Charlotte, North Carolina • www.infoagepub.com

Library of Congress Cataloging-in-Publication Data

Challenges in volunteer management edited by / Matthew Liao-Troth.
    p. cm. -- (Research in public management)
  Includes bibliographical references.
  ISBN 978-1-59311-924-9 (pbk.) -- ISBN 978-1-59311-925-6 (hardcover) 1. Volunteers--United States--Management. 2. Voluntarism--United States--Management. 3. Nonprofit organizations--United States--Personnel management. I. Liao-Troth, Matthew Allen.
  HN90.V64C43 2008
  658.3--dc22

2008013272

ISBN 13: 978-1-59311-924-9 (pbk.)
        978-1-59311-925-6 (hardcover)

Printed in the United States of America

CONTENTS

SECTION II: THE CONTEXT OF VOLUNTEER MANAGEMENT

FOREWORD

Mathew Liao-Troth

This volume began as a conversation at the 2003 meeting of the Academy of Management in Seattle. Nancy Roberts, coeditor of this series and a former chair of the Public and Nonprofit Division of the Academy, announced the series at the Division's annual business meeting and invited proposals from the membership. I saw a need for a book on the challenges of volunteer management targeted at those who could most use the information—the practitioners and academics who are dedicated to improving nonprofit management. I began soliciting contributions to an edited volume investigating both the challenges in organizing volunteers and the variety of contexts in which volunteers work. The goal was to have a meeting of like-minded folks at the 2004 Academy of Management meeting in New Orleans. As program chair for the Public and Nonprofit Division's program that year, I had the opportunity to review manuscripts that potentially could contribute to this volume.

Additional meetings at the 2003 Association for Research on Nonprofit Organizations and Voluntary Action conference in Denver and Internet inquiries ultimately attracted a core cohort of contributors. The 2004 Academy of Management Meeting in New Orleans enabled us to "work-shop" the papers and to integrate our overall efforts for the volume. We then prepared full manuscripts, and made a symposia presentation with a majority of the papers at the 2005 Academy Meeting in Honolulu. After additional editing, Victor Murray joined our efforts and graciously wrote the concluding chapter of this volume.

I must say that all of the authors have been splendid to work with. For readers who have had the opportunity to collaborate with these individuals in the field or in the classroom, I know you will share my enthusiasm for the contributions they have made to this volume. For those of you who have yet to meet them, I hope this volume exposes you to the important ideas they offer us on volunteer management, a critical issue for all organizations.

Finally, I need to thank a few more individuals who contributed to this endeavor. Jacie DeLaruelle, Christine Wright, Michelle Seman, and Meghan Krauss provided excellent departmental support. In addition, all of us owe thanks to several anonymous reviewers who provided important feedback and insights to the chapter authors. And of course for myself I thank my family that grew by one during this endeavor: I love you all.

INTRODUCTION

Challenges in Volunteer Management

Matthew Liao-Troth

Volunteer management has many challenges, not the least of which is how we study it and view it. Academics examine it from a variety of disciplines and practitioners experience it in a variety of contexts. However both approaches have limitations. In academia we go to public administration schools to learn about public and nonprofit management, to business schools to apply the principles of private enterprise to nonprofit management, to sociology departments to study the phenomena of volunteerism, to psychology departments to understand the motives of volunteers, and economics departments to examine the value or economic worth of volunteerism. The liability of the academic approach is the segmentation of study and research into departmental areas. The study of volunteers and volunteerism needs to cross all of these organizational and discipline boundaries to be fully appreciated and understood as a field of interest. Occasionally, academics speak across disciplines (for example during meetings of the Association for Research on Nonprofit Organizations and Voluntary Action), but most of the time we do not. Some interdisciplinary exceptions are the graduate program in Public Service Management at DePaul University, the Nonprofit Management degree at the New School, and the Master of Nonprofit Organizations program at the University of San Francisco, but these are not the norm.

Practitioners view volunteer management from their own unique experiences. They try to gauge success in volunteer management based on what they have encountered in particular organizations, towns, cultures, and countries in which they work. As important as these insights are, they are difficult to generalize beyond local settings. Just because an individual has been successful in working with volunteers, it does not mean that the lessons learned in one situation can be translated to others under all conditions. Put another way, even if one manages volunteers in one type of organization, and everything works splendidly, one cannot automatically assume the same would hold true for all volunteers in all organizations across all types of situations.

The challenge in managing volunteers is their simultaneous similarity and dissimilarity to paid workers in an organization. Like paid workers, volunteers pursue some end that is part of a group effort. Snyder and Clary (1999) have shown that motives vary among volunteers and paid employees alike: volunteers may not be paid but they still receive something of value for volunteering. The psychological contract (Rousseau, 1989)—workers' beliefs about their relationship with their organization—can be quite similar for volunteers and paid employees (Farmer & Feder, 2001; Littleton, 2002; Smith, 2004). I have demonstrated that an organization's culture and its norms governing the treatment of volunteers and paid employees have a large impact on how the workers behave and perceive their roles in the organization (Liao-Troth, 2001). So not only is the status of the worker (paid versus volunteer) important, but also the relationship between the organization and the individual. Building on Pearce (1993), who argues for using different management approaches for volunteers and paid employees, I believe it is important to understand both the unique challenges of managing volunteers and the organizational context in which they work. Of course, unlike paid workers volunteers are not compensated, at least not with the normative trappings of employment.

The target audience for this volume is anyone who manages volunteers. Often the person who is working with volunteers does not see herself or himself as "managing" as much as they are "coordinating," but I use the term "manage" broadly in keeping with the term as defined by Henri Fayol (1916/1949) as the range of processes that include planning, organizing, commanding, controlling, and coordinating activities for an organization. So in whatever capacity those working with volunteers find themselves, including current professionals and volunteers themselves, they will find value in these chapters. Graduate students in professional fields (such as MBA and MPA) and traditional humanities and social sciences (such as history, psychology, and sociology), as well as undergraduate students (such as those in American Humanics bachelors and certificate programs), will benefit from these readings. The goal of the volume is to offer chapters that demonstrate the breadth of thought on volunteer management, both across disciplines and a wide range of settings in which volunteers work.

Peter Drucker (1990) first sparked an interest in volunteers from a management perspective when he referred to the competitive advantage of volunteers in nonprofit organizations. His important observation led to multiple disciplinary interest in the topic and a stream of contributions over the past two decades from public management, public administration, sociology, and economics. Across all publications on the topic the best selling book dedicated solely to volunteer management, according to Amazon.com, is Fisher and Cole's (1993) *Leadership and Management of Volunteer Programs*. Although the book is 14 years old, and the organization (Association for Volunteer Administration) that sponsored the certificate program on which the book is based went insolvent in 2006, it is still arguably the foundational text for volunteer management from the academic and practitioner perspective.

Fisher and Cole focused on five competency areas for a certified volunteer administrator: program planning and organization; staffing and directing; controlling (monitoring and evaluating the program); individual, group and organizational behavior; and grounding in the profession. In a book review at the time, Steve McCurley (1995) wrote "As an overview of and introduction to operating a service volunteer program, this is certainly the most generally useful text available and is an excellent supportive tool for any person or organization beginning to work with service-providing volunteers" (pp. 439-440). However, he also comments that the "criticism with the managerial approach is that it leaves one with a mechanistic view of how volunteering works, and with very little notion of the intangible psychological aspects of those who volunteer" (p. 440).

The managerial approach is no longer that narrow. Some, such as Helmig, Jegers, and Lapsley (2004) have even argued that the disciplines generally associated with business are making the greatest contributions these days to our understanding of management in the nonprofit sector (see for example the works of Britton, 1991; Liao-Troth & Griffith, 2002; Thompson & Bunderson, 2003). The managerial approach to volunteer management has been informed, either directly or indirectly, from observations by those such as Bush (1992) who believes that nonprofit sector values need to be drawn into management and administration practices of volunteer programs. The focus of our book is to look at the next set of issues, challenges, and implications of volunteer management as it moves beyond this narrow mechanistic view.

Looking at the administration of nonprofit organizations broadly, the most influential book subsequent to Fisher and Cole's work has been Robert Herman's edited volume on nonprofit management and leadership. First published in 1994 and revised in 2004, it examines the entirety of nonprofit management. However, neither edition received recognition in contemporary reviews for contributing to our understanding of volunteer management (Bograd, 1995; Letts, 2005). Our goal in this volume is to advance our knowledge of the topic and present it in one volume. From our initial discussions we realized that there are two broad issues that the manager of volunteers needs to consider: the challenges of volunteer management that cut across all organizations, and the unique issues that the manager faces within specific institutional contexts.

SECTION I

ORGANIZATIONAL CHALLENGES IN VOLUNTEER MANAGEMENT

INTRODUCTION

Matthew Liao-Troth

Section one of this volume addresses the organizational challenges of volunteer management. The chapters here are concerned with the issue of managing volunteers across organizations, and understanding what makes the management of volunteers unique. On this topic we need to know a few things. The first issue is how do organizations manage volunteers; that is, what systems are in place that managers can and do use. A second issue is how is volunteer work designed. The third issue is looking forward to how things change. What follows is a review for how chapters in this section address these issues, and how each fits into the greater work that has been published since Fisher and Cole's (1993) book.

Looking at the stream of work since Fisher and Cole's work, a large proportion addresses the organizational design of nonprofit and public organizations, and how different features of organizing impact volunteer management. Jeffrey Brudney and Beth Gazley (2002) have found that a volunteer corps has a more synergistic rather than cannibalizing effect on paid staff when looking at the U.S. Small Business Administration and the Service Corps of Retired Executives. Likewise Keven Kearns, Chisung Park, and Linda Yankoski (2005) find similar synergistic value in volunteers in faith-based organizations. The latter is not as generalizable as the former, however, as Prescilla La Barbera (1992) has found that religious organizations view these volunteers as a sacred, rather than a secular, asset.

Michael Martinez (2003) has argued that with increased liability comes increased formalization of a volunteer workforce. Indeed several have looked at this issue of formalization and work environment. They include: Margaret Kelley, Howard Lune, and Sheigla Murphy's (2005) analysis of how a change to a more formalized work environment undermines volunteer commitment in a needle exchange program; Michael Zakour and David Gillespie's (1998) work on how the focus of the organization on local rather than broader issues in social service versus emergency management organizations is related to lower levels of volunteerism; and Anne Standley's (2001) documentation that moves towards a more national focus in major health related nonprofit organizations focused on the development of trust and the promise of scale of economy efficiencies.

This issue of formalization, as well as organizational design and job design for volunteers, is an important theme of this book's first section where we look at several organizational challenges in volunteer management.

Management Capacity and Retention of Volunteers (Mark Hager & Jeffrey Brudney)

Fisher and Cole covered many key issues on the topic of management practice, but we have not known how widespread these practices are, or where they are most likely to occur. Rob Paton and Jane Foot (2000) showed how the nonprofit sector implements human resource systems in ways different from the public section, but Emma Parry, Clare Kelliher, Tim Mills, and Shaun Tyson (2005) gave some inkling how similar the nonprofit and public sectors are in terms of human resource practices, and the validity of some of these practices when applied to volunteers.

In the first chapter of this section Mark Hager and Jeffrey Brudney review what nonprofit organizations (specifically public charities) currently use in terms of volunteer management practices, and how different aspects of the organization impact those practices. In addition, they look at how different practices impact the retention of the volunteers. It is quite interesting that they did not find widespread use of similar practices across all organizations—that the unique characteristics of the organizations impact the use of different practices. They also find that practices that enrich the volunteer experience lead to greater retention of volunteers, but again, these practices are not widespread. There is also a two-way impact, of both the organization on volunteer management practices, which in turn impacts the characteristics of the organization. Their work not only presents academics a road map of where additional research can be conducted, but also gives the practitioner a benchmark and a sense of common practices that can be adopted.

No "One Best" Volunteer Management and Organizing: Two Fundamentally Different Approaches (Lucas Meijs & Ester Ten Hoorn)

Another challenge within volunteer management is how volunteers and their relationships with organizations are viewed. The second chapter in this section can be seen as a comparison of the grassroots membership model of Europe and the human service administration paradigm of the United States. Lucas Meijs and Ester Ten Hoorn's contribution demonstrates different models for organizations that are useful and can complement each other. The membership management model they discuss provides one way of addressing an enriched experience for the volunteers, although it will not be easy for organizations designed to pursue purely programmatic ends to shift to a model that places more emphasis on the volunteers.

Meijs and Ten Hoorn's chapter parallels the social enterprise work of Janelle Kerlin (2006) in which she argues that the strengths of the U.S. address the weaknesses of the European model, and vice versa. She writes that "the United States can learn from Western Europe by following, to the extent possible, its practice of involving the program recipient or beneficiary in the social enterprise activity" (p. 259), while "Europeans interested in expanding the range of services supported by social enterprise can learn from these working models in the United States" (p. 260). It also should be noted that not all see the European sports organization as a monolithic institution. Ørnulf Seippel (2002) argues there is a great variety of volunteer work functions in these organizations that is dependent, not only on the volunteers and structure, but also the economics of the organization.

A Typology of Short-Term and Long-Term Volunteers (Linda Hartenian)

Since Fisher and Cole's book (1993), significant advances have been made in understanding volunteer motivation. A research stream begun by Gil Clary and Mark Snyder (1991), followed by an instrument designed with Robert Ridge (1992) known as the Voluntary Function Inventory (VFI), has had a significant impact on our understanding and application of the motivation to volunteer. Recent work by Elena Marta, Chiara Guglielmetti, and Maura Pozzi (2006) has also demonstrated the strength of the VFI by generalizing its applicability to Italian teenagers. Others have continued to develop new models of volunteer motivation, such as Anna Birgitta Yeung's octagon model (2004) and Walter Rehberg's model based on Swiss young adults (2005), but there is at least some indication that managers have a sense of volunteers' motives even if they are not schooled in the theories across national cultures (Liao-Troth & Dunn, 1999).

Linda Hartenian's contribution looks at how an organization's processes interact with a volunteer's motivation and goals in differentiating between long term and short term volunteers. Integrating several fields of study, Hartenian differentiates between those who are long term volunteers across organizations and within a single organization, and short term volunteers for a single organization. She examines how the goals and values of the volunteer impact their desires in the relationship with the organization, and gives insight to managers on how to management the relationship. Earlier work by Mary Tschirhart, Debra Mesch, Theodore Miller, and Geunjoo Lee (2001) has already pointed out how the goals of incoming stipended volunteers impacted outcomes related to those goals one year later, and how that attainment reinforces future volunteering. However Hartenian points out that this goal setting and attainment is also related to the nature of the relationship the volunteer has with the organization. Hartenian's chapter also demonstrates the VFI's versatility and application to the volunteer and organization relationship.

Streamlining Volunteer Management Through Information Communication Technologies (Valentina Mele)

Technology has had a significant impact on organizational processes since the early 1990s, especially the widespread adaptation to Internet access. Entire organizations are enabled by information communication technologies (ICTs) and many of the volunteers never meet face to face with each other or with "clients." Vic Murray and Yvonne Harrison (2005) have done an overview of the phenomena, but Valentina Mele's rich case study in this volume demonstrates how ICTs completely change coordination and control issues for the manager, and produce an organization-wide impact. Although Mele focuses on a case study of one organization, her insights on how ICTs impact efficiency and effectiveness are applicable to any organization with ICTs. For a manager of volunteers, the impact goes in two directions. First, there is the impact of these tools on how to manage volunteers. Then there is the issue of how these tools will impact their organization.

Volunteer Management in Community Currency Systems: An Examination of Time Banks (Bruce Clary)

A final concern in volunteer management is how the work of volunteers is accounted for by the organization. This more formal view centers around the topic of social accounting (see for example Laurie Mook, Betty Jane Richmond, & Jack Quarter's 2003 article) and economic evaluations of the net benefit of volunteer work, such as those done by Femida Handy and Narasimhan Srinivasan (2004 & 2005).

Bruce Clary's work on time banks provides a utility measure that allows economists and accountants to measure the value of volunteer work. In his chapter he looks at social exchange, the heart of many models of volunteering. He examines two time bank programs, one in the United States (New England Time Banks), and the other in the United Kingdom (Fairshares located in Gloucester). Time banks are community currency systems that facilitate transactions by matching peoples' services to others' needs and facilitating community-building through empowerment of residents who provide and receive services themselves. He looks at three broad areas of volunteer management: recruitment (the role of the Time Bank philosophy, the interview process, participant background), tasks (identification of tasks, and types of services provided), and administrative issues (legal liability, management information systems, and quality control). This method of studying volunteer systems, while somewhat unique, gives every manager a model with which to examine the networks of people with whom their volunteers engage and serve. Many a reader may claim that time banks are bartering systems, not systems of volunteers, but the reader is referred to the cross-cultural net-cost study of Femida Handy, Ram Cnaan, Jeffrey Brudney, Ugo Ascoli, Lucas Meijs, and Shree Ranade (2000). They show that the social construct of volunteerism is not absolute, and volunteering in one context is not volunteering in another, based only on the perception of costs and benefits that accrue to the "volunteer." Thus, Clary's research likely will inform any stream of research attempting to place a value on volunteer work in the future.

CHAPTER 1

MANAGEMENT CAPACITY AND RETENTION OF VOLUNTEERS

Mark A. Hager and Jeffrey L. Brudney

Many charities have less money than they need to effectively carry out their missions. These organizations have to make hard decisions about where to cut corners so that they can make ends meet. Too often, the volunteer program gets short shrift. Such functions as accounting, fundraising, and service delivery are judged as essential to the organization's operations, whereas volunteer management may be viewed as incidental to operations. Charities employ accountants and fundraisers before they employ someone to manage volunteers. When an organization staffs all three functions, the volunteer program administrator almost certainly gets paid less than her or his financial management and development counterparts. Resource constraints, the "expendability" of volunteers, and the lack of professionalization of the volunteer management field conspire against volunteer administrators.

Perhaps we should not be surprised, then, to learn that many U.S. charities possess rudimentary and underdeveloped management structures for their volunteer workers. These management structures, comprised of both professional staff and adoption of a range of

Challenges in Volunteer Management, pp. 9–27

management practices, are what we refer to as *volunteer management capacity*. An organization's capacity to manage volunteers is likely related to a host of outcomes, including the productivity and happiness of the volunteers. In this chapter, we explore the relationship between volunteer management capacity and the ability of an organization to retain its volunteers over time. The chapter proceeds in five parts. First, we review the sparse literature regarding volunteer management practices. Second, we introduce a national study of volunteer management capacity. Third, we explore how adoption of commonly accepted volunteer management practices is affected by the size, scope, and industry of charities. Fourth, we document the relationships between adoption of these practices, various organizational characteristics, and retention of volunteers. Fifth, we offer a range of conclusions for both managers and policymakers who are interested in maximizing the value of volunteers.

RESEARCH ON VOLUNTEER MANAGEMENT

The field of volunteer administration has long promoted a range of commonly accepted practices, including supervision, data collection, recognition, and training (e.g., Ellis, 1996; McCurley & Lynch, 1996; for recent reviews of this literature, see Boyd, 2004; Safrit & Schmiesing, 2004). However, like many areas of inquiry in the nonprofit sector, the extent to which these practices have been adopted has not attracted much research. Therefore, the calls for better management of volunteer programs have largely prescriptive, based on an accumulated wisdom among observers that effective management could bring gains to volunteer productivity in the same ways that scientific management has brought gains to commerce and industry. The prevailing wisdom is that unless organizations pay attention to issues of volunteer management, they will not do a good job of recruiting, satisfying, retaining, and mobilizing volunteers for service.

The importance is underscored by the findings of a study commissioned by the UPS Foundation in 1998. That study revealed that two-fifths of volunteers had stopped volunteering for an organization at some time because of one or more poor volunteer management practices. Reasons included the organization not making good use of a volunteers' time or good use of their talents, or that volunteer tasks were not clearly defined. The study warned, "Poor volunteer management practices result in more lost volunteers than people losing interest because of changing personal or family needs" (UPS Foundation, 1998, p. 15).

Administrators of volunteer programs are not without tools to recruit and retain volunteers. As the field of volunteer administration has become more professionalized, public and nonprofit leaders, agency managers, and field experts have turned their attention to improving the capacity of host organizations to accommodate volunteers. In a report prepared in cooperation with the Points of Light Foundation and the Association for Volunteer Administration, the UPS Foundation (2002) advocated adoption of 23 volunteer management practices. In general, the practices center on providing funding to support volunteer involvement, especially for a designated leader or manager to oversee volunteers, and having a set of appropriate practices and procedures to administer the volunteer program.

Other studies echo these views on effective means for supporting and retaining volunteers. Grossman and Furano (2002) identify three elements as crucial to the success of any volunteer program: screening potential volunteers to ensure appropriate entry and placement in the organization; orientation and training to provide volunteers with the skills and outlook needed; and management and ongoing support of volunteers by paid staff to ensure that volunteer time is not wasted. They conclude,

> No matter how well intentioned volunteers are, unless there is an infrastructure in place to support and direct their efforts, they will remain ineffective at best or, worse, become disenchanted and withdraw, potentially damaging recipients of services in the process. (p. 15)

A research report on volunteer service and community engagement in selected state agencies and organizations in Texas focuses on many of these same practices and procedures, including screening of volunteers and matching them to positions, training and orientation, management and communication, and recognition and evaluation (Rehnborg, Fallon, & Hinerfeld, 2002). In another study, paid staff time allocated to the volunteer program, as well as an array of recommended practices for volunteer management, were related statistically to the benefits these programs realized from volunteer involvement (Brudney, 1999). The accumulating evidence suggests that volunteer management capacity is a function of both *staff support of volunteering* and *adoption of administrative practices necessary for the management of volunteers.* However, to this point, the lack of a national, systematic study of volunteer management practices in the United States representative of a variety of programs has limited our understanding of the prevailing conditions in the field.

A NATIONAL STUDY OF VOLUNTEER MANAGEMENT CAPACITY

In the fall of 2003, we undertook a national survey of the practices, challenges, and benefits of volunteer management. The data were generated from conversations with a representative sample of U.S. public charities (Urban Institute, 2004). We drew a sample of 2,993 of the 214,995 organizations that filed Form 990 with the Internal Revenue Service (IRS) in 2000. Since charities with less than $25,000 in annual gross receipts are not required to file with the IRS, these small organizations are not part of our sampling frame. We selected our sample within annual expenditures strata and major subsector of operation, such as health, social services, and the arts.

We conducted telephone interviews with volunteer administrators or executive managers in sampled charities. We called all organizations to verify their existence and to obtain the name of a volunteer administrator or someone else who could speak authoritatively about the organization's operations. We mailed an information letter to the 80% of sampled organizations with which we completed the initial call. We then called named representatives up to 30 times to collect study information. Interviews averaged 20 minutes. Adjusting for organizations that were defunct or could not be verified as working organizations in the initial call, the response rate was 69%. With the application of appropriate weights, the results can be used to describe overall conditions in the working population of public charities with at least $25,000 in gross receipts.

Although members of boards of directors are important volunteers in virtually all charities, we asked respondents to exclude them when answering our questions about volunteers and volunteer management. We also asked respondents not to count special events participants as volunteers unless the participants were organizers or workers at the events. Study results are based on the nearly four out of five charities (1,354 out of 1,753 survey respondents) that engage volunteers in their operations, either in service to others or in helping to run the organization. We excluded charities that engage no one who fits our definition of a volunteer, as well as charities whose primary purpose is to recruit and place volunteers in other organizations (such as volunteer centers). The study does not include government agencies that involve volunteers, such as schools, libraries, parks, and prisons, although we believe that our findings can inform the operations of these kinds of agencies.

Responding charities were weighted to represent the expenditure and subsector strata from which they were sampled. Weights were further adjusted to account for organizations unreachable in the precall. These weights helped to ensure that our respondents reflected the characteristics of the working population of organizations from which they were drawn. Based on the weighted responses, the results of this study were representative of the population of nonprofit organizations in the United States with annual gross receipts of at least \$25,000 which filed IRS Form 990 in 2000.

ADOPTION OF VOLUNTEER MANAGEMENT PRACTICES

The nine management practices listed in Figure 1.1 are the ones that we presented to those survey respondents who told us they involve volunteers in their operations. We asked them if they have adopted each practice to a large degree, to some degree, or not at all. The bars indicate the percentage of charities that say they have adopted a practice to a large or some degree. The most striking finding is that only one practice, regular supervision and communication with volunteers, has been adopted to a large degree by more than half of charities. Large degree adoption of training for either volunteers or for paid staff in working with volunteers is particularly rare; these practices are more likely to have been adopted only to some degree, if at all.

The likelihood that a charity adopts a particular management practice depends on its specific needs and characteristics. Not all practices can or should be adopted by all charities. While the practice of screening

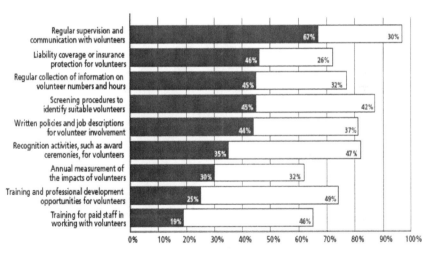

Figure 2.1.   Management practices that charites say they practice to a large degree or to some degree.

volunteers and matching them with appropriate tasks is important when volunteers are mentoring or tutoring children, such screening and matching may be unnecessary when a neighborhood association mobilizes residents to clean up a local park. Training paid staff in how to work effectively with volunteers may be a fruitful practice for many organizations, but it is not relevant to those charities that have no paid staff. The critical question is whether charities that *should* be adopting a particular practice have the resources and other institutional support necessary to put the practice in place.

The following four figures document how adoption of these nine practices vary by important organizational characteristics, such as the size of the organization or the way they use volunteers. These differences provide some clues into which conditions make certain practices particularly relevant, and suggest other kinds of circumstances that inhibit charities from adopting these practices.

Management Practices and Size of Charity

Figure 1.2 illustrates the average level of adoption of management practices by charities of different sizes. For each practice, we assign a

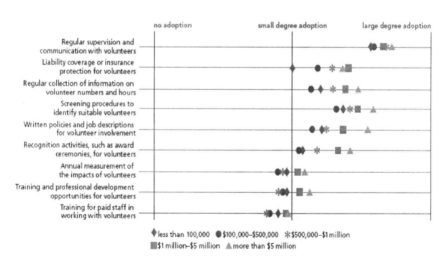

Note: We divided charities into size groups depending on how much total money they say they spent in a year. This figure is taken from Forms 990 reported to the IRS in 2000 by charities in the study.

Figure 2.2.   Average level of adoption of volunteer management practices, by size of charity.

value of 0 if a particular charity has not adopted the practice, a value of 1 if the charity has adopted the practice to some degree, and a value of 2 if the charity has adopted the practice to a large degree. We then calculate the average for all of the charities in a particular group.

As we might expect, the size of a charity matters in whether most practices have been adopted or not. The largest charities (those with over $5 million in annual expenditures, denoted) consistently fall furthest to the right on the scale, indicating highest average levels of adoption. In contrast, the smallest charities (those with less than $100,000 in annual expenditures, denoted) tend to fall furthest to the left, indicating lowest levels of adoption.

In Figures 1.2 through 1.5, the bunching of symbols indicates little or no difference between charities of different types in the adoption of a management practice, while greater spreads indicate greater differences in likelihood of adoption. Figure 1.2 shows, for example, that liability coverage or insurance protection for volunteers is about equally likely for organizations in the top two size classes (those with annual expenditures of $1 million to $5 million, and those with over $5 million in annual expenditures), and that both are substantially more likely than the smallest charities to have adopted this practice.

On the other hand, the rare practice of training paid staff in working with volunteers is not influenced by organization size. Despite our expectation that this practice would be practiced more often by larger charities than by smaller ones, we observe no differences across size classes.[1] All other management practices display differences in adoption level across categories of organization size. Even the apparent bunching of symbols on "regular supervision and communication with volunteers" represents a difference between the smallest and largest charities. This practice is by far the most commonly adopted practice among small charities, but the largest charities are still more likely to have adopted it.

Management Practices and Scope of Volunteer Use

We divided charities into four groups based on their scope of volunteer use. Our categorization of scope is based on both the numbers of volunteers that charities engaged in the past year and the number of hours that volunteers collectively worked in a typical week. If a charity engaged at least 50 volunteers over the course of the year, we defined them as having "many volunteers"; otherwise, we defined them as having "few volunteers." If volunteers collectively worked at least 50 hours in a typical week, we defined a charity as representing "many hours"; otherwise we considered them to represent "few hours."

The cross-classification results in four categories of charities. The group with "few volunteers, few hours" is the largest group, and we expect that they are least likely to have adopted most volunteer management practices. "Many volunteers, few hours" includes those charities that engage many volunteers for predominantly short term or episodic assignments; in contrast, "few volunteers, many hours" includes those charities that use volunteers in more sustained ways. "Many volunteers, many hours" is the smallest group, but represents those charities with the largest scope of volunteer involvement.

Figure 1.3 shows how adoption of management practices varies across scope of volunteer use. As expected, charities with large scope of volunteer involvement are significantly more likely to have adopted the various practices when compared to charities that engage comparatively fewer volunteers for fewer hours.

Comparisons of the two middle categories show that charities that use episodic volunteers ("many volunteers, few hours") have the edge in recognition activities, collection of information on volunteer numbers and hours, and measuring the impacts of volunteer activities. In contrast, charities with more sustained use of fewer volunteers ("few volunteers, many hours") are more likely to have liability coverage or insurance protection, training and professional development for volunteers, screening and matching procedures, and regular supervision and communication. As might be expected, the former group tends to focus on the results of

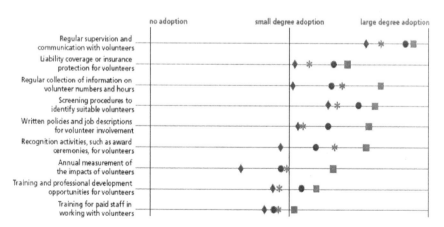

Figure 2.3.   Average level of adoption of volunteer management practices, by scope of volunteer use.

volunteer involvement, while the latter show greater investment in bringing on and sustaining volunteers.

Management Practices and Primary Use of Volunteers

The work that volunteers do also influences adoption of management practices. We asked survey respondents to describe the main role that volunteers perform, the one to which the organization devotes the most time, money, and other resources. Based on these descriptions, we organized charities into four categories based on their primary use of volunteers.

Most charities use volunteers primarily in direct service activities, such as mentoring or tutoring. Some use volunteers in carrying out services, but not in ways that usually bring them into contact with clients, members, or other beneficiaries of organizational activities; we describe these activities as "indirect service." The other two categories include volunteers who are primarily working to make the charity run rather than providing services. One is an internal administrative role, including such activities as filing, copying, or answering phones. The other is an external administrative role, including such activities as fundraising, lobbying, or public relations (see Figure 1.4).

Charities that primarily use volunteers in direct service roles are furthest to the right on all nine management practice scales, indicating that they are far more likely to have adopted each practice. The result makes

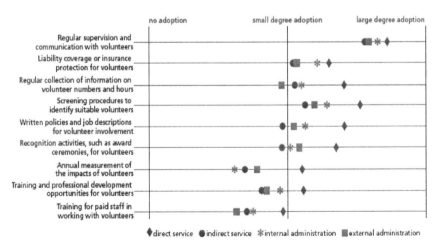

Figure 2.4.   Average level of adoption of volunteer management practices, by primary use of volunteers.

sense because charities that use volunteers for direct client contact must be more careful about how these services are handled. Failure to follow accepted practices for volunteer management may jeopardize service quality, the reputation of the organization, or the quality of the volunteer experience.

In contrast, the average adoption scores for charities that use volunteers primarily in indirect service, internal administration, or external administration tend to group together, indicating that these charities have about the same level of adoption of the management practices and that these uses of volunteers do not distinguish adopters from nonadopters. To the extent that there are differences, charities that involve volunteers primarily in internal administration tend to be second-most likely to adopt most practices. However, these charities are least likely to evaluate the impacts of their volunteers, not surprising given that their volunteer tasks are primarily administrative rather than service-oriented.

Management Practices and Subsector

The charities in this study represent the broad array of nonprofit organizations in the United States. Charities are involved in our daily lives in a rich variety of ways, and their missions touch on almost all issues of public interest. The industry, or subsector, in which a charity works, might be related to how it engages volunteers or which practices it has adopted in managing its volunteers.

We placed our study organizations into categories based on their primary purpose. Three-fourths of them could be placed in one of four major categories: human services; education; health; or arts, culture, and humanities (Figure 1.5). The remaining one-fourth consists of either charities that support the work of other charities or charities that operate in smaller subsectors (such as environmental or animal related). The figure is based only on the three-fourths of the charities that we classified into the major groups indicated.

Charities operating in the health subsector are more likely to have adopted most practices. On average, health charities are more likely to have liability coverage or insurance protection for volunteers, hold recognition activities for volunteers, and to screen and match volunteers to appropriate assignments. This result likely reflects the greater number of resources, the higher level of professionalization, and (in some cases) the greater urgency of volunteer performance in the health field.

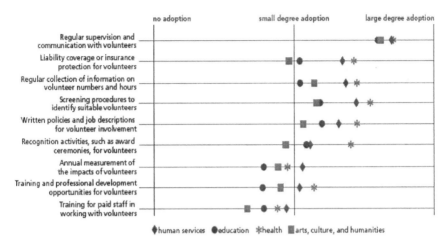

Figure 2.5.   Average level of adoption of volunteer management practices, by subsector.

Human service charities rival health charities on adoption of most items, but charities operating in the education and arts fields tend to lag on most practices. Charities operating in the education and arts fields are substantially less likely to have liability coverage, to regularly collect information on volunteer numbers and hours, to measure the impacts of volunteers, or to screen and match volunteers to assignments. Arts organizations are notably less likely to hold award or other recognition activities for their volunteers.

The only practice that does not vary by subsector is the popular practice of supervision and communication with volunteers, practiced equally by human service, education, health, and arts organizations.

DETERMINANTS OF VOLUNTEER RETENTION

In this section, we explore the relationship between the adoption of volunteer management practices, various organizational characteristics, and the reported rate of volunteer retention among the charities in our study. The goal is to explain statistically why some charities retain more volunteers than others. Retention is a goal for most charities, as well as an indication of the success of its volunteer program. For charities that engage volunteers mainly in episodic or short-term assignments, retention may not be quite so high a priority. Even in these cases, however, most charities would likely prefer to have their volunteers take on new tasks as assignments are completed. Recruiting volunteers is an expensive and time-consuming job, so charities generally like to maximize retention. Retention is also important because volunteers often become loyal financial donors to the organization as well.

To measure retention, we asked respondents, "Of the volunteers that worked with your organization 1 year ago, approximately what percentage would you say are still involved as volunteers?" Nearly 3% said zero, and 17% said all were retained, but most fell somewhere in between. The median charity reported an 80% retention rate; the mean is 73%, with a standard deviation of 28.1.

Our analysis considers how a variety of organizational practices and characteristics are related to the reported retention rate. We employ multiple regression analysis, a multivariate statistical procedure that considers all variables at the same time, so that the influence of one practice or characteristic takes into account all of the other factors in the analysis. The factors are divided into four categories: management practices, investments in volunteer resources, the value that volunteers bring to charities, and various other organizational characteristics.

Management Practices

The variables in this section are eight of the nine management practices discussed on the preceding pages; "annual measurement of impacts" is excluded because it overlaps substantially with "regular collection of information" ($r = 0.65$). This set of variables separates charities that say they have adopted practices to a large degree from those that do not make this claim.

As the model in Table 1.1 shows, four of the eight management practices have an effect on volunteer retention. Charities that say they have adopted to a large degree the practice of hosting recognition activities for volunteers have a higher rate of retention, as do those that offer training and professional development opportunities for volunteers, and those that use screening procedures to identify suitable volunteers and to match them with appropriate jobs or tasks. These volunteer management practices all center on making the experience worthwhile for the volunteer. Other practices, such as liability coverage or insurance protection, regular collection of information on the number of volunteers and hours, training for paid staff in working with volunteers, and written policies and job descriptions, may generate other benefits, but they center on what is important to the charity rather than what is important to volunteers. Not surprisingly, adoption of these practices is unrelated to retention.

Table 1.1.   The Influence of Management, Investments, Volunteer Value, and Other Organizational Characteristics on Retention of Volunteers

	b (SE)
Management Practices Adopted to Large Degree	
– recognition activities	5.54** (1.78)
– training and professional development for vols	3.80* (1.90)
– screening, matching volunteers to assignments	3.30 ~ (1.70)
– supervision, communication with volunteers	−7.54*** (1.76)
– written policies and job descriptions	−1.91 (1.72)
– training for paid staff in working with volunteers	.34 (2.11)
– liability coverage and insurance protection	1.63 (1.59)
– regular collection of volunteer numbers and hours	.25 (1.71)
Investment in Volunteer Resources	
– lack of funds for supporting volunteers	−2.01* (1.01)
– time that paid staffer spends on volunteer management	.06 (.47)
– staff or board members indifferent toward volunteers	−3.10 ~ (1.64)
Value of Volunteers	
– volunteers recruit others one-on-one	4.75*** (1.19)
– volunteer benefits index	1.23*** (.34)
– volunteers absent, unreliable, poor work quality	−3.79** (1.34)
Organizational Characteristics	
– size of charity	−1.41* (.63)
– percentage of volunteers under age 24	−.44*** (.03)
– ratio: number of staff/number of volunteers	−.19 (.12)
– recruitment problems index	−.80 ~ (.48)
Constant (a)	72.72*** (3.58)
R-square	.259
Adj. R-square	0.247
Valid N	1,082

SE = Standard error
Multiple regression model;
 *** $p < .001$; ** $p < .01$; * $p < .05$; ~ $p < .10$

Retention appears to be very much a product of what charities do directly for their volunteers.

Sometimes a practice that is good for the charity may not be popular with individual volunteers. A curious finding is that regular supervision and communication with volunteers is associated with lower levels of retention. This management practice is the most widely adopted among charities, with two-thirds of the charities adopting it to a large degree, and virtually all of them adopting it to at least some degree. We do not suggest that charities stop supervising and communicating with their volunteers! However, some charities may supervise and communicate in a way that volunteer experiences feel too much like the grind of their daily jobs rather than an enjoyable avocation, thereby diminishing the experience for volunteers and reducing their desire to continue volunteering. Of course, increased support and communication may be a response to poor retention. Thus, organizations that encounter retention problems may take steps to alleviate their problems by engaging volunteers more directly-- which would generate a negative relationship between volunteer retention and supervision and communication, as found in Table 1.1.

Investment in Volunteer Resources

The first variable in this section reflects the percentage of time that a paid staff member spends on volunteer management; for charities with no staff or no paid staff member in the role of volunteer administrator, the value is 0. The two other measures come from a series of questions about challenges that charities might face. We asked respondents if lack of adequate funds for supporting volunteer involvement was a big problem, a small problem, or not a problem at all for their charity. We similarly asked whether indifference or resistance to volunteers on the part of paid staff or board members was a problem.

Charities that feel challenged by the lack of funds allocated to support volunteers have lower retention rates than charities that report fewer such challenges. Surprisingly, however, retention rates do not vary according to the percentage of time a paid staff member devotes to managing the volunteer program. Although having a paid staff volunteer coordinator is related to adoption of management practices (as well as other benefits), this support in itself does not necessarily translate into greater retention of volunteers. This finding may suggest that having a volunteer coordinator is not nearly so important as what this person does on the job.

The final issue in the category of investment in volunteer resources concerns organizational culture. That is, has the leadership of the charity invested in creating the kind of climate that welcomes and encourages volunteers? No surprise, the results indicate that charities that experience resistance or indifference toward volunteer involvement are less able to retain volunteers.

Value That Volunteers Bring to Charities

Our first variable in this section indicates whether the charity uses volunteers to recruit volunteers one-on-one to a great extent, to some extent, or to no extent. The second is a Benefits Index, a sum of the reported advantages or values that volunteers bring to charities in the form of increased service quality, cost savings, public support, or specialized skills; higher values reflect greater reported benefits (Hager & Brudney, 2005). The third item is another of the challenges that we asked respondents about; in this case, we asked if absenteeism, unreliability, or poor work habits or work quality on the part of volunteers was a big problem, a small problem, or not a problem.

The value of volunteer participation to the charity affects retention. Charities that use volunteers to recruit other volunteers one-on-one are better able to retain volunteers. Enlisting volunteers as "spokespersons" for the charity in this manner implies a level of trust in these participants, evidence of both a supportive organizational culture and confidence that the charity provides a worthwhile experience to volunteers. The value that charities place on volunteers pays dividends in retention. Similarly, the model in Table 1 shows that the greater the number of benefits charities feel they realize from volunteer involvement, the higher their rate of volunteer retention. Conversely, to the extent that charities perceive that volunteer service is costly to them in the form of absenteeism, unreliability, or poor work habits, they have lower reported rates of volunteer retention. Charities that do not have this perception do a better job of keeping their volunteers.

Organizational Characteristics

Size of charity is indicated by the five size groupings introduced in an earlier section. Percentage of volunteers under age 24 is the reported percentage of total volunteers in this age category. The ratio of staff to volunteers is calculated by dividing the reported number of staff members by the number of volunteers in the past year. A high value on this ratio reflects an organization where most work is done by paid staff; a low value indicates an organization where most work is done by volunteers. The final measure, the Recruitment Problems Index, is a sum of three recruitment challenges probed in the survey of charities (Hager & Brudney, 2005). High values indicate problems with recruiting sufficient numbers of volunteers, recruiting volunteers with the right skills or expertise, or recruiting volunteers during the workday; low values indicate few reported recruiting problems.

We anticipated that larger charities would be better able to retain volunteers due to their greater adoption of various volunteer management strategies (see Figure 1.2), but the results in Table 1.1 suggest the opposite: smaller charities have higher rates of volunteer retention. The survey results cannot tell us why this is the case, but it is easy to imagine several possible reasons for this finding. Since smaller charities tend to have fewer volunteers, they can devote more attention to them as individuals. Or, with less budget to pursue organizational missions, volunteer assistance (and retention) is more critical for them. On the other hand, another measure of the importance of volunteers to the charity, the ratio of paid staff to volunteers, is not related to retention.

The strongest effect in the analysis pertains to the predominant age of the volunteers in a given charity. Table 1.1 indicates that charities with a larger percentage of volunteers under age 24 have lower rates of retention. Again, we can imagine the circumstances that might explain this finding. Young people are newer to work life, their life circumstances often change seasonally and rapidly, and their roots in the community are less deep than for older volunteers. Consequently, they are less likely to maintain relationships with the charities to which they volunteer their time.

Finally, the analysis shows that charities that have problems recruiting volunteers also encounter difficulties in retaining them. Steps toward alleviating one of these shortcomings should also help to address the other.

IMPLICATIONS FOR PRACTICE AND POLICY

In this chapter, we focused on charities' adoption of nine recommended practices for volunteer management. We explored the relationship between adoption of these practices, other organizational characteristics, and the retention of volunteers. The practices under study are supervision and communication with volunteers, liability coverage for volunteers, screening and matching volunteers to jobs, regular collection of information on volunteer involvement, written policies and job descriptions for volunteers, recognition activities, annual measurement of volunteer impact, training and professional development for volunteers, and training for paid staff in working with volunteers. From the analysis presented in the chapter, we draw the following seven conclusions regarding the state of volunteer management capacity in the United States.

1. **Adoption of Volunteer Management Practices Not Widespread:**
   Of the nine practices, only regular supervision and communication with volunteers has been adopted to a large degree by a majority of

charities. We were surprised to learn, for example, that only one-third of charities have adopted to a large degree the practice of publicly recognizing the work of their volunteers. Over 60% have adopted each of the practices to at least some degree, however. This finding suggests that the practices for volunteer management are known, if not always fully implemented, in America's charities.

2. **Likelihood of Adoption Depends on Characteristics of the Charity:** The likelihood that a charity adopts a particular management practice depends on its specific needs and characteristics, such as its size, level of volunteer involvement, predominant role for volunteers, and industry. For example, charities that emphasize episodic volunteer use tend to adopt different management practices than charities that emphasize more sustained use of volunteers. Charities operating in the health field have generally adopted more of the practices as well. Larger charities are more likely to have adopted most, but not all, of the management practices under study.

3. **Some Practices Tied to Greater Retention of Volunteers, Some Not:** Charities interested in increasing retention of volunteers should invest in recognizing volunteers, providing training and professional development for them, and screening volunteers and matching them to organizational tasks. These practices all center on enriching the volunteer experience. Management practices that focus more on the needs of the organization, such as documentation of volunteer numbers and hours, are unrelated to retention of volunteers, even though they help the program to realize other benefits.

4. **Charities Can Do Others Things as Well to Maximize Volunteer Retention:** Volunteer management practices are only part of the picture. In addition to adopting certain management practices, charities can provide a culture that is welcoming to volunteers, allocate sufficient resources to support them, and enlist volunteers in recruiting other volunteers. All of these practices help charities to achieve higher rates of retention. The research shows that adoption of volunteer management practices is important to the operations of most charities. By investing in these practices and by supporting volunteer involvement in other ways, charities enhance their volunteer management capacity and their ability to retain volunteers.

5. **Scope and Nature of Volunteer Use Influences Management Choices:** Different volunteer management practices have different underlying purposes. While all volunteers like to be recognized for their contributions to the organization or community, this kind of

external motivation may not be necessary for charities that have made long-term commitments to their volunteers, a practice that appeals to the intrinsic motivations of individuals. Long-term commitments are exemplified by training and professional development opportunities, regular communication and supervision, and liability coverage. These are precisely the kinds of practices more likely to be adopted by those charities that use volunteers in sustained ways, characterized by having relatively few volunteers who spend a lot of hours working for the charity. Charities that cater to episodic volunteers adopt different strategies, such as providing external validation through public recognition of volunteers.

6. **Charities Must Balance Individual and Organizational Needs:** To sustain the participation of volunteers, charities must create a good experience for them. Charities must be equally concerned with implementing practices designed to make sure that they involve volunteers wisely and well, and commit sufficient support resources to this endeavor. Our study shows that charities that adopt the practices most directly concerned with satisfying volunteers reap the highest rates of retention. Practices that cater more to the needs of the charity than the needs of volunteers are unlikely to motivate volunteers and, in fact, are not related to retention of volunteers over time. Nonetheless, these practices may be critical for the charity to oversee volunteer involvement in an accountable manner, and to generate resources necessary to keep the charity running.

7. **Retention of Volunteers Involves More Than Management Techniques:** Adoption of recommended volunteer management practices can help organizations to retain volunteers, but charities interested in retaining volunteers should not stop there. They should also allocate sufficient funds to support volunteer involvement, cultivate an organizational climate that is welcoming to volunteers, give their volunteers an experience worth sharing, and enlist volunteers in recruiting other volunteers one-on-one. However, neither volunteer management techniques nor these other steps alone will maximize retention. Charities that want to retain these essential human resources should adopt relevant volunteer management practices *and* invest in the infrastructure, culture, and volunteer experience that will keep volunteers coming back.

Charities adopt volunteer management practices for reasons that go beyond the question of whether they can afford them or not. While the resources available to a given charity no doubt play a part in adoption of the management practices under study, the roles that volunteers play in the organization and trade-offs between satisfying organizational and volunteer needs are also important in understanding which charities adopt which practices.

Volunteers are valuable human resources. Four out of five charities use volunteers to help them meet organizational needs for service and administration. Most charities could not get by without their volunteers, and they certainly would be less productive and responsive without them. Turnover of volunteers can disrupt the operation of the charity, threaten the ability to serve clients, and signal that the volunteer experience is not as rewarding as it might be. Charities cannot be expected to keep every volunteer, but building volunteer management capacity to involve and retain them makes sense for both charities and the volunteers upon whom they rely.

ACKNOWLEDGMENTS

This chapter is based on an Urban Institute brief authored by Mark A. Hager and Jeffrey L. Brudney (2004), *Volunteer Management Practices and Retention of Volunteers*. The work was conducted with support from the Corporatiion from National and Community Service, the UPS Foundation, the Urban Institute, and the University of Georgia.

NOTE

1. Conclusions regarding statistical differences (or similarities) between organizations with different characteristics in the adoption of management practices are based on analysis of variance, a statistical test that indicates whether the observed differences are large enough to be considered greater than chance ($p < 0.05$).

CHAPTER 2

NO "ONE BEST" VOLUNTEER MANAGEMENT AND ORGANIZING

Two Fundamentally Different Approaches

Lucas C. P. M. Meijs and Esther M. Ten Hoorn

There simply is no best way of organizing volunteers, neither in volunteer run organizations, in government organizations, in nonprofit organizations with mostly paid staff, nor in businesses. Volunteering, volunteers and the way they are organized and managed differs from context to context. Smith (2000) uses the metaphor of the nonprofit universe to explain that current research misses most of the nonprofit sector by only focusing on the bright stars and omitting the smaller ones and "dark matter." Smith claims, and we agree, that the literature focuses on service delivery organizations dominated by paid staff with (substantial) financial budgets. Little attention goes to *mutual support* and *campaigning organizations* (Handy, 1988), let alone smaller grassroots organizations. Smith (2000) defines grassroots associations as "significantly autonomous, formal nonprofit groups that use the associational form or structure, that

Challenges in Volunteer Management, pp. 29–50
Copyright © 2008 by Information Age Publishing
All rights of reproduction in any form reserved.

are volunteer run and composed essentially of volunteers as analytical members, and that have a relatively small local scope (i.e., locally based)" (p. ix). Smith claims that there exists a larger number of grassroots associations than paid-staff volunteer groups (p. 33). The result is that current research, and to a certain extent even Smith, misses many organizational settings in which volunteering occurs. By this, we claim that only one dominant approach on volunteer management is presented and hence a limited perspective on the position of the volunteer administrator is given (see Figure 2.1).

This chapter will show that this narrow focus leads also to a limited perspective on volunteer management. It seems that a contingency approach is needed to fully understand the dynamics, complexity and diversity of the organizational behavior of volunteers, the relation between paid staff and these volunteers and as a consequence the functioning of volunteer administrators. Therefore, in this chapter we will describe the organizational settings that are given too little attention in contemporary volunteer management literature: (volunteer-run) campaigning and mutual support organizations. We will describe the implications for the management processes and the functions of the volunteer administrator. In order to do this, we look into the role, position and behavior of volunteer administrators in an alternative management approach (see Meijs & Hoogstad, 2001; Meijs & Karr, 2004), which applies mainly to campaigning and mutual support organizations. To understand the position of volunteer administrators in all volunteer or volunteer-run organizations, a better understanding of this "membership management"

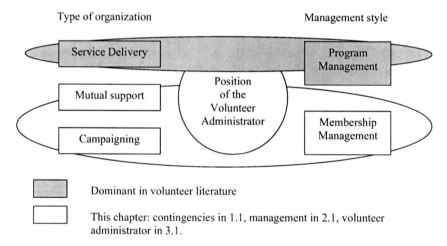

Figure 3.1.

is needed. This is in contrast to some other chapters in this book that primarily focus on service delivery organizations (see Brudney & Hager, in this volume; and Rhenborg & McVey, in this volume) using a more programatic approach.

In the first part of the chapter, we present several organizational contexts which vary the goals of the organization (Handy, 1988) through a focus on mutual support and campaigning organizations. We also describe the relationship between paid staff and volunteers, focusing on all-volunteer and volunteer-run organizations (Meijs & Westerlaken, 1994; Mintzberg, 1993; Smith, 2000). In the second part, of the chapter we look at volunteer management in general. This part builds on the work of Meijs and Hoogstad (2001) and Meijs and Karr (2004) who draw the differences between a membership and a program approach to managing volunteers. We will focus on membership management. In the final part, we link organizational contexts and management systems to volunteer administrators. The question raised is whether the function of the volunteer administrator is different in terms of "quality" and "acceptance" in (volunteer-run) mutual support and campaigning organizations.

VOLUNTEERS IN DIFFERENT ORGANIZATIONAL SETTINGS

Although most literature is only based upon service delivery and paid staff organizations, several additional typologies of volunteer organizations have been developed. Valente and Manchester (1984, see also the chapter by Rehnborg & McVey in this volume) introduce a typology of volunteer program design to describe volunteer management practices, mainly within the state agency context. They distinguish four models: ad hoc, outside agency recruitment/internal agency management, decentralized, and centralized. Rochester (1999) gives four models of volunteer involvement in small voluntary organizations: service delivery, support role, member/activist and coworker. Van Walsum (2001) presents a four stages developmental typology in which small all-volunteer groups develop from a simple structure into a simple-plus structure, into a policy structure, and further into a complex structure.

An important contingency in this chapter is the main goal of the organization as analyzed by Handy (1988). Different goals lead to different organizational cultures and maybe even to fundamentally different volunteers. The second main contingency is the relation between volunteers and paid staff. Looking at how the organizational behavior of volunteers seems to differ from paid staff (see Pearce, 1993), we follow Liao-Troth's (2001) explanation that in Pearce's research there is also the possibility that her findings are more the "result of the work environment rather than the employment status of the workers" (p. 424). Where Pearce (1993) compared all-volunteer versus all-paid-employee organizations, Liao-Troth states that in reality many organizations use both. This leads to the contingency of the position of paid staff in relation to the volunteers, introducing the concept of volunteer-run organizations.

FIRST CONTINGENCY: THE GOAL OF THE ORGANIZATION

Handy (1988) states that the organizational practices, especially the organizational culture, differs between three basic types of voluntary organizations: "service delivery," "campaigning" and "mutual support." In this study, we concentrate on the last two although we start with a short description of service delivery organizations.

Service delivery organizations aim to provide a service to an actual customer or client outside the organization. The volunteers and employees of these organizations usually try to deliver a good service to the customers. This means that volunteers and employees are prepared to submit to management, selection, recruitment, training and coordination. Service delivery organizations are characterized by a high level of professionalism and customer orientation. Basic volunteer administration books such as Brudney (1990a), Ellis (1996) and McCurley and Lynch (1994) are predominantly oriented to this type of organization. It is also the type of organization in which volunteers seem to function much like paid staff, so it seems logical to develop a volunteer management model based upon the workplace metaphor (see Carroll & Harris, 1999).

The *campaigning organization*, or advocacy (see Carroll & Harris, 1999), does not have individual customers or clients, but aims to convince or take on the entire world. For this type of organization, anyone who supports the cause can be accepted as a volunteer. Campaigning organizations are the topic of research in the tradition of resource mobilization, social movements and collective action, and the discipline of political science. Management seems to be more complicated in campaigning organizations (see also Meijs, 2004). One explanation is that campaigning organizations face a fundamental dilemma. On the one hand, they seek to have as many (more or less official) supporters as possible for their ideas. On the other hand, they seek to divide the world as neatly as possible into "friends and enemies," in order to keep their ideologies as pure as possible. The inherent ambiguity of campaigning organizations poses a true management dilemma. Another factor contributing to the management dilemma appears to be that the work of campaigning organizations, perhaps to an even greater extent than other organizations, revolves around core volunteers. In campaigning organizations, the work never stops and it sometimes becomes an integral part of a volunteer's life (Carroll & Harris, 1999, p. 14). Their recommendation is to proceed from the enthusiasm and commitment that exists among the volunteers.

There are several more management challenges for campaigning organizations (some apply to service delivery organizations as well but our impression is they are more volatile in campaigning contexts). Research by Hyde (2000), on volunteerism in feminist social movements suggests that "when ideological commitment is more orthodox and the member relationship more intense, the greater is the difficulty with volunteer recruitment and retention" (p. 40). Hyde states that "those nonprofits that wish to recruit a broader range of volunteers need to entice them by offering a mixture of incentives, including purposive, solidarity, material, instrumental, humanitarian and status-enhancement" (p. 41) (see also Carroll & Harris, 1999; Chinman & Wandersman, 1999; Knokes, 1988). There also is high turnover and many complaints from volunteers about the managers. This ideological tension between volunteers and paid staff is a typical problem of campaigning organizations. Hyde recommends program oriented measures to nonprofits, such as the integration of volunteers into the organization, clear lines of communication, and support for volunteers. Also "normative practices may need to be put aside, in favor of structures and processes that are more inclusive" (Hyde, 2001, p. 41; see also Brudney & Hager, in this volume; and Hartenian, in this volume).

The *mutual support organization* exists because a certain group of people have come together around an issue that binds them: for example, a particular illness (such as a Diabetes Patients Support Organization), a sport (such as a local hockey club), or a shared interest (such as collecting teacups). Mutual support organizations are, in many cases, grassroots organizations. They often have less than one full-time equivalent paid staff and are quite autonomous. As most grassroots organizations, mutual support organizations have an informal tax-exempt status (in several countries including the United States), tend toward informal organization and more internal democracy, are more likely to be a "member benefit group" than a "nonmember benefit group," are often polymorphic, have substantial sociodemographic homogeneity and have few economic resources (Smith, 2000, pp. 107-123). A lot of the volunteering takes place outside office hours, which means that volunteering for grassroots associations often happens during the weekend and evening hours (p. 127). Solidarity and camaraderie are the most important qualities. There is a clear relationship between volunteers, members, and clients in mutual support organizations (Meijs & Van der Linden, 1999, p. 3). Mutual support organizations have a culture of "doing things together"; the people involved work together to organize all. This means that the recruitment of volunteers is in fact membership involvement. Managers are likely to be members as well. In theory, it should make volunteer recruitment easier compared to service delivery organizations because the potential volunteers are all known to the organization. Therefore, there is less of a need to "flyer the whole city." This leads to probably the most prevailing main management challenge as described by Hoogendam and Meijs (1998, p. 31): a misfit between organizational capabilities and ambitions. In theory and practice, the competencies of the volunteers are limited to the competencies of the members. So mutual support organizations, especially those located in deprived neighborhoods, face the problem of not having certain skills, even more so if they have a very small membership basis. Another characteristic of mutual support organizations that distinguishes them from volunteer-supported organizations is the role of the manager. In mutual support organizations, where an active board of volunteers is present, the managers' role can be reduced from "executive director" to a more coordinating role or an enlarged "executive secretary" role.

At healthy mutual support organizations, organizing among volunteers becomes "the hobby," the contribution of the volunteer becomes almost unlimited. Working overtime is an unknown concept. Managers, both paid and unpaid, may think on the one hand that this unlimited "hobby energy" is wonderful, because people no longer need to be motivated to go to extremes to do the job. However, the question comes up how to control and guide this activity (Meijs, 1997). For example, a volunteer of a sports club can decide that this year's tournament should be even bigger than last year's, but is that what you want as a manager? Therefore, mutual support organizations can be weak if they lack enough resources and diversity in their membership, but they are strong if resources are available and the culture is strong. They are indestructible like weeds if they form a group of "last-heroes" who decide that they will survive.

In mutual support organizations, paid staff can be seen as a threat. According to Boessenkool and Verweel (2004, p. 30), the increasing influence of volunteer administrators and other professionals in Dutch sports could threaten the current way of involving members and replace member volunteering by membership fees. Associations should have a core task of pleasing their members for the benefit of building social capital (Putnam, 2000). Only the support and advice structure may be professionalized (Boessenkool & Verweel, 2004, p. 34).

Contextual Sidebar

It is not always possible to make a clear distinction between the three types of organizations identified by Handy (1988). Therefore, organizations should choose what type of organizations that they mainly want to be. For example, what kind of organization is a church?

The nature of a church is a campaigning organization, especially evangelist churches trying to attract new believers. Nevertheless many churches function as turned in upon hem selves. A self oriented mutual support organization in which members come together on Sunday. In other churches, church members experience the "order" to perform services to the outside world (based upon Meijs, 2004).

SECOND CONTINGENCY: THE POSITION OF PAID STAFF IN RELATION TO THE VOLUNTEERS

A simple type of organization is an all-volunteer one, such as many grassroots or other small local organizations in which there is no paid staff. Meijs and Westerlaken (1994) call this, *volunteer-run organizations* in which the goals of the organization are set and realized by volunteers. By calling these organizations volunteer-run, they acknowledge that these all volunteer, local groups are not simply "all-volunteer" organizations, but are either part of a national (multilevel-) organization or network that has paid staff or are supported by external paid staff organizations such as volunteer centers.

Smith (2000, p. 80) distinguishes two kinds of grassroots associations, monomorphic and polymorphic organizations, which in most cases are volunteer run organizations. Monomorphic grassroots are not vertically affiliated with an (other) organization. This kind of volunteer run organization is autonomous, but can be tied to a foundation or government agency. Polymorphic organizations are part of a national organization, resulting in limitations on decision making, but have better access to (funding) resources. These polymorphic organizations are part of the national organizations researched by Meijs (1997) and Sills (1957). Meijs (1997, 1996), following Sills research, describes that national organizations have a regional structure and a national level with headquarters (paid staff, sometimes volunteers), a national board and some representation of the whole organization ("annual membership meeting"). The local units may be legally part of the organization (chapters) or independent (affiliates). Meijs (1997) shows that, at least in the Netherlands, the hierarchical power of national headquarters to achieve change at local level is limited, even in organizations with chapters. Local volunteers can easily decide not to react to formal correspondence and "wait to see what happens" (such as "vote with their hands") or they can decide to continue a local independent organization with a (slightly) different approach (and "vote with their feet"). In terms of Mintzberg's (1993) *Structure in Fives*, the position of paid staff is more like the support staff and techno structure (with limited power) than like the strategic apex or middle line. Paid staffs in these organizations are not classical volunteer administrators that direct their "own" volunteers.

In *volunteer-supported organizations* (Meijs & Westerlaken, 1994)—or "paid-staff voluntary groups" as Smith (2000) refers to them—such as hospitals, museums, and schools, volunteers are not connected to the setting of policy and, in many cases, do not perform the primary processes. A volunteer board with limited connections to the direct "service" volunteers, together with paid staff, formulates goals and policy. They function as the strategic apex and middle line of Mintzberg (1993). Paid staff performs the primary processes and a volunteer administrator runs a (kind of "separate") volunteer program. Volunteers are only involved to a limited extent in carrying out specific tasks. This is the classical organizational setting for the volunteer administrator. Of course, there are many organizations in gray areas between models, such as small museums with very few paid staff or churches with small budgets, for example, those with itinerant pastors. However, the model is clear; the policies are still established by others and carried out by volunteers.

In contrast to volunteer-run organizations, volunteer-supported organizations will continue to operate even when there are no volunteers present. If the volunteers disappear, the quality of service may deteriorate, but the organizations themselves will not be in danger. This makes possible a more demanding approach to managing volunteers. In these organizations, the metaphor of the workplace is and can, in many cases, be used (Liao-Troth, 2005). In volunteer-run organizations, the situation is different. Carroll and Harris (1999, p. 16) describe that in the campaigning and volunteering organization context of Greenpeace in the United Kingdom the workplace model simply does not work. As Meijs and Westerlaken (1994) make clear, volunteer-run organizations face discontinuity when volunteers drop out.

The Consequence for Management

Following the picture of Smith (2000), it becomes clear that the nonprofit management literature is dominated by service delivery organizations with paid staff. We argue, as a consequence, one management style with volunteers (program management performed by a volunteer administrator) is also dominant. As stated in the introduction, this chapter takes a closer look at membership management oriented organizations. For information on program oriented organizations, we refer to the chapters in this book by Brudney and Hager and by Rehnborg and McVey. In order to shed some light on the consequences of the two contingencies (goal/position paid staff-volunteers), we will present a short summary on volunteer management. Following that, we examine the differences in style for the contingencies presented.

Volunteer Management

Volunteer Management in General

Based upon a small, Anglo-Saxon dominated literature study on volunteer management, Paull (2002) states that the current line of thinking is that the business management theory can be applicable to voluntary organizations (p. 21). The main point of difference seems to be that volunteers have different characteristics and recognition needs than paid staff. Research by Paull (2000) indicates, "volunteers do not wish to be managed as if they were employees, but that they do expect their work to be well organized" (p. 22). Volunteers like to be valued for their contribution by all members of the organization, not just by their managers (Paull, 2000). Volunteers are aware of the fact that they give their time and therefore expect proper management of their contributions (Hedley, 1992). "To waste a volunteer's time--ever" is one of the deadly sins of managing volunteers (Ellis, 1994). As Paull (2002) states it: "The manager must therefore find a balance between providing guidance and organizing the work so that the organizational outcomes are achieved, and treating the volunteer in a manner appropriate to their volunteer status" (p. 22). It becomes increasingly important to offer volunteers a well-organized work place because of the competition for volunteers (Farmer & Fedor, 1999; Wilson & Pimm, 1996).

It is argued that managing volunteers is more difficult than managing paid staff (Hedley, 1992, p. 115). Paull (2002) mentions that the tensions between volunteers and managers are also a reflection of the complex context in which volunteering takes place. McCurley and Lynch (1994) state that the key to managing tensions is to meet volunteers' "personal mixture of motivational needs" (p. 61). McCudden (2000) identifies six main volunteer areas that are influenced by managers: expectations, relationships, role management, support structures, evaluation and monitoring, and volunteer person specification (p. 71). King and Lynch (1998) add that administrators need to know volunteer motivations in order to effectively recruit volunteers. In many cases, volunteers also act in their own self-interest (Cnaan & Cascio, 1999; Pearce, 1993). Based upon Cnaan and Goldberg-Glen (1991) research, it is useful to assume that volunteers all "use" their activities to their own advantage. Such an assumption lies at the base of the functional approach to volunteer motivation, as developed by Clary and Snyder (1991).

Regarding the management challenges described above, the practical implementation and execution will be different for mutual support/ campaigning (all-volunteer) organizations than for service delivery (paid-staff) organizations. This is consistent with Rochester's (1999) observation that "many voluntary agencies have adopted a bureaucratic approach to the organization of volunteering" (p. 9) as well as his assertion that this "one size" workplace model does not fit all organizations, especially what he calls "member/activist" and "co-worker" organizations (p. 15). Smith (2000) translates this into an interest gap for nonprofit and volunteer management: "Grassroots associations (GA) tend not to be interested in the nonprofit management profession, the volunteer administration profession, or complicated GA (grassroots associations) leadership tactics" (p. 130). However, Smith does mention several aspects of grassroots incentive systems that are still in place despite the shunning for professional management, such as sociability, purposive, service, informational, developmental, utilitarian, charismatic, lobbying, and prestige incentives (pp. 95-102).

In order to address these differences in organizations, we take a look at a different management approach (Meijs & Hoogstad, 2001).

A Different Approach: Membership Management

Meijs and Hoogstad (2001) observe that some (Dutch, in particular) volunteer organizations take a fundamentally different approach to the management of volunteers. In their typology, management systems most often focus either on the volunteers themselves (membership management) or on specific operational tasks (program management). To illustrate the difference between program and membership management, we will use a metaphor. Program management can be compared to an assembly line in a car factory, where every mechanic performs a predetermined task for which he is recruited. Mechanics can easily be replaced; changing a small part of the car only involves changing one mechanic. However, a failing mechanic leads to constructing cars improperly. Membership management, on the contrary, can be seen as a self steering team of mechanics who make their own decisions on how to organize themselves. Individual mechanics can not easily be replaced without the consent of the others. Furthermore, replacements are not necessary because the others will step in. Acceptance for episodic mechanics (for episodic volunteers see Cnaan & Handy, 2005; Macduff, 2005) is low. External attempts to change the car lead to long group discussions. This has a basis in job design and compensation models that distinguish between a person-centric and a task-centric focus (Lawler, 1990).

Membership management starts with the possibilities and needs of the volunteers, a priori. The decision on what is done and by who is made by the people involved. The focus of membership management is to assign tasks to the volunteers preferably based upon their preferences instead of volunteers to the tasks. Each member must be asked what he or she wants to do. The distance between the management/executive committee and the volunteers is small, with many personal links. Membership management is usually characterized by a strong organizational culture; "the volunteer feels strongly involved in the organization and the other volunteers, making it harder to find a good fit with other organizations" (Meijs & Hoogstad, 2001, pp. 49-51). The social costs of exit and entry are high, due to the need to develop trust and build friendships. There is a considerable homogeneity among active volunteers, mostly because of shared goals, ideas and history. The motivation is highly socially oriented and the status of the volunteer is more internally oriented. The social culture and organizational process create high solidarity among the volunteers.

Social mobility can be hindered, however, because people tend to stay in the organization. Expectations of volunteers are not explicitly formulated since volunteers can do what they want to. Recognition is based on the number of active membership years. Membership managed organizations usually have a strong internal drive, which makes it difficult to adapt to changes in the environment. On the other hand, there is also less need to adapt, because the ideology and/or internal goals need to be accomplished and are nonnegotiable for the in-crowd. "Membership management is capable of generating broad, multifaceted involvement of volunteers, leading perhaps to a greater overall satisfaction with the volunteer experience" (Meijs & Karr, 2004, p. 178).

Management and Contingencies

In the previous section we discussed general management theory and to some extent its applicability to nonprofit organizations. We also examined a different model for managing volunteers. The question is to what degree organizational contexts, goals, and the relationship between volunteers and paid staff matter for management. This issue will be discussed in the next section.

Differences in Management Based Upon the Goal

The effects on managing volunteers in the different organizational settings can be analyzed from the point of the possible and needed use of more or less ridged management approaches. Service delivery organizations are predominantly program managed, which has been discussed in most contemporary literature. Mutual support organizations benefit greatly from membership management. For the board of directors (core volunteers), membership management involves charting what all of the members are able and willing to do and developing appropriate arrays of volunteer tasks to match. Components of membership management can be useful for cultivating a good pool of volunteers who are willing to assume these tasks. If groups of volunteers are used to carry out operational or policy preparation tasks, mutual support organizations, in which paid staff members are dominant, can work well with program management.

Clearly, the situation is more difficult for campaigning organizations. In these organizations, boards and managers are constantly deliberating which management approaches are beneficial for the two types of volunteering processes: decision formation and realization. These two processes require a different management approach. As decision formation is the work of limited elite who adopt strict selection criteria, membership management works adequately. For the process of realization, "people" may be better organized according to program management, in which "ordinary citizens" are encouraged to (episodically) take part in the forms of activism that have been thought and prescribed by the organization.

Differences in Management Based Upon the Relation Between Paid Staff and Volunteers

Membership management is of great importance in volunteer-run organizations, as program management calls for too much organization. This in turn calls for strong professional, instead of personal, leadership. A large paid-staff structure works better within volunteer-supported organizations.

In a volunteer-supported organization, volunteers perform tasks that are less crucial to the continuity of the organization. Also, volunteers perform tasks that are less integrated into the organization. The risk of volunteers walking out "en mass" is limited, but also not critical for the survival of the organization. This opens possibilities for a more rigid and formalized volunteer management. In volunteer-run organizations, the risk of volunteers walking away is also limited. However, in this case, they might consider staying but not listening. Therefore, the team approach of membership management is more appropriate.

There are differences among the three types. For service delivery organizations, the idea that there is a customer outside the organization, and the desire to do a good job allows for more rigid managerial approaches such as targeted programs. This is in contrast to the mutual support organization in which the social relations between the volunteers are more important. Campaigning organizations, with their dual processes, can use both. Thus, different management approaches are suitable for different types of organizations, based upon goals and decision structures (Table 2.1).

LINKING TO DIFFERENT VOLUNTEER ADMINISTRATORS

In the previous section, we have shown that volunteer management varies in different organizational contexts. However, "how does this influence the functioning of the volunteer administrator?" First, we need to analyze the formal position of the volunteer administrator. After that, we will elaborate on the effectiveness of the volunteer administrator, which will be divided in quality and acceptance.

The Position of the Volunteer Administrator

In the dominant service-delivery, paid staff literature, the volunteer administrator is the link or liaison between the paid staff and the volunteering part of the organization. An important issue is the organizational place for this volunteer administrator. Ellis pledges for "a separate, independent department head" instead of a position in the public relations or human resource management department (Ellis, 1996, p. 28). As described by Meijs and Westerlaken (1994), volunteer-run organizations have no direct supervising paid staff and consequently, clear director of volunteers. This means in many cases the volunteer

Table 2.1.   Management Styles Matching the Goal of the Organization (Based Upon Meijs & Hoogstad, 2001, p. 59)

| | Decision Structure | |
Goal	Volunteer-Run Organization (Volunteer Organization)	Paid Staff Organization (Volunteer-Supported Organization)
Mutual support	Membership management	Program management
Service delivery	Program management	Program management
Campaigning	Membership management, or program management with strong membership management component around decision making	Program management with membership management component (of a sort) around decision making

administrator tasks are part of core volunteer duties or that paid staff
perform more supportive tasks to the volunteers, where the administrator
position is equal or "less" important when compared to the role of
volunteers (an example would be an administrative support person rather
than a manager). These groups sometimes also have paid staff
functionaries in there surroundings (national offices, local supporting
organizations) that perform supporting and counseling functions, which
are supposed to have managerial influences.[1] This kind of position brings
about a different juridical environment for the administrator. The position
of volunteer administrators within associations (most mutual support and
many campaigning) is an integral part of the whole organization because
the volunteers, in many cases, are (formally) also the employer. One of the
consequences is that this paid staff does not see him/herself related to those
in the volunteer supported organization. "A volunteer administrator in a
work organization is far more likely to be a member of the Association for
Volunteer Administration (AVA), for example, than is a grassroots
association leader" (Smith, 2000, p. 153).

Effectiveness of the Volunteer Administrator

As a rule of thumb, the effectiveness of any supporting, managing,
counseling or managing professional can be seen as a function of: (a) the
"quality" of the professional and (b) the "acceptance" of the professional
by the client.

The "quality" of a volunteer administrator can be described in terms of
applying effective and efficient instruments of volunteer management,
for example, understanding the concepts of volunteer motivation and
being able to use them in the organization. Part of the quality of the volunteer administrator is having the ability to alter practices for different
situations (contextualization). Organizations such as the former AVA (the
international professional membership association for individuals working in the
field of volunteer resources management) provided with their credential-
ing systems an understanding of this quality issue.

An extension of this quality of the professional, and in many cases
fundamentally different than simply using effective and efficient
instruments of volunteer management, is the need to make personal
contact with clients. Acceptance is achieved by either being very good on a
content level or by being part of the team, for example, having the same
kind of characteristics as the rest. Acceptance is much more subjective. In
mutual support organizations, this means also having played soccer in the
same local soccer association or having the same illness, for example being

a problematic alcoholic in an Anonymous Alcoholics association. In campaigning organizations, one must be a believer as well.

We propose that "objective" quality is more important in service delivery organizations while "subjective" acceptance is more prevalent in both mutual support and campaigning organizations. The same applies to quality being important in paid staff dominated organizations while acceptance is important in volunteer-run organizations.

Quality of the Volunteer Administrator

In this section, we will elaborate on the quality of the volunteer administrator and on some management issues that influence the work of the manager that arise from achieving quality in a membership environment. Exploratory research by Aggidou (personal communication, September 19, 2002) to establish an "association for all professionals working with volunteers" in the Netherlands failed, resulting in solely the formulation of three abstract, basic skills for volunteer administrators: "managerial," "ideology" and "voluntary." These basic skills must be translated into less abstract competencies and practices.

Therefore, which competencies and practices are different in membership management? For a volunteer administrator in a membership environment, it is necessary to start by exploring what volunteers want instead of starting with formulating tasks to match to volunteers. Basically, this means getting to know them through such activities as informal meetings. From their first introduction, volunteers and managers negotiate on the role of the volunteer in the organization and what the manager may expect from the volunteer (Liao-Troth, 2005, pp. 512-513). Managers should negotiate from the perspective of the volunteers and not the perspective of the organization or staff. Implicitly, the focus needs to be on the assets (or need to develop these) and availabilities of the volunteers, which could for instance be filed in a skills database. This is related to the new conceptual model of matching volunteers presented by Meijs and Brudney (2004).

A second management issue pertains to the interaction between the volunteers. In many mutual support or campaigning organizations, not all of the volunteers will be active volunteers. There will always be members who do less or refrain from action. The very inactive are an extension to Pearce's (1993, p. 49) "core" and "peripheral" volunteers. In a membership environment, there is a different perspective on these "free riders" (Van Tulder, 1996, p. F4). They are not wanted by the active volunteers. Meijs and Van der Linden (1999) report that the potential area of frustration for mutual support organizations is then unsurprisingly the frustration of seeing others doing nothing.... This leads to a built-in feeling of their being a shortage of active functionaries, a feeling that is sometimes valid, but also sometimes not. Mutual support organizations are more inclined to doing the same (or more) with more volunteers rather than more with fewer volunteers. Efficiency plays no part. (p. 4)

In service delivery organizations, free riders do not exist, because of these discrete roles. For example, not every Red Cross donor is expected to also be an active volunteer, let alone every beneficiary. In mutual support organizations, free riders are known to the other members, because they benefit from the organization without volunteering. For management, this means that managing the free riders is important. Free riders should at least become peripheral volunteers (Pearce, 1993). The volunteer administrator could make a roster to include all members in, for example, the bar duties. Actively managing the inactive members fosters feelings of commitment and unity among all members. On the other hand, the active volunteers may become too active (explosion of "hobby energy" (Meijs, 1997). Burn-outs should be avoided, for example by establishing a sabbatical for core volunteers.

An issue connected to managing the interaction between the different groups is whether some active core volunteers should get extra benefits compared to the other members. Acknowledging and rewarding volunteers is important in any organization. However, in mutual support organizations an issue that arises is that although all members contribute in some way (time, money and/or means), a small group of members contributes extra time. In practice, these volunteers sometimes receive benefits in return for their time that the other members do not receive. For example, in Dutch Scouting most core volunteers do not pay their membership fee. This fee is covered for them by the children (Karr & Meijs, 2002, p. 43). Volunteer administrators need to know how to manage the members that contribute with both time and money and how to manage the ones that contribute only money.

A fourth implication is that a volunteer administrator in a mutual support or campaigning organization should always manage by organizational culture. Pearce (1993, p. 115) mentions the concept of control through shared values. Shared values (derived from the mission) are even more important than the management of the organization. In other words, behavior norms in local chapters may vary and could be more important than the values propagated by the national organization. Meijs and Van der Linden (1999) mention "almost everybody who is involved with a mutual support organization, whether as volunteer or professional must share the culture that binds the members of the organization" (p. 4)

There is a lot of normative (see DiMaggio & Powell, 1987) pressure on many mutual support organizations to become service deliveries. Especially in Dutch sports, the idea that members (should) become clients or even customers is widely spread. Since 2001 the NOC/NSF (Dutch Olympic Committee/Dutch Sports Federation) started with "PRinS," a project to increase the quality within sport associations through professionalization of (volunteer) management (www.nocnsf.nl, 10/12/05). Since the beginning of the PRinS project, together with the rise of commercial and unorganized sports, a growing market for sports managers has been created. In order to begin an educational program to cater to this need, the Academy for Physical Education (Academie voor Lichamelijk Opvoeding) has done research on desirable competences of managers in sports. Their findings are that sports administrators need 10 competences (Academie voor Lichamelijk Opvoeding, 2005, p. 20) as shown in Table 2.2.

A second illustration of how volunteer managers can act in a membership environment is given by Hoogendam (2000). He advises managers with four strategies to reduce the workload for the current volunteers within local sport associations.

First, Hoogendam (2000) suggests to discard tasks or activities. Organizations should make a critical appraisal of the present parcel of tasks. Tasks that were introduced some time ago and are now carried out largely as a matter of course should be dropped.

The second strategy is obligation. Members should be obliged to take on some of the less pleasant routine jobs, such as serving at the bar or cleaning. Although this method has been criticized as conflicting with the true spirit of volunteering, studies have shown that it is increasingly being

Table 2.2.   Ten Competences That Sport Administrators Need (Academie voor Lichamelijk Opvoeding, 2005, p. 20)

- Expresses passion for sports in word and deed
- Stands for the quality of the sports program
- Develops and realizes sports policy
- Creates a positive sport- and work climate
- Is an active player on the sport market
- Is an inspiring leader
- Initiates and implements changes
- Develops and preserves a network
- Directs financial matters
- Works and develops proceeding from a vision of sport.

applied, particularly in sports clubs. The percentage of sport associations using obligation rose from 43% in 1998 to 62% in 2000 (Janssens, 2000). Remarkably, many members took a positive attitude toward this obligation: 42% were in favor, 15% neutral, 40% against and 3% undecided (Janssens, 2000).

The third strategy is flexibilization. The principle behind this recommendation is that the organization should use the talents and potential of the members as efficiently as possible. For example, the situation often arises where certain members are only available for short periods to help with large one-off jobs. This means that the "permanent" volunteers do not have to concern themselves with these jobs.

Professionalization is the final option. This means assigning tasks to paid staff, who can either be hired for the occasion or employed on a project basis. This should take place only if no volunteers are available for the task.

Based upon our analysis, we postulate some differences (see Table 2.3).

These changes in organization and management practices are not only evident in mutual support organizations as illustrated by the Dutch chapter

Table 2.3.   Sport Associations[1] Between Service Delivery and Mutual Support (Meijs, 2005, Speech for National Conference of the Royal Dutch Field Hockey Association)

	Service Delivery	Mutual Support
Emotion of volunteering[2]	Unpaid labor	Active membership
Flexibility of approach	From tasks to members	From members to tasks/ assignments
Consequence of not volunteering	Member needs to pay higher dues	Member becomes "outcast"
Mandatory volunteering	To ensure that all make a "gift in time" or pay a higher due	To ensure that there are no "free riders," but also that people who have a good reason are "protected" (the idea of a sabbatical)
Volunteer administrator	Coordinates, plans, and schedules	Organizes, negotiates, and guards the "fun"
"Motto"	Doing more with fewer volunteers	Doing the same with more volunteers (all members)

Notes: 1.   Research by the Social Cultural Planning Bureau (SCP, 2003a, p. 117) shows that 1.1 million (8.2%) Dutch residents are volunteering in the Dutch sport sector out of 25-33% volunteers in total (SCP, 2003b, p. 8).
2.   See for a discussion on differences in emotions of volunteering Dekker (2002) and Meijs and Karr (2004).

of Amnesty International. Research (Gonesh et al., 2004) shows that Amnesty International Netherlands (AIN) is shifting from membership management to program management for many of its activities. This has implications for the way administrators manage the volunteers. There are two kinds of volunteers within AIN. The first type can be seen as a "core" group of volunteers who perform most of the work and who are closely involved with achieving the goals of the organization. An implication for management is that this "core" group performs all of the tasks rather than the tasks being split into groups who concentrate on one specific task. However, there seems to be a shift toward the second type of volunteers, which are peripheral volunteers. In Pearce's (1993) words "peripheral" volunteers are those who do not wish to commit to the organization. They engage only in short-term activities that ask for little effort. To reach this group of "new" volunteers, business-like words such as "market orientation," "positioning" and "target group segmentation" are becoming more important to volunteer administrators within AIN.

Acceptance of the Volunteer Administrator

The second aspect that influences the effectiveness of a volunteer administrator is the acceptance of the administrator by the volunteers. This mainly has to do with interaction, attitude and personality of the administrator in the organizational context. We found that there is very little information available on the acceptance of volunteer administrators. The literature that we have found primarily regards the effects of personality of the manager on employee motivation in the business context. Judge and Ilies (2002a) demonstrate that every manager should know how personality type helps drive employee motivation. The authors use five personality traits: neuroticism (poor emotional adjustment, often depressed or anxious), extraversion (sociable, positive thinking, and dominant), openness to experience (creative, curious, and unconventional), agreeableness (kind, warm, and trustworthy) and consciousness (deliberate, achievement-oriented, and dependable). These five traits tend to appear in every culture (Wright, 2003). Judge and Ilies (2002a) found that neuroticism is negatively related to employee motivation and consciousness is positively related to motivational perspectives, meaning that these traits are associated with respectively lower and higher performance motivation. Judge and Ilies (2002b) also found that extraversion is the strongest correlation to the effectiveness of leadership. Neurotic personalities are not likely to become effective leaders. Consciousness and openness to experience have a slight positive effect on the effectiveness of leadership. This outcome is of great importance to volunteer administrators, because personality has influence on the effectiveness of a leader. We propose this also goes for volunteer administrators, who can be seen as leaders within voluntary organizations. The finding is most important to volunteer administrators in mutual support organizations because acceptance also depends on the personality. Unfortunately, personality is hard, if not impossible, to alter. Bradley and Hebert (1997) suggest that personality types are an important factor in successful team performance. It must be noted that their study is based on information systems development teams in a business context. However, it can be assumed that their suggestion also goes for nonprofit teams, such as a volunteer administrator who steers a team of volunteers.

Acceptance in a mutual support organization, to a large extent, cannot be influenced by the volunteer administrator. The volunteer administrator either "has it or not." One could question if the acceptance of a volunteer administrator really is influenced by having the specific characteristics the members share in the mutual organization. We expect that the conspicuousness of the characteristic is of importance. For example, anyone who can see clearly stands out in a blind persons' association and will less easily be accepted. Acceptance in campaigning organizations depends on how convincing the volunteer administrator is a "true believer." This means the volunteer administrator is constantly "walking on eggs." Just imagine what would happen to the acceptance of the volunteer administrator in the association of vegetarians who is caught while eating meat. So, in mutual support organizations, the volunteer administrator needs to blend in, without overdoing it. In campaigning organizations, it is important to "walk the talk" and always stay "in your function." Also in private life, the volunteer administrator needs to live up to the mission of the organization because deviation will not be tolerated. Just to make the point, an anecdote is provided about one of the authors of this chapter, who once gave a presentation at the Animal Protection Front in the Netherlands. Before he started, he was making small conversation about a great diner the day before that included a sublime lobster. After hearing this, three paid staff members immediately started yelling at him with their concerns regarding lobsters being cooked alive. Fortunately for the presenter the rest of the audience did not hear this exchange.

CONCLUSION

The aim of this chapter is to explore the influence of different organizational contexts on the functioning of the volunteer administrator. The dominance of paid staff service delivery organizations in the literature has led to a dominant volunteer management model in which volunteer management is more or less explicitly based upon a workplace metaphor. This chapter has described another approach to volunteer managers that places the volunteers at a central point.

Looking at the volunteer management literature, it appears volunteers want the best of both worlds: (1) professional organizational practices of the workplace that lead to efficient processes and effective outcomes and (2) the relatively freedom, fun and mutual respect of the leisure time inefficiency. It is the task of the volunteer administrator to balance these worlds. This balancing act is not only influenced by such factors as competition for volunteers, but also by organizational contingencies such as goals of the organization (service delivery, mutual support, or campaigning) and the relation of volunteers with the volunteer administrator (volunteer-supported, volunteer-run). A membership management approach as described by Meijs and Hoogstad (2001) and Meijs and Karr (2004) seems to be much more appropriate when placing volunteers at a central point. Volunteer administrators that work in these types of organizations need to understand that they basically have to start with the assets and availabilities of the volunteers to build the assignments (see Brudney & Meijs, 2004; Meijs & Brundey, 2004 on how to build winning volunteer scenario's by combining availabilities, assets, and assignments), which is very much like the employee based job design and compensation models of Lawler (1990). Each type of organizational context generates different management issues for the volunteer administrator. The practical implementation and execution of these management challenges will be different for mutual support / campaigning (all-volunteer) organizations than for service delivery (paid-staff) organizations. Understanding these sometimes small but important differences in management is part of the quality of the volunteer administrator. For a volunteer administrator in a membership environment, it is necessary to start by exploring what volunteers want instead of starting with formulating tasks to match with the volunteers. This leads to specific management issues and a special set of important competences. For example, in sports passion for the activity is crucial. Social skills are probably even more important in this membership management than in program management.

Next to quality, the more subjective issue of acceptance is important. In mutual support and campaigning organizations, the fit between organizational characteristics and the personal characteristics and beliefs of the volunteer administrator play an important role. In many cases, this is a kind of "dummy or dichotomous variable" for volunteer administrators. However, in this public part of their private lives, it also means that volunteer administrators have to blend in and be aware of the "glass house" they are living in.

A last issue concerns the professional development of these volunteer administrators. The statement of Smith (2000) that volunteer administrators in grassroots associations are not linked to the professional associations of the volunteer administrators in paid staff organizations is supported by an experience in the Netherlands. Although it has been tried many times, an overall association of professionals (paid and unpaid) working with volunteers in direct supervision, consulting or in a supporting role was not viable in the Netherlands. Internationally, the AVA has provided a (knowledge) network for volunteer administrators. Hopefully it successors, the Association of Volunteer Resources Management and the Directors of Volunteers in Agencies, will continue this tradition.

NOTE

1. For simplicity reasons these are all called "volunteer administrators."

CHAPTER 3

A TYPOLOGY OF SHORT-TERM AND LONG-TERM VOLUNTEERS

Linda S. Hartenian

Organizations that depend on volunteers for their very existence face two widely recognized challenges—attracting and retaining people who will donate time and talent. From profit/private, to government/public, to nonprofit, these organizations and agencies often develop and implement human resource management systems similar to those designed to attract and retain employees. Reaching into the community to advertise volunteer opportunities, ensuring that individuals understand what is involved when they make a commitment to volunteer, and providing frequent recognition are just a few of the ways that agencies establish and maintain a volunteer pool. While agencies hope that volunteers begin with a life-long commitment to the agency's cause, often volunteers do not. Some people who stop volunteering choose to never volunteer again. These are true short-term (ST) volunteers. Others, often considered ST volunteers, stop out from volunteering due to other responsibilities (e.g., family, job). Still others may quit volunteering at one agency and begin at another. Finally, people may intentionally engage in ST volunteering by volunteering in consultant-type episodes with one or more agencies. A simple distinction

Challenges in Volunteer Management, pp. 51–68

between ST and long-term (LT) volunteering typically does not capture these nuances. As a result, agencies are not able to adequately recruit or retain these different types.

Previous research and theory on personality, social and role identity, motivation, psychological contracts, and commitment are used to develop a typology of ST and LT volunteers. This 2 x 2 typology makes distinctions between Misfit, Consultant, and Missionary type volunteers using (1) length of service with a particular agency (short, long), and (2) length of service overall (short, long).

INTRODUCTION

Volunteers represent a valuable resource to nonprofit, governmental, and for-profit organizations. When they donate their time and talent, multiple benefits accrue to the organization, the individual, and society. The obvious organizational benefit is that volunteers work without pay; they can provide indirect support services (e.g., serving on boards and committees) and direct delivery of service (e.g., staffing crisis lines) that offset the overall workload for staff and use their talents. As a volunteer, the individual may develop an appreciation for the social issues/challenges facing a resident; volunteering may strengthen the social fabric that binds the community.

Attraction and retention of volunteers represent two challenges for agencies. Yet, the intensity of an agency's efforts to address these challenges should vary depending on the type of volunteers sought. Understanding why and how people volunteer in the first place helps to explain, in part, why they stay (or not). The remainder of this chapter will examine individuals' choices to volunteer on a ST or LT basis, considering the reasons why they volunteer, the experiences they have when volunteering and what contributes to their choice to continue to volunteer. Implications for the agency are explained throughout the following discussion. (The terms agency and organization are used interchangeably, below.)

A PROCESS OF ATTRACTING AND RETAINING VOLUNTEERS

The process model in Figure 3.1 reflects a staffing model that applies to both employment and volunteer contexts. With similar goals of attracting, motivating, and retaining labor talents, the agency is aware of: (1) multiple individual, organization, and cultural influences at each of three stages (cf. Penner & Finkelstein, 1998), and (2) the sequential nature of the

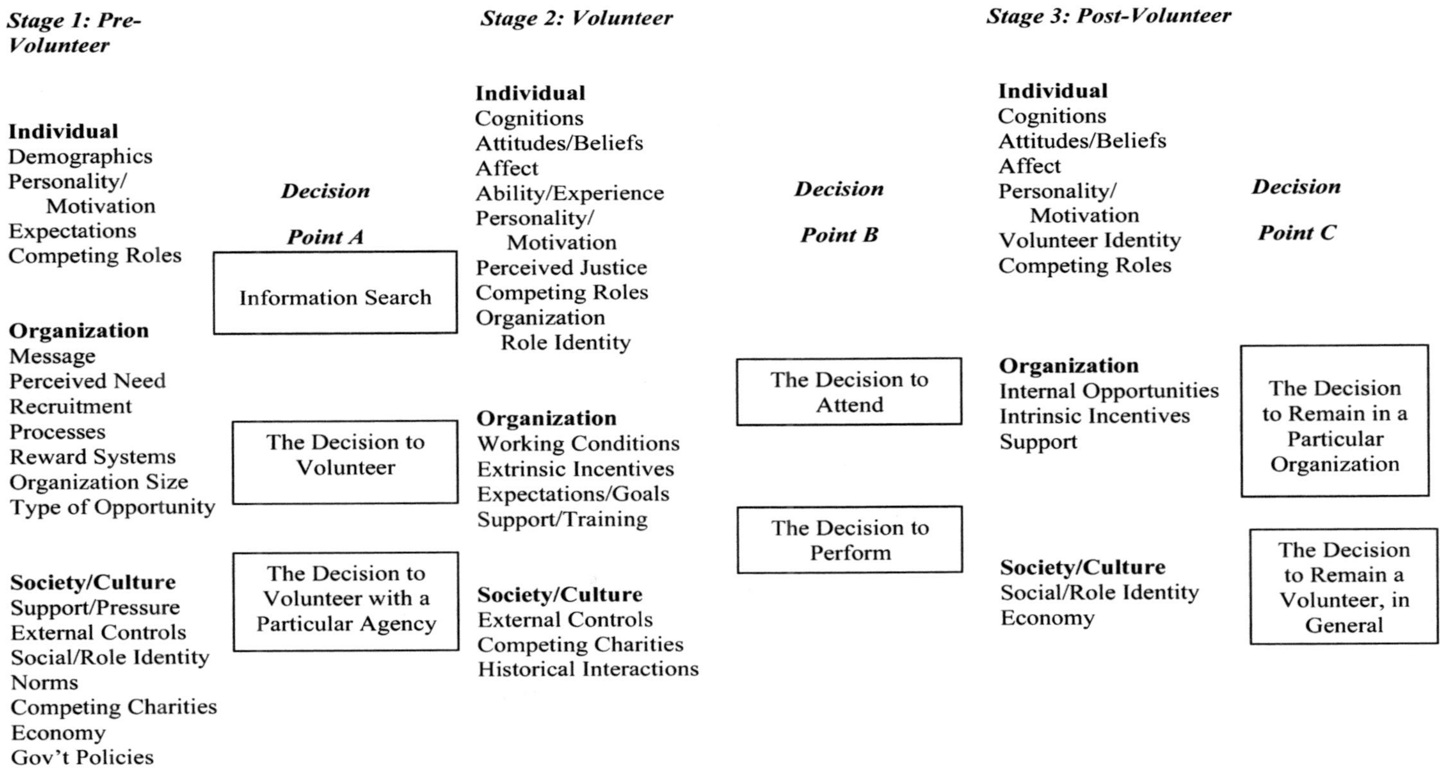

Stage 2: Volunteer

Stage 3: Post-Volunteer

Individual
Demographics
Personality/
  Motivation
Expectations
Competing Roles

Individual
Cognitions
Attitudes/Beliefs
Affect
Ability/Experience
Personality/
  Motivation
Perceived Justice
Competing Roles
Organization
Role Identity

Individual
Cognitions
Attitudes/Beliefs
Affect
Personality/
  Motivation
Volunteer Identity
Competing Roles

Organization
Message
Perceived Need
Recruitment
Processes
Reward Systems
Organization Size
Type of Opportunity

Organization
Working Conditions
Extrinsic Incentives
Expectations/Goals
Support/Training

Organization
Internal Opportunities
Intrinsic Incentives
Support

Society/Culture
Support/Pressure
External Controls
Social/Role Identity
Norms
Competing Charities
Economy
Gov't Policies

Society/Culture
External Controls
Competing Charities
Historical Interactions

Society/Culture
Social/Role Identity
Economy

Decision

Point A

Decision

Point B

Decision

Point C

| Information Search |

| The Decision to Attend |

| The Decision to Remain in a Particular Organization |

| The Decision to Volunteer |

| The Decision to Perform |

| The Decision to Remain a Volunteer, in General |

| The Decision to Volunteer with a Particular Agency |

Figure 4.1.   Volunteer decisions with antecedents.

individual's decisions to join (prevolunteer stage), to attend and perform (volunteer stage), and to remain with an agency (postvolunteer stage).

In the prevolunteer stage, the organization can influence the individual to apply by advertising its particular need. This begins the organization's search process. Messages communicated to the two potential applicant pools are typically different. The organization advertises for people to fill job openings when hiring employees. To attract volunteers, the agency advertises a need for a particular skill set or for someone to complete a particular task. This is the first point in the staffing model where the agency has the opportunity to be clear about the volunteer opportunities that exist and the type of volunteer characteristics that match best.

The application process continues with a review of applicant credentials. The organization wishing to hire an individual into a paid position carefully examines applicant knowledge, skills, and abilities to ensure that it will be getting the best talent for its compensation dollar (a person-job fit). To bring in a volunteer, organizations should be simultaneously assessing what are volunteer interests (i.e., why are they volunteering) and whether the agency can provide the type of opportunity that can bring about outcomes to satisfy that initial purpose. When agencies look for a good fit between their own need and volunteer characteristics, they may first examine whether an organization-person fit exists rather than a job-person fit [an exception is the individual who is performing direct delivery of service]. This stage represents a second chance to clarify the needs of the agencies and the requisite volunteer characteristics.

If agency advertising is successful, the volunteer likely is faced with multiple volunteer opportunities because the number of community agencies seeking volunteers is greater than the number of available volunteers. The volunteer's decision to join an agency is undoubtedly an individual one. While volunteer applications can be denied, rarely is free time and talent ignored. The benefits of volunteer assistance usually out-weigh the costs to the agency, and accepting volunteer efforts contributes to good community relationships. Turning away free talent does not make sense because it implies the agency does not need volunteers. (Little is known about volunteer decision processes when multiple choices are available.) Once an agency is selected, attention shifts to establishing an understanding of the exchange relationship.

For the employee, organizational entry is formalized with a contract clarifying the job responsibilities and the salary/benefits paid for perform-ing the job. While employees expect this level of formalization, the agency-volunteer exchange is primarily implicit. Without a contract or other explicit methods for establishing expectations, both the agency and volunteer are left to assume each other's needs. Agencies continue to improve the way they communicate expectations and transmit what it is like to volunteer with an agency. Beyond the personal appeal to remain for 6 months or a year, however, little exists in stage one to ensure a volunteer will stay with an agency. The agency recognizes that volunteer satisfaction with his/her agency experience in stage two will keep the volunteer coming back (Clary & Orenstein, 1991).

The second stage focuses on an individual's experiences in the agency (Phillips, 1982). The volunteer makes two main decisions: the decision to attend and the decision to perform. Volunteer management systems are designed to influence these decisions. Some of the same best practices for employees are adopted with volunteers. For example, agencies provide realistic job previews so that the actual experience closely reflects the actual volunteer situation. Videos of a typical volunteer day may help to encourage attendance by welcoming the new volunteer and by demonstrating activities in a way that they are achievable. Mentors (whether volunteers or staff) help to facilitate a smooth transition into the agency.

Satisfaction is the level of a positive affective response toward the [volunteer] situation (Locke, 1976), which plays an important role in explaining attendance (Clary & Orenstein, 1991). Factors that contribute to volunteer satisfaction include:

- good internal company relations and well-defined skill requirements (Thompson, Bono, & Rybeck, 1993)
- procedural and distributive justice (Hendrix, Robbins, Miller, & Summers, 1998)
- the opportunity for self expression (Bonjean, Markham, & Macken, 1994)
- a high level of functionally relevant benefits (Clary et al., 1998)
- training (Eckert, Falvo, Crimando, & Riggar, 1993)
- a helping disposition (Omoto & Snyder, 1995)

Satisfaction, in turn, leads to a greater number of hours devoted (Jenner, 1982) and time spent, though a causal relationship has not yet been established (Penner & Finkelstein, 1998).

Despite agency efforts in stage two, the unique relationship between the agency and the volunteer continues to provide a widely recognized challenge for managing volunteers. Neither is bound to the other through the type of contractual relationship that exists between organization and employee. One outcome of a poor volunteer experience is the decision to leave an agency (postvolunteer stage). Following a brief overview of definitions of ST and LT volunteering, the remainder of this chapter focuses on a framework that organizations might use when considering that people volunteer for different reasons.

RETAINING VOLUNTEERS

For the most part, volunteer turnover is defined similarly to employee turnover—when a volunteer leaves an agency, they have "quit" working for that agency. Length of service is the standard by which volunteers are judged to be ST or LT. At one end of this continuum is the person who does not last for 6 months; at the other end are volunteers who support an agency throughout their lifetime. Conceptually, length of service is a continuous variable though researchers have defined length of service as:

- Attendance—a frequency count of the number of times a person volunteers—once per day ... to ... once a year (Okun, 1994)
- Intent to volunteer (IntV) in the future (near-term): will the volunteer show up again
- IntV in the future (distant-term): will the volunteer continue for a length of time (Clary et al., 1998; Farmer & Fedor, 1999)
- Length of time (sustained altruism) (Clary & Miller, 1986) and greater amount of help (Clary & Orenstein, 1991)
- Length of service (in months) (Gidron, 1984)
- Length of participation (Rubin & Thorelli, 1984)

Only the last three in the above list reflect length of service; yet, the first three are particularly useful as the agency establishes work schedules and forecasts labor needs into the future. For example, "frequency of episodes with an agency" is important when an agency has to schedule staff around volunteer times. Knowing whether someone will volunteer once a day, or once a week, or far into the future allows the agency some predictability about the labor pool. From the organization's perspective, a level of certainty and stability about the labor pool is created enhancing the management of the internal labor force (Katz & Kahn, 1978).

While the decision to quit is more delicate for the employee who depends on the income-generating aspect of a job, usually when they quit, they do not return again to that same organization. Volunteers may quit for the same reasons as employees—lack of recognition for a job well done, poor relationship with a supervisor, or unmet expectations. A volunteer, however, may make what seems to be a rather quick decision to quit when volunteering is not convenient or when family or other commitment must take precedence. An individual could "come and go" as a volunteer—something an employee would not do. Volunteers need to feel a broader sense of commitment to an agency (see Penner & Finkelstein, 1998) and see how their work impacts organizational goals (Hackman & Oldham, 1976).

Whether or not a volunteer remains with an agency is influenced by the individual's socioeconomic context, type of positive or negative agency experience, and level of satisfaction with task assignments. Unknown is the extent to which individuals who quit volunteering do so with no intent of ever volunteering again. A closer look at the distinction between ST and LT volunteering is necessary—agencies can reclaim ST volunteers and nurture LT volunteers. How, then can the volunteer process model be reframed to reflect stopping and starting?

Typology of ST and LT Volunteers

People differ in their hoped-for outcomes from volunteering (Miller, 1985), leading to different levels of participation in agency activities (Anderson & Moore, 1978). To explore the distinctions between ST and LT volunteers, research, and theory on personality, social, and role identity, motivation, psychological contracts, and commitment are examined. Those who intend to do LT volunteering participate for different reasons than ST volunteers. LT volunteers are believe to have altruistic reasons for volunteering, such as helping those less fortunate and giving back to the community.

The individual's decision to volunteer could be a response to the agency's message, or it could be driven by an internal need. Generally, if individuals initiate an information search about volunteering alternatives, they are seeking to address an internal need to volunteer. When people respond to an organization's request (and they have not volunteered before), the reason they volunteer is externally driven. These reasons are linked to LT and ST volunteering, respectively. Individual characteristics, including: personality, motives and motivation, individual needs, and demographics influence the decision to volunteer (see Clary & Orenstein, 1991; Culp, 1997; Harrison, 1995; O'Driscoll, Ilgen, & Hildreth, 1992). Referred to as the individual's motivation to volunteer, reasons have been classified as egoistic or altruistic. Egoistic reasons include economic incentives, building a resume, getting hands-on organizational experience, and determining if a career in the field is feasible. Altruistic reasons include doing something for others, like helping a community agency.

The typology introduced in Figure 3.2 incorporates these theories in a 2 × 2 typology that considers length of service for one agency and length of service through life. Cell 1 shows the ST volunteer with one agency who decides to quit volunteering altogether, never taking on volunteering again (the Misfit). The volunteer in cell 2 contributes time and talent to one agency and then another (ST) and is considered to be a LT volunteer over his or her lifetime (the Consultant). Cell 3 represents the individual

| | | Length of Service: Volunteer, In General | |
		Short	Long
Length of Service: Particular Agency	Long	(0)	(3) **Natural Missionary** --------------------------- **Cultivated Missionary**
	Short	(1) **Misfit**	(2) **Project Consultant** --------------------------- **Contingent Consultant**

Figure 4.2.   Volunteer decisions to remain with a particular agency and a volunteer in general.

who stays with one or more agencies over his or her lifetime (the Missionary). [The cell labeled (0) would not occur; one could not be a ST volunteer with many agencies and ST altogether.] Each cell is examined below.

MISFITS

Volunteers in the first category (Figure 3.2, cell 1) discover that the volunteering role did not fit well. Figure 3.3 reviews characteristics of the misfit. Driven by their own interests, Misfits have an egoistic orientation. For example, people who volunteer to gain job experience (i.e., extrinsic outcomes) have an egoistic orientation (Klein, Sondag, & Drolet, 1994). They have not developed an organizational identity, which would work to keep them affiliated with an agency. They never develop a volunteer identity because the first attempt at volunteering resulted in achievement of their ST goal. For others, the volunteer experience may be so unsuccessful that Misfits do not try again. The Free Spirit identity reflects a lack of a sense of obligation to an agency; this person looks for an activity that feels right

		Contingent Consultant	Project Consultant	Cultivated Missionary	Natural Missionary
	Misfit				
Orientation	Egoistic	Altruistic → Egoistic	Egoistic ←→ Altruistic	Altruistic	Altruistic
Identity/ Role	Free Spirit	Tutor Role	Advisor Role	Volunteer Identity → Goal Identity	Organization Identity → Volunteer Identity
Motivation	Extrinsic	Extrinsic	Extrinsic	Extrinsic → Intrinsic	Intrinsic
Commitment	Normative	Continuance→ Normative	Continuance→ Normative	Continuance→ Constituency	Continuance Affective
Time Frame	Short	Short→ Long	Short→ Long	Long	Long

Figure 4.3.   Individual differences between ST and LT volunteers.

to them. Subsequently, Misfits are moving on to other roles, hoping they will address the needs that the dominant roles in their lives did not satisfy. Their commitment lasts only as long as it has to in order to receive their hoped-for outcomes or determine that those outcomes will not be received.

At two points in time, Misfits could remove themselves from volunteering—following the information search about volunteering (Stage 1) and following a brief volunteer experience with an agency (early Stage 2) (refer to Figure 3,1). Both represent the extreme in ST volunteering.

Stage 1—Failure to Act on Information. For someone who has never before volunteered, perhaps the process shown in Figure 3.1 begins when a friend asks if the individual would consider volunteering, or the individual might receive services from that agency and develops a sense of obligation to help others who are experiencing similar circumstances. The potential volunteer considers: what it means to be a volunteer, available volunteer activities, required level of responsibility, and agency characteristics. Typical criteria used to evaluate whether or not to volunteer include time required, perceived competence to provide the type of needed help, support/acceptance by immediate family, personal expense associated with helping, and anticipated satisfaction from volunteering, to name a few. The outcome of this evaluation may be an economic one—"Working for no pay makes no sense; it's not efficient. I should spend my time earning a wage at a job that uses my skills and talents and make a donation to an agency so it can hire staff with special skills" (see Knox, 1999 for an expanded discussion). The outcome may be a personal one—"I could never do that." When the agency is successful in reaching but not in bringing in new volunteers, it will need to explore whether its message is convincing.

Stage 2—Loss of New Volunteers. In Figure 3.1 (Stage 2), volunteers show up to train and/or to begin to volunteer. Representing the second point at which an individual recognizes a lack of fit, they find that the volunteer experience did not meet their needs or expectations and/or did not fit well with their social and role identity. This conclusion results from an evaluation of their volunteer experience.

Implicit and explicit expectations about what will happen when individuals begin to (and continue to) volunteer form the psychological contract for the agency-volunteer relationship (see Liao-Troth, 2001; Rousseau & Parks, 1993). Volunteers may desire a particular type of assignment, a certain level of social interaction, and to be recognized (or not) for what they do. Reasons for volunteering are also expectations in the sense that volunteers hope for these outcomes:

- to help other people (Kratcoski & Crittenden, 1983)
- to express deeply held beliefs about the importance of helping others (Clary, Snyder, & Ridge, 1992)
- to serve as an advocate (Nathanson & Eggleton, 1993)
- to socialize, expand networks, and apply skills to social issues (Covelli, 1985)
- to meet interesting people, help others, be involved in community politics, learn skills/develop self-confidence, and feel a sense of accomplishments (Daniels, 1988)
- to try new skills or to meet new people (Taylor, 1990).

Not surprisingly, individuals frequently offer, and organizations often ask, why that agency was chosen. If these reasons are verbalized, the likelihood increases that the organization can place the volunteer in a situation where they will be able to accomplish that objective. On the other hand, an individual may join the agency without sharing expectations, such as amount of assistance they will receive from staff or volunteers if needed or if volunteers are respected by the staff. Whether explicitly stated or not, the individual trusts that expectations will be met.

Generally speaking, if individuals primarily perform volunteer activities for their own benefit (e.g., learning a skill, building a resume, contacting key community players), they are considered to have ST goals and are characterized as wanting an immediate receipt of tangible outcomes. The ST relationship is considered to be: (1) an economic exchange—something of value (besides pay) is received by individuals in exchange for their free services to the agency; (2) reciprocal—volunteers continue as long as something is received in return; (3) transactional—costs as well as benefits associated with volunteering are considered; and (4) based on self-interest—volunteers consider primarily "what's in it for me" (see Farmer & Fedor, 1999; Rousseau & Parks, 1993). ST relationships imply the volunteer will leave sooner rather than later. If no costs of quitting exist, volunteers' continuance commitment is low (see Allen & Meyer, 1990, for a discussion of three forms of commitment). According to some, a decrease in any type of commitment is sufficient to lead to an increased intent to leave (Dunham, Grube, & Castaneda, 1994).

However, it is not only the ST aspect of their volunteering that best characterizes the Misfit—some have found that those with self interest reasons will still be volunteering after a year (Omoto & Snyder, 1995). Rather, the Misfit leaves early if it appears something of value will not be received or costs will outweigh the benefits of volunteering.

Identity explains the differences between ST and LT volunteering from two perspectives—the broader social environment and the specific organizational context. The broader sociocultural perspective may explain the parameters around individual decisions to begin and/or stop volunteering. When asked, "does the individual receive support at home and among friends," most likely we are discussing the fit, or congruence, between volunteer behaviors and the values and expectations for behavior based on membership in a larger social group (see Callero, Howard, & Piliavin, 1987). Continuing to volunteer is difficult in the face of opposition by an educated family member (e.g., "why do you do such unsophisticated volunteer work when you have an advanced degree?") or challenged by the religious or cultural community for engaging in activities that run counter to its values or beliefs (e.g., volunteering at pro-choice community agencies or in the inner city). Role theory also suggests that if volunteering activities are undertaken to compensate for something that is missing from the dominant roles in their lives (e.g., social interaction, feeling in control of choices), a person would quit if those feelings and activities become realized in their dominant roles (Rubin & Thorelli, 1984).

Finally, agency efforts to integrate the individual may not be successful. As will be noted shortly, volunteers cannot develop an organizational identity if they do not spend time in the organization. Successful transition into the agency takes time—holding onto the volunteer is difficult when the role as well as the organizational experience are new. As the agency addresses issues under its control, it can seek more information about volunteer expectations. Knowing that volunteers have preentry expectations, the volunteer recruitment and hiring process takes on a different quality, exploring why the volunteer wishes to help this particular agency and what they hope to gain from the experience. Efforts to make this contract more explicit may mean that the agency can successfully provide the necessary opportunities and, hence, influence the attitudes that will keep the volunteer coming back.

When volunteers quit after 6 months, the typical agency would view them to be ST volunteers. If that person now enters and stays at another agency, in the larger realm of things, that person is a LT volunteer. Hence, any model distinguishing between ST and LT volunteering must allow for this possibility. If the agency cares about retaining lost volunteer talent, programs will be created to encourage their return (e.g., call back systems).

A LT volunteer is one who remains a volunteer over time. There are two ways to become a LT volunteer: (1) to have many sequential organizational experiences over time (the Consultant, Figure 3.2, cell 2), or (2) to stay with one or more agencies over time (the Missionary, Figure 3.2, cell 3). When volunteers have many sequential volunteer experiences with different organizations, cumulatively their ongoing choices to volunteer would reflect a decision to remain a lifetime volunteer. The Consultant has a volunteer identity, but not an organizational identity. The Missionary not only possesses a volunteer identity, he or she also has a strong identity with the organization. Both types of LT volunteering are now examined.

CONSULTANTS

Consultants are LT volunteers who come to an agency with a specific talent or personal purpose rather than coming to an organization because of its mission. Consultants are different from Misfits primarily in their intent IntV. Misfits are low on IntV; Consultants are high on IntV. Once Consultants complete an assignment with agency A, they intend to return to that agency (Contingent Consultant) or another (Project Consultant). The Project Consultant is discussed first.

Project Consultants (PCs)

These individuals come into an agency to volunteer for a specific task, activity, or project. PCs may have a particular expertise, such as working with boards of directors or crafting operating policies and procedures. When they feel they are no longer making a value-added contribution at agency A, they move on to agency B (Champoux, 1978). In general, when PCs switch from one organization to another, they still remain a volunteer. However, why would PCs switch from one agency to another?

Van Tripj, Hans, and Hoyer (1996) found that people who were more likely to become bored or satiated quickly (and extrinsically motivated) were more likely to seek variety. Examples of other reasons for jumping from agency A to agency B include lack of opportunity for rewards that correspond to the person's values (Champoux, 1978), perceived unfair agency-individual exchange (Organ, 1988), unmet compensatory roles, and the realization that costs exceeded benefits at agency A. Relatively speaking, PCs may have more egoistic reasons than altruistic, switching agencies for personal reasons, not because the agency no longer needs them. With ST projects, the PC is likely to be in relationship with an agency because of self-interest—perhaps developing a reputation for their expertise in writing policies.

Despite the negative connotations, egoistic orientations have been linked to positive consequences for agencies (Omoto & Snyder, 1995). When individuals bring special expertise, they serve in an Advisor Role (see Figure 3.3). As advisors, they mentor and guide agencies using proven theories and best practices. Their initial commitment reflects the intent to remain as long as needed (continuance commitment); however, at some point, their sense of obligation to the agency wanes (normative commitment) (Allen & Meyer, 1990). Perhaps perceived obligations change (Robinson, Kraatz, & Rousseau, 1994). Perhaps interactions between the volunteers and staff change over time because the agency is not successful in achieving its objectives (Knoke & Wood, 1981). When volunteers question their involvement and the agency's intent, the relational contract that was once based on the trust that LT outcomes will be received, becomes ST and transactional (Rousseau & Parks, 1993).

The main distinction between the PC and the Contingent Consultant (CC) is the consistency and frequency with which they are involved with an agency. The individual's reasons for shifting from one agency to another may reflect the same reasons people quit altogether (needs and expectations were not met) as well as feeling they have contributed all they can to the agency. The PC has a higher level of both, regularly volunteering in different agencies; agencies who need help will call the PC before the CC. The CC will help, if possible, but agencies cannot count on a "yes." To retain the PC, an agency must find suitable additional projects (refer to Figure 3.3).

Contingent Consultants

These individuals have characteristics congruent with LT volunteering (e.g., motives, good volunteer experiences at agency A) but find they need to put volunteer responsibilities on hold. Most likely, personal illness or other roles interrupt volunteering, but not permanently—a family emergency, a tough semester at school, or ongoing business travel cause a volunteer to resign rather than disappoint an agency with frequent absenteeism. Longer absences from volunteering are explained by the need to return to work and time conflicts (Bacharach, Bamberger, & Conley, 1991; Tiehen, 2000). They resolve the stress associated with role conflicts, such as helping others (Clary et al., 1992) versus a work-related value such job security (Wittmer, 1991) by temporarily stopping-out. The CC intends to volunteer in the future with that same organization perhaps because they are aware of that organization's need for volunteers (see Clary & Miller, 1986). Their previous volunteer experiences lead to a higher IntV and result in actual return to volunteering (Frisch & Gerrard, 1981; Snyder & Clary, 1999). The smart organization puts in place callback systems, on-call arrangements, or emergency staffing volunteer programs designed to keep in touch with the CC.

Their orientation is more egoistic than altruistic, stopping out for personal reasons (see Figure 3.3). As previously noted, ST relationships are transactional in nature and based on self-interest. As an unpredictable source of volunteer labor, agencies call on a CC only when the Consultant's schedule permits. They serve a Tutor Role, occasionally returning to help those in need. CCs may also begin with a higher level of continuance commitment that wanes as dominant roles begin to use up discretionary time (Herzog & Morgan, 1993). Their previous volunteer experiences lead to a higher IntV and result in actual return to volunteering (Frisch & Gerrard, 1981; Snyder & Clary, 1999). The potential exists, therefore, for CCs to develop into Cultivated Missionaries (discussed next).

Consultants differ from Missionaries based on the strength of their identity with the organization. Consultants primarily participate because they have a talent that the organization needs. They do not have as strong of an identity connection with the organization as do Missionaries. Stopping and starting is easy for the Consultant because loyalties lie in other roles (for the CC) or in maintaining an active consulting agenda (for the PC). Agencies must recognize the potential—careful, planned education about the agency's mission may guide a Consultant into the Missionary role.

MISSIONARIES

In a basic sense, all Missionaries buy into the mission, goals, and objectives of the agency, reflecting what most would call an identification with the organization. This identity, however, has two levels—one that reflects a commitment to the goals that are espoused by key players who champion the successes of a given organization, and one that reflects a total integration with the identity of the agency. This progression through these levels might well characterize what happens to the Consultant-turned-Missionary (also described as the Cultivated Missionary, below).

The first type, the Natural Missionary (NM), is a zealot for the agency's mission. Little, if anything, would divert the NM from serving that agency and its purpose. The second type, the Cultivated Missionary (CM), evolves from the ongoing decisions that a Consultant makes to stay with one agency. Gradually, the CM's identity shifts from an Advisor and/or Tutor role to a constituency identity, where an individual identifies with the organization's goals (Reichers, 1985). As one's connection becomes a deeper fusion of oneself with the organization, he or she has developed an organizational identity (Ashforth, 1998). CMs develop an organizational role identity over time as they have the opportunity to judge whether their trust in the agency is well placed (see Phillips, 1998). Trust comes from being treated fairly and with respect (Konovsky & Pugh, 1994). What distinguishes CMs from NMs is the initial strength of their commitment and devotion to the agency's cause.

Agencies may confuse volunteer identity with organizational identity, thinking that people will stay with an agency if they have a LT altruistic orientation. Since one's connection to an organization is distinct from one's connection to a broader role (Ashforth & Mael, 1989), to keep volunteers, the agency must encourage the volunteer's development of an organizational identity. It is the CM that the agency needs to nurture. CMs first have a volunteer identity—the broader role—and then develop an organizational identity. The NM has both a volunteer identity and an organizational identity. Each is briefly described.

Cultivated Missionaries

Volunteer attachment to a particular agency and its cause develops over time for the CM. Perhaps PCs (Figure 3.2, cell 2) are influenced by their experience in the agency, resulting in their embracing agency values, supporting its purpose, and remaining organizational volunteers. Or, people looking for a way to help in the community might contact a local volunteer center and are directed to an agency.

How do agencies develop CMs? The first step is to achieve a good match between the person and the organization (Sergent & Sedlacek, 1990). When the screening process provides a realistic picture of what it is like to volunteer with that agency and the organization is able to determine that a potential volunteer's knowledge, skills, abilities, and personality characteristics fit well with the organization, retention will be enhanced. Once individuals becomes volunteers, the availability of internal volunteering alternatives, providing clear roles for volunteers, and training may help individuals to develop a sense of purpose to their volunteering (Barlow & Hainsworth, 2001; Kirschenbaum & Mano-Negrin, 1999; Wandersman & Alderman, 1993). Finally, successful outcomes, both individual and organizational, and the rewards that accompany success may lead to feelings of pride and identity with the organization (see Farmer & Fedor, 1999; Murnighan, Kim, & Metzger, 1993).

CMs begin with a volunteer identity (see Figure 3.3). Consistent with their initial reason for volunteering, this identity is based on the rewards and outcomes provided for the investment (of time and talent) that they have made (Homans, 1976). Now the agency must determine how to keep them coming back. Organizations work the hardest to positively influence levels of volunteer satisfaction and commitment because these may be the only things that retain volunteers (Dailey, 1986). The longer they remain with an agency, the more likely they will experience a positive change (see Clary & Miller, 1986). As long as agency values are upheld and outcomes accrue to the beneficiaries and the community, the volunteer continues to believe in the agency (Rousseau & Parks, 1993). They develop a commitment to the values of, and an identity with, that particular organization (Knoke & Wright-Isak, 1982; Piliavin & Callero, 1991). In this sense, they possess characteristics of the NM.

Natural Missionaries

These individuals join agencies committed to and engaged in its cause from the outset (Figure 3.2, cell 3). Whereas CMs are developed mainly via organizational initiatives, the LT time frame of the NMs is deeply imbedded. A result of cultural influences on their personality development (Miller, 1999), these persons have altruistic orientations—emotional responses, driven by the perception of the other person's welfare (Batson et al., 1988). A proactive personality (i.e., one who is inclined to take initiative to improve circumstances) is a stable disposition unconstrained by situational forces and is correlated with conscientiousness and extraversion (Crant & Bateman, 2000), two characteristics related to volunteers in some contexts (Dollinger & Leong, 1993). Altruism is shown to predict greater amounts of help (Clary & Orenstein, 1991); and aspects of helping dispositions distinguish ST from LT volunteers (Penner & Fritzsche, 1993).

LT relationships are value-based (Rousseau & Parks, 1993) and relational (Farmer & Fedor, 1999), with trust that [undefined] outcomes will be received, but at a future point in time. To support the NM, agencies must ensure that volunteers see how their contributions lead to valued ends (Rubin & Thorelli, 1984) and communicate to them how the agency's goals have been achieved (Knoke & Wood, 1981). The agency, essentially, is concerned about organizational systems and processes that work to maintain the NM's level of commitment and reinforce their organizational identity. The next section briefly describes how agencies might focus their efforts to appropriately to cultivate Missionaries.

INFLUENCING VOLUNTEER TYPES

By acknowledging that volunteering for an organization is different from being a volunteer over one's lifetime, agencies can now attend to the characteristics that place volunteers into one of three broad categories— Misfits, Consultants, and Missionaries. Of the three, Misfits will be the hardest to influence because they have neither a volunteer identity nor an organizational identity. Their initial ST personal focus should be met, if possible, because research shows benefits still accrue to agencies. Yet, the likelihood is small that additional time with (and education about) the agency will result in the Misfits developing a LT commitment to that agency.

Consultants will be more receptive than Misfits to agency attempts to educate, integrate, and instill in them an organization identity. Consultants come to the agency with a desire to help—a volunteer identity. But, they are not committed to the agency yet. The agency has an opportunity to influence the Consultants in the same way it retains Missionaries— demonstrate success in achieving objectives, treat staff and volunteers fairly, and recognize volunteer efforts. The internal environment that nurtures one's organizational identity is greatly influenced by the organization. In contrast, the agency has little to no influence over factors that compete for the volunteer's time and talent.

Agencies should educate volunteers about the agency vision and mission. For example, explaining the finer nuances of policies that, on the face of it, might appear controversial helps simultaneously to educate the volunteer and to allow volunteers to ask questions. A focus on integration will include task/activity training, support from staff and other volunteers, the opportunity to attend and participate in meetings (as appropriate), and the type of recognition/or outcomes that brought the volunteer to the agency in the first place. Creation of internal "job" markets (see Kirschenbaum & Mano-Negrin, 1999) may be highly motivational to a volunteer; as one becomes more knowledgeable, more responsibility can be earned.

At the other end of the continuum is the Missionary. The Missionary is the type of volunteer that most agencies hope for when an individual indicates he or she would like to help out. Someone who loves animals and has a commitment to volunteering may walk through the doors of the local humane society willing and able to serve the agency in any way possible, despite less sophisticated training programs, negative interactions with staff, and minimal recognition. The walk-in Missionary, however, is a rare type; most Missionaries are Cultivated.

SUMMARY

This chapter has focused on the retention of volunteers, highlighting the distinctions between ST and LT volunteers through application of theories on psychological contracts, personality, motives/reasons, and social/role identity. At one extreme is the volunteer who joins an agency with a specific, personal goal in mind. One of two things occurs—the volunteer quits over the realization that volunteering is not what they thought it would be or once the ST goal is obtained, they leave before developing a volunteer identity or an organizational identity and never plan on returning. This person has an egoistic orientation primarily motivated by personal gain; his or her relationship with the agency is transactional because it is based on a ST gain for each party. At the other extreme is the individual who dedicates his or her life to volunteering, entering the organization with a volunteer identity and strong beginnings for development of an organizational identity. They have an altruistic orientation, helping disposition, and are anticipating the development of a LT relation with an agency. Very little is likely to deter them from supporting the agency's cause. Between these two extremes are the Consultants. These persons enter an organization primarily for personal reasons, yet they intend on LT volunteering. They have a volunteer identity, but not yet an organizational identity. Agencies should focus their best influence and retention efforts with this latter type.

CHAPTER 4

STREAMLINING VOLUNTEER MANAGEMENT THROUGH INFORMATION AND COMMUNICATION TECHNOLOGIES

Valentina Mele

INTRODUCTION

This chapter seeks to understand how Information and Communication Technology (ICT) can be strategically used for managing volunteers in order to enhance the capabilities of voluntary organizations in pursuing their mission. If ICTs create opportunities, it is to be investigated (a) how voluntary organizations can innovate to exploit the opportunities, particularly in terms of volunteers management and service improvements and (b) which changes in the organization and management are necessary to achieve such ICT-enabled results.

In the relative scarcity of literature on ICTs impacts on volunteer management, the work is gap filling in nature. It is intended to contribute to the knowledge of the effects of innovation, technological innovation

Challenges in Volunteer Management, pp. 69–89
Copyright © 2008 by Information Age Publishing

69

particularly, on "the organizational black box of voluntary sector organizations" (Burt & Taylor, 2004, p. 287). Considering that "despite them being possibly the most significant technologies available to contemporary organizations, surprisingly little is known about the ways in which ICTs are shaping, and being reshaped by, voluntary organizations—and to what effect" (Burt & Taylor, 2003, p. 116). The literature scarceness mirrors the field shortage, as recent major surveys have found consistently low levels of uptake on ICTs and of strategic capability in their use throughout the sector, even among large and well-established International nonprofits.[1] Thereby, it seems that an exploratory work on the possibilities that ICTs offer to volunteer management could contribute to a field of studies that, while promising, is still underdeveloped

After reviewing the literature on ICTs impact on nonprofits and the voluntary sector, and discussing the choice of an instrumental case study to address the research questions, this chapter analyses the experience of Sidelines. Founded in 1991, Sidelines is a U.S. nonprofit which helps sustain women with high-risk pregnancy. It was the first nonprofit to provide support to patients via e-mail and was the prototype for many organizations that followed its lead. The case of Sidelines is investigated in order to contribute to the practitioners' debate about the role of new technologies in shaping the organizational structure and in fuelling organizational change. The use of ICTs for increasing the organization effectiveness is also investigated.

My analysis of Sidelines' experience encompasses two main phases. The first phase (1991-2001) witnesses the evolution of Sidelines from its foundation to the development of a nation-wide 30-chapters nonprofit heavily relying on the telephone and Internet to accomplish its mission. The second phase (2001-2005) shows the ICT-enabled restructuring of the organization. By establishing a centralized toll-free number and reshaping the organization, Sidelines has shifted the matching of volunteers and patients from an approach based on location to an approach based on the types of complications in high risk pregnancy. Online support has become more in demand than the phone support and the weekly online chats have become extremely popular. These changes have enabled Sidelines to serve more patients and to match them with the volunteers more efficiently and rapidly. These changes, on the other hand, have been burdensome since they have challenged the organizational and cultural status quo, making redundant local chapter coordinators and leading to the centralization of the managerial functions. This choice disconfirms much of the conventional wisdom on voluntary organizations willingness to preserve values-driven organizational arrangements even at the cost of missing efficiency and effectiveness opportunities.

The final remarks address the theoretical issue of ICTs impacts on volunteers' motivation, challenging the claim that volunteering declines as a country becomes a knowledge society. The ICT-enabled possibility to choose channel and timing of the voluntary activity might represent a decisive tool for revitalizing and encouraging the "vocation" of potentially interested individuals.

NEW TECHNOLOGIES AND VOLUNTARY SECTOR: AN OVERVIEW

The works investigating the impact of ICTs on voluntary organizations follow chronologically the wave of research on ICTs and private organizations (Castells, 2000; Orlikowsky, 1992) and ICTs and public administrations (Dunleavy & Margetts, 2000; Mele, 2005; Kamark & Nye, 2002; Norris, 2001; Snellen & van de Donk, 1998). They do not represent a well-integrated body of literature, and, more important for this chapter, are not explicitly focused on ICTs and volunteer management. Still, they offer a variety of methodological and conceptual frameworks, as well as empirical findings to drawn on. Mapping these works allows to identify and locate the specific contribution of this chapter in the stream of volunteer management literature.

A rather fertile literature started to investigate the links between new technologies and nonprofit sector in general, recognize the increasing adoption of ICTs by nonprofits (Johnson, 1998, 2001; Pargmegiani & Sachdeva, 2000; Wagner, 1999), and then questioning the effectiveness their usage by nonprofits (Cravens, 2000; Hall, 2001; Spencer, 2002).

On the economic theory side scholars have predicted the changing role of nonprofits in the network economy (Ben Ner, 2002; Te'eni & Young, 2003), claiming that the spread of ICTs is likely to erode the relative advantages of nonprofits, compared to businesses and government agencies, in providing services and public goods characterized by information asymmetry. At the same time these studies recognize that nonprofits might play the role of trusted intermediaries to "help people cope with a delude of complex information" (Te'eni & Young, 2003) in the network economy.

This chapter narrows the study of ICT strategic usage to volunteer management, which has a restricted definition compared with nonprofit management in general. While acknowledging scope and variability of volunteering as a concept among scholars[2] and across countries,[3] the work adopts the definition of Dekker and Halman (2003). This definition collapses the vast array of interpretations and perspectives into a set of four apparently unambiguous conditions: "volunteering or voluntary work is nonobligatory, is carried out (among other things) for the benefits of others: society as a whole or a specific organization; it is unpaid, and, somewhat less common, it takes place in an organized context" (Dekker & Halman, 2003, p. 1).

It should be specified that, while providing this definition, the authors are quite aware of the difficulty in drawing clear-cut lines between what is and what is not volunteering. For example, the requirement of producing "public good" (Wilson, 2000) or of the unconnectedness between the paid and unpaid work might exclude volunteers working for their own organization or their own group. Also, community service as an alternative for imprisonment or military service creates the oxymoron of coercive nonobligatory service. Furthermore, one could question whether voluntary includes the activity performed by students in order to obtain credits for their study and to gain the necessary experience to find a job, or performed by the long-term unemployed to be reintegrated into the labor market. Also, there is an even more subtle question about the nature of voluntary activities performed to avoid social exclusion and isolation, or to fulfill moral and religious obligation.

The requirement of being an unpaid worker is also disputable, as there seems to be a continuum among completely unpaid work, reimbursement of expenses, small material tributes of appreciation, acceptance of payments below the market honorarium and work not being undertaken primarily for financial gain. While this debate is of importance to the larger scholarly practitioner world, Sidelines is a case where ICTs and the Internet in particular affected the work of *completely unpaid volunteers* we need not be too caught up in these definitional debates.

A research area which significantly overlaps with the concerns of this chapter is the use of Internet and other ICTs for advocacy and policy related issues, variously labeled as "electronic advocacy" (McNutt, Rowland, Keaney, & Howard, 2002), "e-advocacy" (Bennett & Fielding, 1999), and "Netactivism" (Schwartz, 1996). The use of tools, which range from e-mail and discussion lists to advanced Web-based techniques, enable advocates to access, process and store data, educate and sensitize public opinion, mobilize constituencies and put policymakers under pressure through mass campaigns and online petitions. Though most of the literature on these practices is mainly oriented toward practitioners and has little or no methodological and empirical foundation, there is a promising research base that looks at the use and effectiveness of these methods in a variety of organizational settings. These settings include professional associations McNutt & Boland, 1999), environmental groups (Gilbert, 1999; Zelwietro, 1998), health care advocacy organizations (McNutt & Boland, 2000), and child advocacy organizations (McNutt et al., 2002).

A substantial contribution to those studies has been recently provided by the Brainard and Brinkerhoff (2004) writing on how information technology affects the forms and possibilities of voluntary efforts, enabling the emergence of grassroots organizations in cyberspace. Grassroots organizations are considered a subset of voluntary organizations. They are more specifically defined as "locally based groups working to improve and develop their own communities either through communitywide or specialized membership" (Fisher, 1993, p. 21),[4] and depending on "direct, in-person relationships" (Smith, 2000, p. 249).[5] Such features have been progressively reinforcing the common perception of grassroots as "small, informal and geographically based" (Brainard & Brinkerhoff, 2004, p. 34) organizations. The article builds on the work of Smith (1997, 1999, 2000) who first described the heterogeneity of voluntary organizations and identified a "dark matter" typically crowded by hardly visible, informally organized associations that are significant nonetheless. Through the conceptual framework of social constructivism, the authors distinguish between static Web sites and "sensemaking" (Weik, 1979, 1995) cyberorganization where people create and enact the organization by debating ideas, rules and values. The analysis of two concrete cases concludes that in a networked world, technologies permit the rise of large, global organizations with asynchronous, remote interaction, but which retain the highly personal communication character of grassroots. Last, the authors argue that "global changes and technological changes blur the demarcations between communities and categories, thereby facilitating the cyber grassroots organizations' ability to provide multiple benefits simultaneously to members and nonmembers" (Brainard & Brinkerhoff, 2004, p. 50), a phenomenon which, *mutatis mutandis*, can be observed also in the case of Sidelines.

More relevant to the concerns of this chapter, recent studies have explicitly examined the impact of ICT on volunteer management. Saidel and Cour (2003) investigated how ICTs have changed the nature and distribution of work and workplace relationship in the voluntary sector.[6] The research focused on ICT-driven changes on the workplace, in terms of transformation in jobs, migration of work tasks within working units, shift in the distribution of power and effects on job satisfaction. Nonetheless, the definition of volunteer workers according to Saidel and Cour (2003) definitively include paid workers. Thereby, only some of the findings are significant for the purpose of this chapter, namely the ones on satisfaction. Saidel and Cour's conclusions confirm early insights on managing work tasks from Kraemer and Danzinger (1990), which found computerization as having increased employees' sense of control over certain aspects of the job, including mastery over relevant information and improved communications.

Harrison, Murray, and MacGregor (2004), explore the factors that affect ICT use and effectiveness in the management of volunteer programs in Canada. Their research questions focus on what affects the amount and type of ICT used in Canadian volunteer management programs, and what affects managers' perceptions of volunteer resources effectiveness of these ICT applications. From the analysis, interesting conclusions emerge. Organizations that rely solely on volunteers tend to use ICTs in ways that meet the needs of volunteers but might fail to meet organizational demand. However, in contrast organizations that rely on professional managers for their volunteer programs may give priority to organizationally driven goals in their ICT implementation, failing to meet volunteers' needs. Also, managers of volunteer resources may want to rethink their work to ensure that they are making the most of what ICT has to offer. This holds even when using ICT to replace some of the traditional tasks that managers perform. The report, in this case, suggests that tasks could be divided between managers and volunteers, with managers focusing on developing ICT capability and infrastructure, for example, using Web sites to a greater degree, while volunteers perform volunteer-related tasks (Harrison, Murray, & MacGregor, 2004). This is evident in the Sidelines case. The authors also stress that in a time of rapid technological change, increased competition for scarce resources, and accountability demand from many stakeholders, some voluntary organizations are put at a disadvantage relative to organizations that have successfully adopted these tools of modern management.

Burt and Taylor (2003) addressed the issue of ICT-driven strategic change in volunteer organizations in a research note that drew evidence from two case studies conducted in the United Kingdom. Their insights are extremely pertinent to this work, which to some extent builds on Burt and Taylor's findings and tries to address some of the interrogatives left open by the authors for further research. Like Sidelines, the organizations selected are "universal service" providers. Their services are available to all who want to use them, regardless of geographic location, economic status or demographic profile. In the conclusion, the authors state that "universal service provision brings new imperatives toward centralization, standardization, and control for organizations seeking to manage their resources effectively, in conditions where there is intensive pressure on volunteers" (Burt & Taylor, 2003, p. 126) and this suggests analogies with Sidelines.

In both cases that Burt and Taylor (2003) analyzed, the nonprofit is organized in local branches. Internet-based technology in one experience and advanced networked telephony systems in the other challenge the historically discrete structure that is based on such atomistic local branches. By repositioning around the capabilities allowed by electronic networks, their strategic choices are delimited by the deep historical commitment to local autonomy, which prevents the ICT-enabled shift toward a more centralized regime. Thus, the organizations do not fully achieve the potential benefits of an integrated approach. Such holistic approaches would be very useful for tackling the societal problems these organizations are trying to solve and which increasingly need a multifaceted answer, involving many players and various approaches. In order to achieve these reforms, it is crucial to advance internal management systems, particularly in terms of significant resource economies and "quality control (on) the information and expertise on which reputation and credibility depend" (Burt & Taylor, 2003, p. 121).

There are significant similarities between Burt and Taylor's (2003) account of the two cases and the evidence from Sidelines. Pinpointing them might help identify which of the tensions that Sidelines has faced are common features among nonprofits adopting cutting-edge ICTs applications.

In one of their cases, by using Internet and Web technologies, local groups were increasingly able to share information, expertise and experiences with others. The knowledge was previously "isolated within each individual group," with few opportunities for regular or rapid knowledge cross-transfer. "By making information available centrally, data can be consolidated, trends can be identified and ... resources can be more effectively focused as a result" (Burt & Taylor, 2003). In the second case they analyze, the nonprofit organization was able to direct calls to networks of local chapters in ways that were not possible prior to the introduction of the toll-free number. However, for both experiences, the technological changes brought about the need to redesign the organizational structure. This ultimately raised fundamental questions about the continuation of core values such as the combination of personal local service and local autonomy. The following sentence, quoted from Burt and Taylor's account of the two U.K. cases, is perfectly tailored to depict the situation Sidelines had to confront:

> As the atomistic organization gives way to networked clusters at local and national levels, ... the high level of operational autonomy traditionally enjoyed by branches with regard to workload, services offered, and quality assurance is usurped in the interest of the movement as a whole. (p. 123)

There is, nonetheless, a crucial difference between these two cases and the experience of Sidelines. When facing the crossroad between a radical ICT-driven transformation and a milder adaptation of the status quo to new possibilities, the first organization interpreted the technologies by relying heavily on their previous arrangements and embedded values. It could be said that their evolution toward an ICT-enabled structure was pulled back by the existing cultural and organizational setting, as in both cases "the power of the ... founding vision and the institutional arrangements that have developed around this, make more radical solutions and alternatives to localism inconceivable at present time" (Burt & Taylor, 2003, p. 123). The second organization, instead, pushed through new ICT-enabled organizational configuration and management systems, as will be later discussed. Thereby, Sidelines represents an original context in which to study pioneering changes and answers this chapter's research questions, while also broadening the spectrum for the analysis suggested by Burt and Taylor (2003).

PROCESSUAL ANALYSIS AND CASE SELECTION

The chapter uses the conceptual lenses of institutionalism, and particularly of "processual institutionalism" an approach that is ascending. However, the approach is still relatively underdeveloped compared to other neo-institutionalist approaches, such as the cultural fringe that, so far, has been typically used for investigating organizational and managerial changes.

Cultural institutionalism states that institutional choices made when an institution is formed will have deep impacts on future decisions, and will heavily constrain the spectrum of alternatives that an institution selects (Steinmo, Thelen, & Longstreth, 1992). "Processual institutionalism," a recently coined label (Barzelay, 2003; Barzelay & Gallego, 2006), is an approach which seeks to attain a causal understanding of processes, including organizational decision making and organizational change, thereby fitting this chapter's research questions.[7]

Looking at Sidelines' experience entirely through the cultural perspective would have likely reinforced stereotypes about the possibilities of ICT-driven managerial changes in volunteer management. According to the cultural approach, nonprofit organizations with strong autonomous, local traditions would not alter their core values and organizational traditions to exploit the potential adoption of ICTs. Instead, analyzing the case from a "processual institutionalism" perspective captures the true dynamics of the change that took place at Sidelines. This approach also expands the knowledge about managing ICTs-driven innovation in nonprofits in general, and specifically when volunteers represent the core resource of the organization.

The distinctive research methods of institutional processualism are case studies with narrative explanations[8] where the particular case is an episode and the explanations often take the form of event turning points, trajectories, and outcomes (Abbott, 2001). This instrumental case-study, coherent with Stake's (1995) definition, has been designed as "a particular case examined to provide insight into an issue or refinement of theory … (where) the case … plays a supportive role, facilitating the understanding of something else" (Stake, 1995, p. 237).

As for the case selection, Sidelines was chosen as it provides "descriptive, exploratory" and, to some extent, "explanatory"[9] evidence of ICTs impact on volunteer management. First, it meets the case selection criteria since it is a nonprofit whose mission is entirely pursued by volunteers and is providing universal services to its beneficiaries—a feature which is proven to be crucial in accounting for ICT-enabled changes. Second, Sidelines is a pioneer in ensuring online support to its patients, which enabled them to experience the advantages and hindrances of new technologies because, since the start of the organization, volunteers have been flexible in the time and place of their activity. Third, the experience of Sidelines demonstrates cumbersome managerial and organizational adaptations that, ultimately, enable volunteers and patients to fully benefit from ICTs.

To sum up, nonprofits' ability to exploit ICT-enabled opportunities is considered, particularly through the cultural neo-institutionalist lenses, irreversibly bounded by its values and organizational arrangements. This chapter uses institutional processualism as the conceptual framework, case study as research method, and Sidelines as the experience: this mix is expected to shed light on the innovation process embraced by voluntary organizations to exploit ICTs opportunities. By doing so, it provides counterevidence to conventional wisdom in mainstream literature, telling the story of a nonprofit that did not leave the arena of deep ICTs-driven modifications which challenged the status quo. Instead, the organization altered its organizational and management practices.

The data collected for such a longitudinal analysis are primarily gathered through structured and semistructured interviews with Sidelines management and staff and, secondarily, assembled through documents and literature relevant to this research. An analysis of virtual devices to recruit, train, and gather volunteers, as well as the virtual spaces where volunteers and patients exchange experiences and opinions has also been conducted. The drafted case study report has been reviewed by the key informants.

General research design is divided up into the first phase (1991-2001) and the second phase (2001-2005), as summarized in the timeline of the ICT-driven organizational and managerial changes.

Table 4.1. Timeline of the ICT-Driven Organizational and Managerial Changes Experienced by Sidelines

Phase	Year	Main Events
First Phase	1991	Sidelines is founded to fill the gap in the assistance to high-risk pregnancy women. Early 30 local chapters are created throughout the United States. Volunteers and patients communicate via phone.
	1995	Internet is introduced as an additional channel for the patient/volunteer communication.
	1997	Internet usage grows and so do the online patient/volunteer e-mail communication. The first online chat is launched.
	1999	In order to deal with the growing number of online volunteers and patients, five group coordinators and one group coordinator floater are hired. They work at the central level and manage the entire Internet-only volunteers and patients data and matching. Local coordinators keep managing data and matching of telephone volunteers and patients.
Second Phase	2001	The 30 chapters throughout the country are closed out, and the management of all the phone support is turned to the central office, already in charge of managing the online support. A national toll-free number is established. Online and offline support management is unified at the central level. Volunteers and patients are matched only by complication, regardless of their location. Volunteer training is turned into an open and distance training, supported by restricted sections of the Web site.
	Today	As the population in general has greater access to the Internet and many hospitals are making wi-fi networks available to their patients, online support has become the core channel of the approximately 5.000 Sidelines volunteers. Online chats grow in attendance rate and frequency. The Internet has been crucial in attracting and informing prospect volunteers.

THE EXPERIENCE OF SIDELINES: FIRST ACT

Sidelines was founded in 1991 by two women, Candace Hurley and Laura Maurer[10] (who had both experienced high-risk pregnancies) realized that ad-hoc support for women with high-risk pregnancies was missing. Indeed, "no community-based association, nor national group, dealt with this crucial time."[11] The founders contacted hospitals and physicians throughout the country. Hurley and Maurer also got in touch with other women who had shared the experience of complicated and high-risk pregnancies. The founders involved these people in what became, after only 6 months from the germinal idea, a national nonprofit organization with 30 chapters across the United States.

Most of the patients and volunteers of Sidelines were women. However, there was a very small number of husbands, typically partners of high-risk mothers, who were also participating as beneficiaries or volunteers. Since the beginning, Sidelines was conceived as a telephone support group because most mothers were unable to commute or find transportation to the meetings.

Initially, the telephone was the only feasible remote communication device, but by 1995, Sidelines had launched a Web site and provided support online. The Internet was introduced primarily to increase contact with potential patients and volunteers and to decrease the enormous telephone costs. The shift to online participation was gradual, mirroring figures on Internet use during this time in the United States, because few patients/volunteers had computers and Internet access at that time. "Initially only 10-15 percent of volunteers and patients moved online ... we were doing it so early that many women just didn't know about it."[12]

In 1997 the ICT applications had a considerable increase, and the first online chat was launched. Management, matching, and monitoring of volunteer and patient data functioned in this phase according to two main systems. There was a central section that managed fundraising, recruiting and training for the Internet section. The Internet section was handled from 1997 until 1999 by Annie Douglas, the online coordinator. In this period, she handled all the matching; patients were not broken into groups by pregnancy complication. The online coordinator was responsible for e-mailing volunteers and records. The 30 local sections throughout the country were managing local telephone volunteers and patients. Telephone volunteers were matched with telephone patients by local medical complication criteria. They met as much as the limited geographical spectrum allowed.

Internet-only volunteers who wanted only to offer their help online were matched with virtual patients according to medical complications at the central level. They had to file the forms online and were trained via a Training packet from the central office. Initially, they communicated with the online coordinator at the central office via e-mail and later communicated with the group coordinators.

An example of communications from the central office was an "Action Alert." An "Action Alert" recruited volunteers to send letters, e-mails, or make phone calls to their congressman on behalf of legislation directly affecting the high risk pregnant women. One such alert was directed to the U.S. Food and Drug Administration, addressing a proposed ban on the use of a specific medication prescribed to stop preterm labor. Sidelines was successful in stopping the ban within 1 week. An additional example involved working to find volunteers for women with rare medical conditions. Before the merger, online volunteers were e-mailed with a request to support a patient with a rare complication. Those who replied would agree to support the patient by phone and report the outcome of the pregnancy to the local coordinator in the patient's area. As the number of Internet users increased throughout the country, the Internet became a strong tool of Sidelines in attracting volunteers and patients, as well as ensuring cheaper and more flexible contact between them.

By June of 1999, five group coordinators and one group coordinator floater were hired. The volunteers and patients were then broken into groups according to pregnancy complication. This system was further refined in 2000, with the addition of both volunteers listed solely in the separate state chapters and additional fields for more pregnancy complications and treatments.

However, the use of double sections on the central and local level generated some problems. For example, in a case where a patient was initially matched with an Internet volunteer, selection and checking were run at the central level while the matching was done by complication rather than by geographical proximity. Supposing the patient had to switch for any reason to the telephone support, she had to be rematched with a volunteer at the local level, as local offices only ran the telephone support selection and checking. This and similar occurrences were frequent, especially when wireless networks and laptops, at home or in the hospitals, were not so widely used. Moreover, the information was dispersed in the local databases. This generated some unnecessary passages, which was particularly cumbersome when information and data had to be provided quickly and precisely to actual and prospect donors. The so-called delivery information was previously available online for online-supported patients, but later needed to be retrieved from each local chapter for all the telephone-supported patients.

As the number of volunteers and patients increased, the possibilities offered by new ICTs and the expectations in terms of case and information management grew over time, causing the organizational arrangements of Sidelines to become inadequate. To give an idea of the organization's size, for the year 2000, Sidelines listed the total number of volunteers at 3,500. This included volunteers who provided support at the local level via phone and possibly e-mail volunteers as well. To staff and track the local managers was time-consuming and not always successful, in part due to the fact that many were telecommuting. The weak control mechanisms were leading to heterogeneity in the management of phone volunteers. Of more concern, these mechanisms led to unnecessary chapter work due to the lack of a central database and to the weak online database orientation of many chapter managers. Consequently, in June 2001 Sidelines was totally restructured.

The Experience of Sidelines: Second Act

The restructuring of Sidelines in 2001 determined the centralization of both the organizational structure and of the management systems by using ICTs. From a symmetric perspective, the restructuring determined the adoption of ICTs by centralizing the organizational structure and the management of volunteers and patients. These remarks do not fall in the realm of the chicken and egg questions, but rather acknowledge the reciprocal influences of volunteer organizations' evolution and ICTs' developments. Therefore, whichever perspective one wants to embrace, during 2001 deep changes occurred at Sidelines. After informing the local coordinators, all thirty chapters throughout the country were closed out and the management of the entire phone support was turned to the central office, which was already responsible for managing the online support.

Establishing a national toll-free number (888-447-4754 or HI-RISK4) made it possible. Since the national toll-free number has been launched, incoming patients in search of phone support have been recorded and matched with a volunteer no longer according to the geographical area, but rather by complication; the same criterion which was already in place for the online matching. The patients who were already receiving telephone support at the local level continued to receive the service until they delivered. A 6-month transition period allowed the organization to complete the local phone support service for women already in the system, as well as to complete the migration of patients/volunteers' data from the community chapters' databases to the central office database. The great majority of volunteers remained with Sidelines, with only a 10% rate of attrition.

Volunteer training was restructured. Before, all training was done in person and "packets" were used to teach the volunteers, including a checklist of items they had to read. "In the very early days of Sidelines, training was done by the state coordinator to a group of potential volunteers. It took one day. They followed along with the packets in this training."[13] After the direct training became too difficult, a videotape was created and sent to each volunteer in training for viewing. Following the video, the packets were updated and used to train volunteers. The big change occurred when more than 99% of the potential volunteers had Internet access, and after the elimination of the state chapters. Then, all of the outdated materials were substituted by revised ones and located in a password-only accessible area of the Sidelines Web site. The online access to training materials through this restricted Web site section reduced training costs by over 95%.[14]

Today, online training is done once a very detailed application is received, reviewed, and accepted. Potential volunteers are then given access to the materials where they can study at their own pace. Usually volunteers are given 2 months to complete the training. After a volunteer is trained, she/he can access an additional private area of the Sidelines Web site for volunteers only. The volunteer section of the Sidelines Web site has materials to refresh and reinforce what the volunteer has already learned.

Today, the reputation of the nonprofit and the multichannel approach seems to ensure a positive volunteer turnover. "We don't have to recruit, we get volunteers who are either doing an online search, are former patients, or read about us in news chapter and magazines,"[15] and the Internet has been crucial in attracting and informing prospect volunteers: "it plays a huge role as that's how they (volunteers) find us and learn what we do."[16] The attendance rate and frequency of online chats has grown through the years, and currently three chats are hosted by volunteers on a weekly basis, with an average of 15-20 chatters. Once per month specialty chats with volunteer obstetricians and/or authors who specialize in pregnancy are offered. The online communication with the volunteers does not rely on a proprietary Intranet, but has always been organized through a series of Yahoo groups that are closed and private. The online manager has the ownership to all of the groups, meaning she can access, change or delete them. The volunteer training coordinator has access, without modifying options, to all the groups, and each group coordinator manages his/her group.[17]

As the population in general has greater access to the Internet and many hospitals are making Wi-FI networks available to their patients, this reinforces the shift from telephone to Internet. In 2000, roughly 70% of the volunteers and patients were in contact via e-mail, and roughly 30% via telephone. Today, Sidelines provides 85 percent of its contacts by e-mail and 15% via phone. It should be added that the distinction has never been clear-cut, as volunteers often offer to do both online and telephone support. "By use of the Internet, we can allow a potential volunteer flexibility in their work and in their training. The training is available 24/7 and is updated as necessary to keep the material current as our nonprofit organization grows and changes."[18]

AN ANALYSIS OF THE SIDELINES EXPERIENCE

Considering the difficulties emerging from the original organization and management arrangements, on one hand, and the appealing options ICTs were opening on the other, Sidelines founders have faced a crossroad.

However, they have opted not to preserve the status-quo, as the conventional perspective on nonprofit would suggest. It is worth emphasizing that the turning point has not been a single event such as an external shock or an internal emergency, and the solution for the institution was not to adopt a specific application or technology. Rather, a careful design has led to a complete reorganization of the structure and of the internal functioning systems in order to maximize the possibilities. The central managers evaluated the opportunity costs of maintaining the original conditions when ICTs-enabled systems were potentially allowing far more efficient arrangements, and decided accordingly. Particularly restructuring the organization and management systems implied:

- Firing the local coordinators who had been independently running community offices[19] ("we needed to fire quite a few people and that was hard. But we knew it was for the best of the organization").[20]
- Reallocating responsibilities among the central staff, composed by three directors (executive director, administrative director, online director) and eight coordinators (one national online coordinator, one national intake coordinator, one group coordinator floater and five group coordinators divided by type of pregnancy complications).[21] Now all of the directors and coordinators work from home and outside accounting is employed in order not to overstaff the nonprofit.
- Moving to a main database to store all of the data on volunteers and patients, which is sorted according to the existing online criteria. This enables an effective matching by complication.
- Standardizing and streamlining all the procedures, particularly the delivery form in which local coordinators previously gathered the information from the volunteer and from the patient. This enables an extremely efficient collection of outcome information and the possibility to calculate statistics in real time. Attaining stats quickly and accurately, indeed, has proven to be a crucial tool for successful fundraising.
- Standardizing and improving the check and balance systems, both *in itinere* through an *ad hoc* extension within the toll-free telephone line, and *ex post* by randomly checking back patients satisfaction through an interview after the delivery. The "let us know" message is emphasized in all the communications between Sidelines staff and the patient, so that the latter can be easily re-matched, should any personal or practical problems arise in her contacts with the volunteer.

Updating the training program, now completely delivered online. It provides the volunteers with the tools they need to work with Sidelines, and they can train at their own pace and at any time they chose. Thanks to the new online system, the training costs have been cut by over 90%.

The overall perception of the changes Sidelines experienced according to the central staff is effectively captured by the comments of the online director:

> New technologies (e-mail, Internet, toll-free number, and database programs) have allowed us to use the system already in place to refine and better service the needs of our volunteers and our patients. It has cut costs for the organization, allows complete tracking of every patient/volunteer, and provides to every patient a system of feedback on the quality of services.[22]

She continued:

> This also allows us to train volunteers anywhere in the world potentially expanding our services to women who would otherwise not be able to have Sidelines support.[23]

The latter quotation sheds light on the ICT-enabled possibility to choose channel and timing of the voluntary activity. By addressing specific needs and attitudes, online volunteering might represent a decisive tool for revitalizing and encouraging the "vocation" of potentially interested individuals.

CONCLUSIONS

Two kinds of conclusions flow from the analysis of this case. The first, central set of conclusions have to do with the main research questions, namely (a) how can voluntary organizations innovate to exploit the opportunities offered by ICTs, particularly in terms of volunteers management and service improvements? and (b) which changes in the organization and management are necessary to achieve such ICT-enabled results?

As for the research question (a), traditionally the literature has been more concerned with the single act of innovation than with the organizational settings in which those acts take place. A number of authors, though, shifted the emphasis of innovation management studies to the organizational components and tools that an organization should develop to facilitate the innovation process.[24] Evidence from Sidelines fits these frameworks on how organizations systematically manage innovation.[25] Process needs existed within Sidelines and new technological knowledge emerged outside as a source of opportunity.[26] Sidelines' managers, then, have been diligently and persistently adopting such new knowledge since 1995, when the Internet was an emerging channel of uncertain success, because

> what innovation requires is hard, focused, purposeful work.... There is, of course, far more to entrepreneurship than systematic innovation ... in the established enterprises, the public service organization, and the new venture. But the very foundation of entrepreneurship—as a practice and as a discipline—is the practice of systematic innovation. (Drucker, 1985, p. 72)

As for research question (b), several changes in the organization and management were needed in order to achieve ICT-enabled results. At a first glance, Sidelines' reorganization was disruptive, while a closer look at the process sheds light on the adaptive nature of such changes rather then on the abrupt shift toward a centralized structure. Online volunteers were already recruited, trained, and managed online, as they were matched with the patients online, by complication. This method and rationale was effective for both volunteers and patients. The organization-wide adoption of the central managerial practices was less onerous than the local ones. Moreover, as a subsidiary effect, the retrieval of delivery information and outcome stats for the purpose of internal control and external accountability proved to be immediate and easy. Change implied the extension to the whole organization of methods and routines already in place for the online section.

This account of the evolutionary nature of the change process should not be taken at all as a *diminutio* of the remarkable consequences it generated. Sidelines fostered the challenges posed by Internet-based technology and advanced networked telephone systems to the autonomous local branches. By repositioning the capabilities allowed by electronic networks, their strategic choices were not delimited by commitment to local autonomy. Unlike the account from Burt and Taylor (2003), this experience shows that an ICT-enabled shift toward a more centralized regime resulted in more significant resource economies and "quality control (on) the information and expertise on which reputation and credibility depend" (p. 121).

The case seems to confirm the mutual influence between new technologies and autonomous change efforts in voluntary organizations, in the research stream of nonprofit organizations being shaped by, or rather shaping, ICTs (Mele, 2005; Orlikowsky, 1992).

Research and articles about ICT adoption in the private and public sector, indeed, typically endorse the leitmotif that organizational change is the *condicio sine qua non* for a successful adoption of ICTs by organizations.

While sharing this view, the contribution insists that it works also all the way around: ICTs cannot work without a proper organizational change, but, at the same time, they often provide the momentum and represent the catalyst for such change. This view of the reciprocal flow of action builds on the literature on the reciprocal influence between public sector autonomous reform and ICTs (Mele, 2005; Snellen & Van de Donk, 1998).

The last set of conclusions concerns the management of volunteers' motivation, and is intended to contribute to the lively debate on modernization and volunteering (Dekker & Halman, 2003; Inglehart, 2003; Salamon & Sokolowski, 2003). There is, indeed, a burgeoning social sciences literature "on the (assumed) decline of civic community, the crumbling of civil society, and the erosion of social capital" (Dekker & Halman, 2003, p. 1), and a claim that volunteering declines as a country becomes a knowledge society (Putnam, 1995, 2000). Some scholars challenge (Inglehart, 2003; Salamon & Sokolowsky, 2003) this view arguing that

> This is only part of the story and a second major dimension of cultural change—a shift from Survival values to Self-expression values, lined with the emergence of the knowledge society—is conducive to higher levels of activism in general, and volunteering in particular. (Inglehart, 2003, p. 57)

While agreeing with the view that volunteering is changing in nature rather than being eroded, this work affirms the need for both definition and mapping of volunteering, volunteering motivation and volunteering practices that include ICTs and their impacts. In the studies on volunteer definition, for example, some authors (Cnaan, Handy, & Wadsworth, 1996; Meijs et al., 2003) address the issue of divergent perception among the public of different countries regarding the definition of volunteering. Typically, the public perception of a volunteer is connected to the net costs incurred by the individual in the voluntary activity. The individual incurring higher net costs is likely to be perceived as more of a volunteer than someone with low net costs, defined as total costs minus total benefits to the volunteer. The costs include the time spent on volunteering, the effort involved, and the loss of income incurred. Considering "virtual volunteering," as experienced by Sidelines' members, could challenge or, at least, add complexities and facets to these dimensions, thereby increasing the understanding of current practices. Also, the inclusion of ICTs' impacts may clear up some perceived ambiguities and help assess possible trade-offs between "the decline of voluntary associations with intensive face-to-face contacts" (Dekker & Halman, 2003, p. 5) and new forms of volunteering.

Furthermore, surveys on volunteer motivation often include clusters of motivation based on the personality of individuals, while "an alternative explanation for pro-social behavior emphasizes the circumstances" (Dekker & Halman, 2003, p. 3): the basic idea being that people tend to do things because of where they are, not who they are. Within the latter category, ICTs-enabled interactions and distance communication could be explored as possible sources of motivation and thereby should be included in these kinds of surveys (Clary et al., 1998; Cnaan et al., 1996; Eliasoph, 2003; Pearce, 1993; Wilson, 2000).

Finally, ICT-enabled freedom and flexibility could also add depth to studies on the new generations and the need for organizational change in voluntary organizations (Wollebaek & Salle, 2003) as well as on postmodernized volunteers and individualized new volunteers (Hustinx, 2001), which "appear to be less interested in doing regular board work and prefer more specific goals and greater freedom" (Dekker & Halman, 2003, p. 8).

ACKNOWLEDGMENTS

The author would like to thank Candace Hurley and Nancy Veeneman, at Sidelines, for sharing their experience and Matthew Liao-Troth, Western Washington University, for his valuable insights and observations. This chapter is part of the research project "Impacts of ICTs on Nonprofit Organizations," conducted by the author and supported by the Public Administration Division at Bocconi School of Management.

NOTES

1. For a review of the surveys on ICT penetration and strategic use among voluntary organizations see Burt and Taylor's (2004) paragraph on The technological deficit, from "Voluntary Organizations in the UK: Repositioning Within the Information Polity?" (p. 296).

2. For a comprehensive review of the literature on, and the definitions of, volunteering, see Cnaan, Handy, and Wadsworth (1996). In their review they present a typology based on four dimensions, namely free will, the availability of tangible rewards, formal organization and proximity to the beneficiaries. The two latter dimensions are of chief relevance for this chapter, as they are deeply affected by ICTs in general, and the Internet in particular. Furthermore, their work suggests that the public perception of the term volunteer is the outcome of people's conception of the net-cost of any given volunteer situation, which they define as total costs minus total benefits to the volunteer.

3. Dekker and Halman (2003) pinpoint the difference between the German perspective of volunteering as an honorary work, to some extents synonym

of civic engagement necessary for the political community, and the Anglo-Saxon perspective of volunteering as "unpaid work in the sphere of charity and service for the community (which) sees politics and advocacy as somewhat exceptional cases" (p. 2). For an extended cross-country comparative analysis of volunteering, see also Meijs et al. (2003) and Hodgkinson (2003) in the same volume.

4. For a comprehensive review of the literature on, and the definitions of, volunteering, see Cnaan, Handy, and Wadsworth (1996). In their review they present a typology based on four dimensions, namely free will, the availability of tangible rewards, formal organization and proximity to the beneficiaries. The two latter dimensions are of chief relevance for this chapter, as they are deeply affected by ICTs in general, and the Internet in particular. Furthermore, their work suggests that the public perception of the term volunteer is the outcome of people's conception of the net-cost of any given volunteer situation, which they define as total costs minus total benefits to the volunteer.

5. The authors conducted semistructured interviews with 23 respondents in three nonprofits agencies with an extensive history of involvement in contracting relationships with multiple government bureaucracies.

6. Institutional processualism's preferred form of knowledge is a consistent and interesting body of historically grounded analytic generalizations (Abbott, 2001; McAdam, Tarrow, & Tilly, 2001; Ragin, 1987; Yin, 1993). The distinctive theoretical perspective of institutional processualism is the focus on flows of situated interaction, as well as on the subtle interplay between belief and action as experience unfolds. The institutional strand is especially attentive to how situated interaction is influenced by context, whether structural or temporal in kind.... Institutional processualism construes social reality and causality as stories (Barzelay & Gallego, 2006).

7. Narrative explanations typically attribute the analytically significant facts to flows of interaction among individual and collective actors. Such interactions take the shape of conjunctural combinations of influences, rather than being the mere sum of separate pressures exerted by single facts. Narrative explanations involve some degree of formalization of

In exploratory case studies, fieldwork, and data collection may be undertaken prior to definition of the research questions and hypotheses. This type of study has been considered as a prelude to some social research. However, the framework of the study must be created ahead of time. Pilot projects are very useful in determining the final protocols that will be used. Survey questions may be dropped or added based on the outcome of the pilot study.... Explanatory cases are suitable for doing causal studies. In very complex and multivariate cases, the analysis can make use of pattern-matching techniques.... Descriptive cases require that the investigator begin with a descriptive theory, or face the possibility that problems will occur during the project. (Tellis, 1997, p. 4)

8. Laura Maurer's role was subsequently taken on by Tracy Hoogenboom, due to Ms. Maurer's family circumstances.
9. Interview with Candace Hurley, February 8, 2005.
10. Interview with Candace Hurley, February 8, 2005.
11. Interview with Nancy Veeneman, February 10, 2005.
12. Training with an updated packet is still available if a volunteer does not have Internet access.
13. Interview with Candace Hurley, February 8, 2005.
14. Interview with Candace Hurley, February 8, 2005.
15. Interview with Nancy Veeman, April 26, 2005.
16. Interview with Nancy Veeman, April 26, 2005
17. The chapter leaders used to receive a small stipend, approximately a part-time work stipend, which would mainly cover the office expenses.
18. Interview with Candace Hurley, February 8, 2005.
19. The five groups divided by complication include "preterm labor" group, "incompetent cervix/cerclage" group, "placenta previa/PIH" group, "multiples" group and "all other complications" group.
20. Interview with Nancy Veeman, April 26, 2005.
21. Interview with Nancy Veeman, April 26, 2005
22. This is conjured up by titles such as "The Discipline of Innovation" (Drucker, 1985) or "Sustaining Innovation: Creating Nonprofit and Government Organisations that Innovate Naturally" (Light, 1998).
23. "The key to stimulate innovation lies in the mundane work of organisational change" (Light, 1998), and a shift from the innovation-event to the innovation-process is needed. According to Paul Light the organization innovativeness depends on four factors that ignite and sustain new ideas, and which, again, seem to match the Sidelines experience: external environment, leadership, internal structure, and managerial tools. In the case the external environment fuels the innovation, on the one hand since ICT opportunities are the driver of change, on the other because patients and volunteers are increasingly accustomed to communicate and transact online. The internal structure has been redesigned and centralized. Internal management systems such as volunteer management, volunteer training, volunteer/patient matching, information systems have been changed accordingly to ICTs enabled possibilities. A key role, finally, is played by our forth variable, the leadership. Managers are responsible for interpreting and selecting volunteers and patients needs, and, even more important, are in charge of transforming the single user-led innovation into an ordinary practice, by boosting the "learning organization" paradigm.
24. Drucker (1985), indeed, lists as areas of innovation opportunity within a company or industry: unexpected occurrences, incongruities, process needs, industry and market changes. As additional sources of opportunity which exist outside a company in its social and intellectual environment include: demographic changes, changes in perception, new knowledge.

CHAPTER 5

VOLUNTEER MANAGEMENT IN COMMUNITY CURRENCY SYSTEMS

An Examination of Time Banks

Bruce B. Clary

INTRODUCTION

How can volunteerism in society be increased? This question has been widely analyzed and debated within the context of developed democracies like the United States and many countries of the European Union, but also those faced with the initial challenges of creating a civil society. At the base of social capital, a widely discussed issue since Putnam's (1995) first article on the subject, are networks of individuals and groups, acting on a voluntary basis to help each other. By increasing volunteerism, it is argued, the stock of social capital is increased.

Over the last decade, community currency has been advocated as a way to increase this involvement. These are nonmonetary systems of exchange, like alternative currency schemes such as Time Banks, where

Challenges in Volunteer Management, pp. 91–120
Copyright © 2008 by Information Age Publishing

91

individuals earn credits for community service (see Boyle, 1999). These types of programs pose fundamentally different challenges for volunteer management. The key idea is to establish a process of reciprocity whereby an individual provides a service to another and, in turn, earns credits that can be used to obtain goods and/or services that he or she needs. The person who originally received the service has a debit, which is paid back in terms of performing a service for someone else. The ultimate goal of the Time Bank movement is to create social capital in the communities. As a theory of volunteerism, it is the application of a private sector concept, the market, to an activity more commonly associated with the nonprofit sector and to a lesser degree, government. As such, it represents an interesting study of organizational design that spans sectors and raises new issues of volunteer management, that of managing volunteers within a market system of noncurrency, service exchange.

Unlike the vast majority of programs, the volunteer defines what tasks he or she is willing to perform. Similarly, the recipient defines the needs that he or she has, without reference to eligibility or other types of criteria for participation. The management role of the organization is to facilitate these transactions, much like an exchange, whether it deals with stocks, animals or other commodities.

The term, volunteer, is not used to describe persons involved in Time Banks networks. Instead, they are described as "members" or "participants." This distinction flows from how Time Bank organizations view their role. They are set up to facilitate community-building through residents providing and receiving services, themselves. Time Banks emphasize they are not a bureaucracy providing services through a hierarchical structure of administration, where volunteers provide defined services with eligible clients being the recipients. The organizational model which they espouse is flat and horizontal. Time Banks staff and board members share responsibility with the community and its participants. For example, in the East End Exchange in Portland, Maine, a Kitchen Cabinet of ten individuals is responsible for basic policy and programming, but the actual decision on what services to provide and who is to receive them is made by the participants themselves.

In the Time Banks literature, the term "empowerment" is a central theme. The idea is that the community is helping and building, itself, through residents providing and using their own services. The role of Time Banks organizations is to facilitate this process. In this sense, its advocates see it as a part of the community, not a governmental bureaucracy or nonprofit organization providing services on a contract basis. There is also an emphasis on the importance of giving and receiving services. Traditional volunteer concepts are based on giving, not receiving. There may be a variety of reasons a person is willing to volunteer—altruism, skill-developing, commitment to social change—but these are relatively, intangible benefits. In contrast, in the Time Bank model, a person receives an hour's service credit for an hour of services that they provide. In this case, the reward is tangible and demonstrable. The idea is that exchanges of this type result in reciprocation and engenders trust, which leads to the development of networks of relationships within communities, the building block of social capital. It is on this point that Time Bank theory intersects with the social capital thinking of Putnam (1995).

While the concept of "co-dependency" is commonly cited in counseling literature as a major problem that has to be overcome, a goal for Time Bank systems is to foster such relationships through service exchanges. Advocates argue that when service exchanges are looked at from this perspective, it is inappropriate to think of the service provider as a volunteer. Rather, the individual is a participant in community-building. The person who is having his or her needs met is also a participant since they have the responsibility of acting in a provider role to meet the debits they accrue through services they receive. Hence, the community network that develops is a set of codependencies.

RESEARCH DESIGN

The paper examines the aspects of volunteer management as they pertain to this form of community currency. In developing these programs, staff has had to address a variety of issues that are quite different from the traditional volunteer program: earning credits, redeeming credits, removing account debits, personal expenses, and taxation. Others are traditional issues, such as what are volunteer responsibilities, legal liability, and quality control (see Brudney, 1990a).

Emphasis is given to both the differences from and similarities to other types of volunteer programs. In some respects, Time Banks have the same challenges as any other program: how to recruit volunteers, determine their suitability for a position through interviews, conducting background checks, providing supervision and recognition. At the same time, the service exchange between the provider and receiver is largely an independent activity. The Time Bank program provides a match between the services a person is willing to provide and the needs of other participants. However, the performance of that task, described in Time Banks literature as "coproduction," is almost solely a result of the interaction between the provider and consumer (see Cahn, 2004). Supervision is limited, but that is by design. A key value of Time Banks is empowerment, helping residents take responsibility for their own welfare, not just as individuals but also as members of a community. Recognition (of volunteers) is a common activity for most nonprofits, but, for Time Banks, it raises some difficult volunteer management problems. Is it appropriate to recognize the individual for his or her service time when the philosophy places equal emphasis upon reciprocation, both giving and receiving services? Can the recipient of services be ignored in terms of recognition for service to the organization? It is these considerations that frame the analysis of volunteer management in Time Banks.

The paper examines these specific areas of participant management as they relate to Time Banks and volunteerism in general.

Recruitment

Most nonprofit organizations recruit based on a match between their mission, the functions they perform and what individuals seek as volunteers. In this respect, Time Bank organizations are quite similar to other nonprofit organizations. They have a well-articulated philosophy, which serves to attract both individuals and organizations committed to community-building. Two topics will be examined within this context. The first is philosophy, what is the Time Bank mission and how have potential participants responded to it? A second focus is the interviewing of participants. How are participants interviewed in the Time Bank process, particularly since every person could bring a different skill or express a singular need? Further, how does the approach differ from the usual volunteer program since interviews are conducted not just with persons who are willing to perform services, but with the people who receive them as well?

Another topic related to recruiting is who actually participates in Time Banks. Given its dependence upon participants for both the definition of supply (of services) and demands (the needs they may have), who participates is an important determinant of the ability of the organization to address community problems and produce networks of residents who are willing to work together. The latter dimension directly relates to the production of social capital, a key element of Time Bank philosophy.

Task Definition

Services are neither standardized nor routine. What services are provided depend upon what individual participants can provide and what their needs are. In this setting, job descriptions are not applicable. Tasks are defined in terms of what individuals are willing to do and the needs of participants. What are the tasks that Time Bank participants perform? What is the range of services and with what frequency are they delivered?

Understanding this dimension is critical to understanding the coverage of Time Bank services relative to the problems that a community faces. Additionally, how do the tasks performed in Time Bank systems compare and contrast with services performed by more traditional human and social service agencies?

Administration

Three current administrative issues are examined. What issues of legal liability arise from Time Bank services? They differ in substantial respects from many volunteer organizations in that the number of services provided can, in theory, equal the number of participants. What type of legal questions might arise when services are individual, as opposed to organizationally-defined? This issue not only has legal implications, but also could significantly affect the cost of volunteer insurance the organization must pay.

A second administrative question is the type of management information system that Time Bank programs use. With each participant potentially representing a different service and the number of service needs also individually defined, how does the system keep track of the supply of services and service demands? A system, called TimeKeeper, is described which is designed to provide the management information system (MIS) data necessary for service exchanges to occur. How is a match made between a potential provider and receiver of services? Participants earn credits through the provision of services. When a service is received, a debit is incurred. How are these accounts maintained?

Given the Time Bank philosophy, the emphasis is on the "empowerment" of participants, not their supervision. Nevertheless, there are concerns about "quality control." How has this question been approached in Time Banks and what mechanisms have been developed to assess service quality? A survey approach is discussed and an example of such an assessment is presented.

Methodology

The paper is based on a number of different data sources. On-site research was conducted for two Time Bank programs. They are located in Portland, Maine (New England Time Banks) and Gloucester, United Kingdom (Fairshares). The time period is from 1998-2004. Research activities included document collection, interviews, focus groups, surveys of participants, and analysis of statistical information on services. Time Bank organizations use a database program known as "TimeKeeper" to track a variety of information on member exchanges. The program records transactions: service provided, producer and recipient, the number of credits earned and debits incurred. This database is a useful source of information on the type of tasks, which are performed in Time Bank systems. Additionally, publications and Web sites for various Time Bank programs were reviewed for information relevant to volunteer management.

RECRUITING FOR TIME BANK PARTICIPANTS

Generally, the recruitment of volunteers in a nonprofit organization is a relatively straight-forward process. There is position to be filled that requires certain qualifications. The position is advertised and an interview protocol developed. If necessary, training is provided. Most volunteer positions can be described in similar terms: title, purpose, responsibilities, qualifications, reporting relationships, time commitments and benefits to the volunteer (Ministry of Agriculture and Food, Province of Ontario Canada, 1996).

Recruiting for Time Bank participants is a very different process. At the core of volunteer recruiting in the typical nonprofit organization is the definition of the task to be performed. In Time Banks, this definition is not made by the organization and its staff, but the participants. Exchanges depend upon the willingness of a person to provide a service and the need an individual has for it. In the Time Bank literature, this process is referred to as "co-production" (Cahn, 2004). The role of the participant within Time Bank systems is highly individualized. The underlying concept is to empower people, letting them define the nature of the transaction.

The lack of defined volunteer opportunities has not proven to be a significant constraint on the recruitment of participants. Discussions with directors of programs indicate that up to 90% of recruitment is through word-of-mouth. The basic concept behind Time Banks is easily understood: giving and receiving services based on skills, abilities and needs. Another element that works in the favor of Time Bank recruiting is that the process of being a participant is straight-forward. Participants do not have to wait for training to become involved, they define what is expected of them and are interviewed if the task has special requirements. They can participate as soon as a match is found between their skills and the needs of other participants. If a person comes to a Time Bank program with a need, then this process begins when they have to perform a service to pay off the debit they incurred in receiving a service.

Problems do arise in communicating the Time Banks concept. Because many of the tasks are basic (e.g., child care, car washing, cooking, dog walking, gardening), potential recruits often view what they can do as relatively unimportant, not really contributing in a real sense to the community. Because of this perception, staffs often emphasize the concept of equality of participation (everyone has something to give and needs to meet) that underlies Time Banks. A participant receives an hour's worth of credit regardless of the nature of the service provided and the same holds true for debits incurred (Technical Assistance Resource Center of the Annie E. Casey Foundation and the Center for the Study of Social Policy, 2004, pp. 10-15).

Another recruitment roadblock is the reluctance among many individuals to redeem credits, especially if they have a middle class background. They simply do not feel comfortable accepting a service in return for what they view as helping someone and/or the community. Time Bank advocates argue that the service exchanges are not charity, but a way to get them to help one another and build better communities. They use the term, "co-dependency" to describe the relationship. The term is usually applied to dysfunctional living environments where the participants develop compulsive and, often destructive behaviors, to survive. Instead, within the Time Bank context, it means that a functional community is based upon its members depending upon each other. They argue nothing is wrong in receiving help from another; instead, it serves to strengthen the bonds among community's members. From a recruitment perspective, it might be more effective to use another term given its presently negative connotation. Reciprocation, a similar concept, could be employed. Already appearing throughout the Time Bank literature, this word lacks the negativity associated with codependency and has been popularized by Putnam in his writings on social capital (Putnam, 2000).

The problem of service credit redemption is evident in Time Bank accounts. It is not unusual for many balances to have a large excess of credits. An analysis of the first 6 months of the Fairshares program in 1999 revealed that a substantially greater number of credits than debits were earned by participants. In total, 221 service assignments were made. It was possible to compute the balance (credits relative to debits) of participants. Only one person had a zero balance. Seven persons had a negative balance and the large majority (82%) had a positive balance. Although interviews with Time Bank staff indicate that the problem of credit redemption is less (now in the 50% range), it still exists and serves as a potential constraint on people willing to become full participants in the system, providing and receiving services.

Like traditional volunteer programs, most people volunteer in Time Banks because they want to help someone, but survey data (from the

Fairshares program in the United Kingdom) indicate 25% join because they have specific needs to be met. A smaller number of participants join through referrals from other organizations. The need dimension is illustrated in a van program administered by the New England Time Banks. The program has two vans that it makes available to other nonprofit organizations on an exchange basis. The vans are used for moving when homeless persons enroll in subsidized housing. The vans collect donated furniture and other household goods. The time it takes for the move is treated as a debit for these individuals. They, in turn, provide services to other participants in the network. At this point, 10 previously homeless persons have enrolled through this arrangement.

Developing exchange relationships with other agencies, including governmental ones, has proven to be important in the United Kingdom. Unlike the Untied States, the national government has shown considerable interest in Time Banks as a way to expand the service delivery network. Giddens (1998), in his widely quoted book on the "third way" in politics, argues for a middle ground between state control and the deregulated market. Time Banks is often cited in the United Kingdom as such an example, leading, its advocates claim, to social democracy. For this reason, the Blair government has taken considerable interest in promoting this initiative. Its active community unit is supporting the development of 120 Time Banks by the end of 2003. The government has also stated that Time Bank credits will not be considered in the calculation of individual benefit entitlements.

Time Bank Philosophy and Recruitment

The key appeal of Time Banks lies in its concept of service reciprocity (Cahn & Rowe, 1995). As described earlier, it is a service exchange whereby an individual provides a service to another and, in turn, earns service credits, which can be used to obtain services that he or she needs. The person who originally received the service has a debt that, is paid back in terms of him or her performing a service for someone else. The ultimate goal of the Time Bank movement is to create social capital in the communities that participate. There are a variety of definitions of social capital, but the one that best captures the Time Bank concept is provided by Hall (1999). Social capital in a community is created through networks of interactions among residents that serve to increase their ability to respond to problems of collective concern. The trust and interdependence that underlie these networks is the social capital within the community and has been shown to be related to the attainment of positive social goods such as lower crime rates.

While it is not the purpose of this paper to test the proposition that Time Banks create social capital, the concept serves as an organizing principle for participant activity. Individuals provide and receive service; thus, a system of reciprocity is created, a form of community networking which lies at the base of social capital creation.

The way Fairshares defines its program reflects the reciprocity theme:

- Members list the services they can offer
- All agree to both give and receive services
- Everyone is interviewed and provides references
- Every hour giving help earns the giver one credit, a Fairshare
- Members "buy" the services they need with their credits
- The computer matches the task, the giver and the receiver
- Every transaction is recorded on a computer "time bank"
- Members receive a regular "bank" statement
- One hour credit regardless of the skills on offer
- Members can donate credits to friends or to the "credit pool"
- Everyone is seen as special with a contribution to make
- All activities maintain set standards of care and a code of ethics

In focus groups and interviews with participants, general knowledge of the Fairshares philosophy and how the organization operates was clearly evident. The concept of a community network is easy for people to understand and almost all consider the value of reciprocation to be important. The idea of service reciprocity is seen as based on common sense, people helping people in a way that reflects abilities and needs. When discussing Time Banks with participants, some of the elements of social capital were definitely evident in their understanding of the program. In this context, the commitment of Time Banks to social capital creation has figured in its ability to recruit participants.

Interviewing in the Recruitment Process

Time Bank programs do use intake forms to collect data on participants, be they providers or recipients. Central to the Time Bank philosophy is that a participant is a producer and receiver of services. This dimension distinguishes Time Banks from the usual program where volunteerism is providing services, not receiving them.

A major purpose of interviewing is to determine what organizational tasks are suitable for volunteers (Voluntary Action-Leeds, n.d.). Time

Banks is quite different in this respect. Participants indicate the tasks they are willing to perform and the services they need. The process is participant, not organization-driven. Therefore, it represents a substantial shift in the focus of interviews, from the needs of the organization to the potential contributions and needs of the participant. All volunteer organizations have to address volunteers' expectations about their role, but Time Banks is almost exclusively driven by that definition. Additionally, it is the organization's role to ascertain what client needs are, not whether they meet eligibility criteria.

In the typical nonprofit organization, an interview serves to communicate the agency mission and the roles that volunteers can play. With Time Banks, the discussion is far more philosophical. The concept of reciprocity (the participant as producer and recipient of service) forms the core of the interview. Emphasis is given to the idea that "everyone has value," resulting in almost all persons being accepted as participants, but legal checks may be necessary in the case of services like child and senior care.

Recruitment and Participant Background

A core element in the Time Dollars philosophy is to bring individuals into a meaningful role in their communities, particularly those whose labor is not valued in the market system (Cahn, 2004). Data from the Timekeeper Program, which tracks participants, allows comparisons to be made between the New England Time Banks and Fairshares in Gloucester, England. The variables are: age, gender, ethnicity, housing, and living group.

Age
Fairshares has more than three times as many persons over 65 than the New England Time Banks Program (26% compared to 8%). To some extent, this difference may reflect the impact of privatization of social services by the British government. In the United Kingdom, the density of nonprofits is much less than in the United States, especially the Northeast region, which has the highest number of nonprofits per capita (Independent Sector, 1999; Kendall & Knapp, 1996). This difference in the availability of nonprofit services may translate into more options in the United States for older persons in need of social services. Time Banks is an alternative, but the lower density of nonprofit agencies in the United Kingdom may make Time Banks a more significant option than in the United States. In this case, participants are involved because of their needs (the demand side of service production within Time Banks) rather than a desire to provide services to the community.

Gender

The participants in both programs are predominantly female, more than 70% in New England Time Banks and Fairshares. Further, many are fifty years or older, 33% in New England and 50% in Gloucester, which results in a larger number being either retired, widowed, or facing health problems. The age difference in female participants could simply be due to how the two regions differ in terms of basic demographic characteristics. However, as discussed within the context of age, there may be disparities across the countries in terms of the availability of social services that address the needs of this group. Again, Time Banks may be a more attractive option in the United Kingdom because of the structure and coverage of its social service system.

This finding underscores the importance of understanding context in terms of volunteer recruitment (i.e., participant within the Time Banks system). There may be general management principles that can guide the recruitment side of volunteer management. At the same time, what it means to volunteer may vary across cultures according to a variety of factors: traditions of volunteerism, the specific reasons for it, and options available for volunteering. Additionally, as the Time Banks example suggests, the overall availability of needed services may well affect the type and extent of volunteer activities. Answering this question is beyond the scope of this analysis, but the data does point to the importance of addressing service availability and how this could affect the success of recruitment efforts.

Ethnicity

Both of the programs in New England and Gloucester draw heavily from the Anglo population. Over 90% of the participants in both cases identify themselves as from this background. To some extent, this pattern can be expected from the demographics of the areas. The United States Census Bureau (2000) indicates that the city from which most of the New England Time Banks draws members is 93% White. In Gloucester, England where Fairshares is located, the proportion of Whites is over 90% as well (U.K. National Statistics, 2001).

The U.S. program indicates a potential to attract a variety of participants from different ethnic groups. Although the numbers are not large, individuals with Hispanic, African American, Native American, Asian, and African backgrounds are listed among the participants. Given the dominance of persons with White backgrounds in the Time Banks programs, a recruitment challenge is to attract individuals from different ethnic backgrounds. To a large extent, the high percentage of Anglos can be predicted from the primary catchment area for each program. At the same time, minority persons, particularly recent immigrants, are likely to be in need of the types of services that Time Banks provides as they face the challenges of living in a new cultural environment. Many do not have automobiles, for instance, so the transportation service that Time Banks provides can be very helpful for activities like shopping.

Housing

Persons in supported housing environments are likely candidates for participation in Time Banks programs. Typically, this type of housing is provided to seniors and individuals with mental health problems and physical disabilities.

However, only a small percentage of Time Bank clients in both programs (New England and Gloucester) are in supported housing, less than 3%. Yet, there are developing relationships between these programs and organizations serving these types of clients that suggest the potential for effective collaborations. For example, the New England program has worked with an agency (described earlier in the paper), the Preble Street Resource Center, to relocate previously homeless persons to subsidized housing through the provision of a van to help move donated furniture and other goods into the dwelling. Through receiving this service, the individual agrees to become a member of Time Banks. As such, he or she incurs service debit that must be repaid through Time Bank service. This service arrangement not only benefits the recipient in a material sense, but though community service, a positive working experience is provided through the necessity to repay the accrued debits.

Living Group

Over one-third of the participant in both programs live alone. Many of the services provided through Time Banks programs are necessary for everyday living that benefit from having multiple members of a household: childcare, grocery shopping, collecting and hauling yard debris, housekeeping, house-sitting, laundry, home repairs, gardening, and transportation. Time Banks aid persons who live alone by providing such services. For seniors and individuals with disabilities, the provision of such services may mean the difference between maintaining an independent living status and having to move into an institutional facility. The United Kingdom program has been particularly effective in recruiting persons within this broad group. Over a third of its participants lives alone and is 65 years of age are older. The figure is lower for the United States program, 15%. The difference may again reflect the fewer social service options available in the United Kingdom as the country moves from a relatively centralized provision of social services to more localized, and especially nonprofit delivery of services. Given the high density of nonprofits in the United States, especially in the New England region (Vita, 1997), other nonprofit agencies represent potential competitors to Time Banks in service delivery.

VOLUNTEER TASK DEFINITION

One of the unique aspects of Time Banks as an organization is that services are neither standardized nor routine. The choice of what the organization does is dependent upon what participants are willing to provide in services and what people consider their needs to be. In this setting, job descriptions are not applicable.

The term, volunteer, is not used to describe community residents involved in Time Bank networks. Instead, they are described as "members" or "participants." This distinction stems from how the organizations view their role. They are set up to facilitate community-building through residents providing and receiving services, themselves. Staff does not view themselves as a bureaucracy providing services. The organizational model, which they expose, is horizontal and flat with staff sharing responsibility with the community.

Types of Volunteer Service

Participant tasks in Time Banks are of two types. One is organizational where an agency participates in the service exchange process. The other is the traditional volunteer model where an individual provides services and, in the Time Bank model, is eligible to receive them as well. The alternative models of Time Bank participation are described below.

Organizational Participants

Time Bank programs are increasingly collaborating with other agencies. For these organizations, Time Bank participation expands their service networks and involves their clients and even their staffs in community service. Participation is seen as a way for clients to develop self-esteem and interpersonal skills and increase their employment marketability. For staff, it is a way to contribute to the community.

Fairshares divides organizational alliances into two types. In the first one, the "collective model," the entire staff of an organization joins. They earn credits in the traditional manner by providing hours of services through the Time Bank. However, instead of exchanging the credits for services to oneself, they are given to the organization to further its services to its clients.

The second model treats the organization as an "individual." It provides services through the Fairshares network in the same way that individual participants do. These services reflect what the organization does, such as distributing public announcements or the resources that it possesses (e.g., meeting space). Through the earned credits, volunteers are rewarded for their service and/or services are obtained by them volunteers through the Fairshares network.

There is also a "client-based model" within these organizations as well. The aforementioned working agreement between the New England Time Banks and the Preble Street Resource Center to aid persons in relocating to subsidized housing is an example. Individual clients of agencies become members of Time Banks. They receive services through their enrollment in the agency programs, and then provide service to pay off the deficits they incur.

Collaborations between Time Bank programs and other organizations is particularly evident in the United Kingdom. This model has proven to be an effective means to elicit volunteer involvement from paid staff within nonprofit, human service organizations. The Time Bank concept becomes part of the recognition process for employees in other organizations. Awards are given to individuals who participate outside their organization in Time Bank activities.

As the approach evolves in the United Kingdom, an important question will be the extent to which the process will become "organizational exchanges" in contrast to the individual ones that dominate today. The former dimension represents a form of collaboration or boundary spanning, widely recognized as a crucial attribute of nonprofit organization (nongovernmental organizations or NGO) effectiveness in today's voluntary sector (see Independent Sector, 1999). Time Banks in the United Kingdom could develop as a significant force in linking organizations in new and different ways, particularly in how they secure resources and utilize them.

Individual Participants

The traditional form of Time Bank participation is for community members to provide and receive services. As the system has evolved, the number of tasks performed has grown significantly. For the year 2004, 148 distinct services were provided by New England Time Banks. Each service can be categorized by the number of hours they were performed. A total of 7,651 hours were provided. In Table 5.1, the services, for which more than 100 hours were provided by participants, are listed. A total of 4,406 hours of service were associated with these 21 services. They make up 58% of the total service hours for the Time Bank program over the year (2004). Even though these services constitute just 15% of the total

**Table 5.1.   New England Time Bank,
More Than 100 Hours of Service Provided, 2004**

SERVICE (More than 100 hours)	Number (Percent) Of Hours
Healthcare services	645 (14.6%)
Clerical	621 (14.1%)
Truck rental	324 (7.4%)
Time bank taxi	308 (7.0%)
Gift certificate	224 (5.1%)
Computer assistance	213 (4.8%)
Purchased item	212 (4.8%)
Taste around the world	166 (3.8%)
Massage	165 (3.7%)
Time Bank help	160 (3.6%)
Workshops	153 (3.5%)
Storage space	139 (3.2%)
Cooking	136 (3.1%)
Aikido lessons	135 (3.1%)
Transportation	134 (3.0%)
Kitchen cabinet meeting	119 (2.6%)
Minor home repair	115 (2.5%)
Chiropractic health care	111 (2.5%)
Bulk mailing	111 (2.5%)
Food for meetings	108 (2.5%)
Monthly gathering	107 (2.4%)
Total	4,406 (100%)

services provided, they make up over one-half of the participant service hours.

This finding indicates that service provision, as measured by hours provided, is concentrated in a relatively small number of activities. Overtime, a management question that Time Bank staff has to ask is whether it is important to diversify the hours of service that the organization provides. A diversification strategy is a way to address more needs within the community; hence, increasing the coverage of Time Bank services. The problem with this type of approach is that it will be difficult to implement since the participants define what services they are willing to provide. To expand service coverage, it may be necessary for Time Banks to pursue a more active strategy for participant recruitment for specific kinds of services. This broadening of activity may be easier to achieve when working with other agencies (i.e., the "organizational participant" model) since they have a defined mission and specific service activities.

Across the 21 services, however, is considerable spread in terms of the hours devoted to activities. Only health care and clerical services constitute more than a double digit percent of the hours (14.6% and 14.1%, respectively). The other 19 services only range from 2.4% to 7.4%.

The overall pattern provision is for a small percentage of activities to constitute the majority of tasks. Within these services areas, there is considerable variability in the hours of service produced.

Data on service activity is also available from the North Cotsworld Time Bank (n.d.). The organization lists 118 services that have been performed by participants. They can be grouped into 14 categories. Most frequently listed are home chores (21%) and activities related to personal and skill development (20%). The other service category in double-digits is personal care and assistance (12%). Taken collectively, these three service areas comprise 53% of the activities that are offered through the Time Bank. Similar to the case in New England, given the concentration of service interest (for a service to be provided there must be a request for it), a planning question for Time Banks is the extent to which they should try to recruit participants with skills in these areas to meet the demand for services of this type.

The question of whether Time Bank programs should adopt recruiting strategies for participants who bring particular skills is an ideological one as well. Central to the philosophy of Time Banks is the concept that all participants have value and can bring some ability needed by others. To employ recruiting strategies for participants with certain backgrounds potentially conflicts with this mission. There may be an inherent tension between Time Banks pursing its core values and the responding to specific needs of communities. Both approaches may be compatible, but Time Banks, if they want to extend their service coverage in communities, may have to look at the demand side of service production and how to increase the supply of participants to meet it.

Despite this issue, Time Banks should not be viewed in the same as governmental agencies or other nonprofits in terms of service delivery. Public agencies are required by law and regulation to address certain social problems and there may be specific statutory requirements for program coverage and effectiveness. Social service agencies are usually formed to deal with a particular social problem. In contrast, the concept of Time Banks is directed at a much broader process, community-building. It is not a social service agency, but a facilitator of community relationships as defined by the group, itself. Given this perspective, volunteer recruitment is not designed to serve the organizations needs, but those of the participants. Volunteer recruitment is premised on a different concept so that efforts such as targeting volunteer recruitment efforts may be less applicable than often the case for the typical nonprofit agency with a focused mission and problem-focused services.

VOLUNTEER ADMINISTRATION

Time Banks present three major administrative issues beyond the recruitment of volunteers and the tasks they perform. One is the question of legal liability. This issue is increasingly important to nonprofits because of the growing litigious nature of society, especially in the United States. For Time Banks, there is the additional problem posed by the nature of the services it facilitates. In theory, the number of services provided can equal the number of participants. What legal issues arise from this process?

A second administrative question is the demands of information management within Time Banks systems. With each participant potentially representing a different service and the number of service needs also individually defined, how can the system keep track of the supply of services and demands for them? The MIS used by Time Banks is described.

Given the Time Bank philosophy, the emphasis is on the "empowerment" of participants, not their supervision. Nevertheless, there are concerns about "quality control." How has this question been approached in Time Banks and what mechanisms have been developed to assess service quality? A survey approach is discussed and an example of such an assessment is presented.

Legal Liability

Legal liability has increasingly become an issue within the nonprofit sector (Herman & Kronstadt, 2003). Given the high profile legal issues surrounding the operations of the International Red Cross and United Way of America, for example, more scrutiny is being paid to the nonprofit organization. For board of directors, recent events such as the Enron and other private sector cases have placed greater pressure on them for accountability. This legal attention has also focused on volunteers. Despite the efforts of many states in the United States to provide immunity for volunteers, there is a welter of different laws and interpretations that apply to liability faced by volunteers (DeWitt, 2004). In the United

Kingdom, similar questions of the legal responsibilities of volunteers have arisen (Hall, 1995).

Time Bank programs have taken steps to address the legal liabilities a participant may incur in the performance of his or her tasks. For example, the Fairshares program in the United Kingdom uses a multistage process to recruit participants. An assessment is done of all potential applicants in terms of their needs and skills. Where appropriate, reference checks are conducted. Since members may do an activity, like providing transportation for errands, in which their ability to do it effectively and safely is critical, a background check is conducted. Another example is child care where persons must be screened for a potential history of abuse. Insurance policies for particular services, like driving, may be taken out if there are specific liability issues associated with the activity.

A distinctive liability problem posed by Time Banks is the large number of tasks that can be performed by volunteers. For example, during the year 2004, participants in New England Time Bank performed 148 service tasks. The vast majority involved little or no risk to the producer or consumer of the service. Activities of this type included bicycle repair, car cleaning, clerical services, computer assistance, English tutoring, grocery shopping, laundry, and plant care. At the same time, some tasks pose substantial liability questions where there is the possibility of injury, either to the person who provides the service or receives it. Examples of these types of services are: acupuncture, aikido lessons, body treatments, carpentry, chiropractic health care, driving rental vehicles, sailing trips, and transportation. Interviews with staff indicated that liability coverage was becoming an increasingly important issue to the organization. Generally, nonprofit organizations that employ volunteers use them for a relatively small number of defined tasks. Time Banks represent a very different model with clearly a more complex set of liability questions associated with its activities.

In many areas of volunteer activity, there are no clear laws relating to volunteer liability. There may be even conflict between federal and state laws (in the case of the United States). Generally, the laws that leave volunteers immune to suit have limitations in the type of activities covered. In Maine (the location of the New England Time Bank), volunteers are immune unless there is intentional misconduct (Maine State Commission on Public Service, n.d.). However, the law does not apply to the operation of a motor vehicle or a vessel. Consequently, a number of activities may not fall under the blanket immunity provision. The organization does provide specific insurance for vehicle operation by volunteers so there is recognition of the need for insurance coverage for specific activities.

An additional complication for Time Bank participants is that they fall into the category of receiving compensation for the service activity. It is a nonmonetary form, but depending upon the state jurisdiction (in the United States), a participant may be subject to a differing interpretation of liability than that of a "pure" volunteer.

Management Information Systems for Volunteers

Although based on a simple concept of reciprocity, the Time Bank system poses substantial information technology demands. The skills of the participant must be recorded. Individual needs must be identified. A method to match provider skills and recipient requirements has to be devised. The credits earned by an individual and what he/she owe the system (services received) require counting.

Time Banks has developed a software program (TimeKeeper) that provides this type of information. The program was designed for the relational database program, Microsoft Access. The variables are:

1. Member background (age, gender, ethnicity, housing language, marital status, mobility, background checks, transportation)
2. Member services (those that the person can provide and needs)
3. Individual transactions (provider, receiver, service)
4. Time dollars (service credits earned and/or owned by participant)

The MIS is fairly comprehensive. For example, the Fairshares program in Gloucester, United Kingdom, addresses the factors that Bozeman and Bretschneider (1986) see as critical to the effective functioning of an information system:

1. SIZE of the organization
2. TIME FRAME it addresses
3. RESOURCES available to implement it
4. MATURITY of the organization

Size

The client network of Fairshares staff is potentially very large. The TimeKeeper system was specifically developed to track a large number of participants spread over different communities. Data can be reported in the aggregate (the Fairshares program) or for each of the individual community sites (e.g., Newert, Stonehouse) separately where Fairshares has small storefront centers.

Time Frame

Fairshares needs to input client data on a regular basis and have this information available promptly. On an average working day, there can be numerous requests for services (requiring a match between provider and recipient) and updated information on the credits earned. The TimeKeeper system has proven to be responsive to this task. It is easy for staff to access this information for individual participants and respond to other questions they have. For example:

- I can mow lawns, but I do not want to offer this service if others are providing it.
- I will have less of a chance to earn service credits if many people are willing to do the work.
- Are there service needs for which there are few providers? Maybe I can do this job.

TimeKeeper can easily respond to this query through a search on the keyword, lawn mowing, which will indicate the number of participants willing to provide this service and how many have actually earned credits.

Resources

The most important feature of TimeKeeper is that it was developed for a small organization where little staff and time are available for the maintenance of the database. Fairshares is an example. It took limited training to instruct staff in how to input data to the system and access the information. The software developer, the International Time Dollar Network, provides periodic notices of program changes to minimize operational problems. The present Time Bank LISTSERVE (for programs) disseminates updates, FAQs (frequently asked questions) and related information. Since many staff have limited understanding of a computer beyond the basics of operation, system support is critical to the full use of the TimeKeeper software.

Maturity

At this stage, most Time Bank organizations often have limited resources for administrative support, including data processing. It was extremely advantageous to Fairshares to be linked to the International Time Dollar Network, which developed and distributed the software. Without that support, an MIS system could not have been developed by the time that Fairshares began its volunteer operation.

The TimeKeeper System is an important component of the ability of Time Banks to run their service exchange program. Without it, programs would have substantial administrative problems tracking participants, especially an accounting of credits and debits and matching community resources and needs.

All volunteer system can benefit from MIS capabilities as a means to track volunteers, their activities and time commitment. Nevertheless, for Time Banks, every participant potentially can produce a unique service and the services that are requested can be equally diverse. It is probably not an overstatement to say that the functioning of the system depends entirely upon an MIS that can effectively track the web of service credits and debits produced by Time Banks.

Quality Control and Volunteer Activities

In a system such as Time Banks, where services are defined by the volunteers, quality control is an issue. How can the organization be assured that the performance of tasks is satisfactory from the perspective of the individual receiving it? Like any organization that relies on volunteers, another question is the satisfaction of the individual producing the service, whether he or she has had positive experiences to keep engaging in the activity.

"Co-production," is a widely discussed concept in economics (Kiser, 1984). It is based upon the proposition that the quality of a service highly depends upon the relationship between the service deliver and who receives the service. An example is a prescription for a medical patient. The doctor brings her or his expertise to bear in prescribing a medicine. However, for benefits to accrue, the patient has to be willing to follow the directions for taking the medication. Action is required on the part of both actors. Extending this concept to Time Banks, effectiveness depends upon what a volunteer does in a service delivery role, but also what a service recipient thinks and feels about the service and how it responds to his or her needs.

Encompassing both of these perspectives is necessary to determine how a service is delivered and whether it is effective or not and should it be continued. As a methodological approach to these questions, a survey can serve as a way to assess both the level of satisfaction of provider and consumer in Time Bank exchanges. Client surveys have been used for some time to evaluate the effectiveness of services (Monette, 1990). Provider (i.e., volunteer) surveys are employed as well.

Surveys provide the advantage of having the persons closest to the service exchange (provider-consumer) rate the activity. At the same time, they are subjective assessments, open to a wide variety of factors that might affect evaluations, many that may not directly result from the provision of the service, itself. Examples of such confounding factors are: whether the client personally likes the volunteer, if the need can realistically be met by the volunteer and is the task what the volunteer expected. Such problems are typical in survey research and have led to questions about bias in their administration (Wentland & Smith, 1993).

Even given these limitations, surveys are an obvious way to assess how the services that are provided through Time Banks. Programs have been experimenting with surveys as a form of service feedback, distributing them to both producers and consumers of services. An example of one such application is described below.

Provider Satisfaction

Beginning in June, 1999, surveys were administered to providers and receivers of services of the Fairshares program in Gloucester, England. These surveys were included as part of the assignment sheets for providers and recipients were mailed a survey to fill-in after a service was provided. Fairshares collected 92 provider surveys. A smaller number of receiver surveys were returned, 26. The likely reason for this difference in response rates is that persons who received services had to mail in a separate survey whereas providers did it as part of the assignment sheet they had to fill-out to receive Fairshares credits. Both surveys focused on attitudes to the service activity, including satisfaction with the process and willingness to do it again.

A total of 92 surveys were returned to the Fairshares office by providers of services. The results clearly show the positive attitude of providers toward their service experience. Over 90% said they were very or fairly satisfied with the assignment. A similar percentage thought their efforts had helped someone (84%) and were willing to provide the service again (91%). Only a small percentage (4%) said they had problems completing the work.

There are a variety of reasons why persons said they would provide the service again. The most frequent explanation (77%) was they felt their involvement made a contribution to their communities, a key Fairshares value. This finding agrees with research in the United States on reasons for volunteering. A variety of national surveys show that a desire to help others is the primary reason why an individual chooses to participate (Brudney, 1990a, pp. 66-72).

This attitude is critical in the development of community networks. Thinking that one can make a difference often leads to a willingness to engage in community problem solving, a factor at the base of social capital creation (Putnam, 1995). The perception is also reinforced by the enjoyment a person gets from working with others. This element is evident among Fairshares providers with 51% saying that interaction with others is a reason why they would perform the service again. Networks are most effective when individuals think they are making a contribution and like what they do. This example suggests that Time Bank involvement has the potential to create these prerequisites for social capital.

Earning Fairshares credits was important to 50% of the providers. Credits are the market analogy in the Fairshares system (Fung, 1995). In the Fairshares system, you may participate for a very tangible reason, to secure basic services for your well-being. Given the number of Fairshare providers who are motivated to earn credits, this factor certainly is important in the willingness to continue their activity. However, at the same time, making a contribution to the community is very important. Taken together, the two findings indicate that Fairshares has the capacity to respond to both sets of motivations, helping the community and personally benefiting from participating. The ability to respond to a variety of motivations is important for the long-term maintenance of any program using community volunteers (Anderson & Clary, 1987).

One reason a person would provide a service a second time is the skills he or she might obtain from the activity. This factor frequently motives volunteers in the United States. Among young people, in particular, volunteering is increasingly seen as a way to build a resume through skill development (Janey, Tuckwiller, & Lonnquist, 1991). In contrast, improving or learning a skill is cited by only 1% of the Fairshares participants. This figure is consistent with the Fairshares philosophy, which emphasizes community-building and individual empowerment, not developing skills. Nevertheless, many individuals who participate in Fairshares are unemployed and outside the market system in terms of the skills they possess. The Fairshares experience gives the opportunity to work with people, something that is transferable to the market system.

The responses on the provider survey are summarized in Table 5.2.

Recipient Satisfaction

Twenty-six participants returned surveys to Fairshares. Questions focused on the level of satisfaction with the service provided and evaluation of the process. The survey data appear in Table 5.3.

The service recipients were overwhelmingly positive in their assessment of Fairshares services. Almost three quarters (73%) said they were satisfied. An even larger number (89%) said they would request it again. Nearly two-thirds (65%) would recommend it to another person and 89% had talked to friends, neighbors and/or others about their Fairshares experience.

These findings are similar to the data on provider attitudes. Both groups are very satisfied with the service process and are willing to participate again. This willingness is the first step toward the development of reciprocity in the Fairshares system. Individuals are willing to provide services and others are willing to use them. Ultimately, reciprocity in Fairshares philosophy means that the same individuals provide and use services. Nonetheless, giving and receiving services in a community, even if

Table 5.2.   Fairshares Program Provider Survey

Question	Yes (Percent)
Personal satisfaction with the assignment (very or fairly satisfied)	94%
Individual thought they had helped an individual and/or organization	84%
Felt it was a job well-done	91%
Person would provide the service again	95%
(If yes) Reasons	
Improving or learning a skill	1%
Enjoy working with people	51%
Want to earn more Fair Shares credits	50%
Making a contribution to the community	77%
Problems in completing the work	4%
(If yes) Reason	
It was too complicated	0%
Finishing the task took longer than I thought it would	4%
I did not have the proper equipment	2%
The instructions on what I had to do were not clear	1%

different individuals are involved, is a form of reciprocity. If it occurs within the context of an ongoing community network, it is a form of social capital.

Another parallel between providers and receivers is their attitude toward their involvement. For both groups, making a contribution to the community is very important. Seventy-seven percent of the receivers said that receiving the service allowed them to participate in a "useful community program." The tangible gains from being able to redeem Fairshares credits is a motivation (listed by 42%), but not nearly as important as community participation.

CONCLUSION

Community currency has been advocated as a way to increase the participation of residents in their own communities. These are nonmonetary systems of exchange where individuals earn credits for community activities that can be redeemed for services that they need. These systems pose new and different questions for volunteer management. This paper focuses on one of these community currency systems, Time Banks, and how it has responded to those challenges.

Table 5.3.   Fairshares Program Recipient Survey

Question	Yes (Percent)
Satisfied with service received	73%
Service provided when you needed it	92%
Request service again	89%
Talked to others about service received	89%
Recommend service to another person	65%
Evaluation of service	
Positive	
Met my individual needs	85%
I like the person who did the work	81%
It allowed me to participate in a useful community program	77%
By receiving the service, I was able to redeem my Fair Shares credits	42%
Negative	
The work was not done well	4%
The person did not do what was supposed to be done	0%
It took too long to complete the job	12%
It was difficult for me to interact with the service provider	0%
The equipment needed for the work was not available	1%

Unlike most nonprofit service agencies, Time Bank volunteers define the scope of their responsibilities, what services they are willing to provide. Recipients identify their own needs without reference to eligibility criteria. The role of the Time Bank is to facilitate these transactions, matching services to needs.

The term, volunteer, is not used to describe persons involved in Time Banks networks. Instead, they are described as "members" or "participants." This definition is a function of the Time Banks mission: to facilitate community-building through empowerment, residents providing and receiving services, themselves.

The paper examined two programs, one in the United States (New England Time Banks) and another in the United Kingdom (Fairshares located in Gloucester). Three broad areas of volunteer management are examined: recruitment (the role of the Time Bank philosophy, the interview process, participant background), tasks (identification of tasks and types of services provided), and administrative issues (legal liability, management information systems for volunteers, quality control).

General conclusions from the analysis and areas of further program development and applied research are described below (in terms of the major research themes):

Recruitment

The lack of defined (by the organization) volunteer opportunities has not proven to be a significant constraint on the recruitment of participants. The basic concept behind Time Banks is easily understandable: giving and receiving services based on your skills, abilities and needs. Like traditional volunteer programs, most people volunteer in Time Banks because they want to help someone.

A topic for further research is the examination of alternative recruitment and marketing strategies that could serve to increase Time Bank membership. Word-of-mouth is an effective recruitment strategy and the one used most in Time Banks, but it is limited in the number of people who are exposed to the organization and what it does. Time Banks have made extensive use of Web sites to not only promote the approach, but also to support existing organizations in terms of materials aimed at recruiting. However, many new and developing Time Banks do not have the resources to use this information, such as funds to print flyers and brochures. Resources have remained an issue with Time Banks and greater success in recruitment will partially depend upon finding alternative means of support from governmental agencies and foundations (since it does not have a fee structure like many nonprofits that charge for services).

Background of Participants

Demographic characteristics of Time Bank participants indicate that the programs have been most successful in recruiting older women and persons living alone. Many of the services focus on the needs of these groups such as companionship and personal support, health care, home improvement, house chores, transportation and personal care and assistance. Neither the U.S. nor U.K. program has been particularly effective in recruiting members from minority and immigrant groups. There are an increasing number of persons with these backgrounds involved in Time Banks, but the numbers are still small. Both programs are in communities where the non-White population is limited, so they do not have a large pool of individuals from which to recruit.

One program question is whether there are lessons from other volunteer organizations about alternative strategies for member recruitment from ethnic and minority communities. For example, personal contact may work best in communities with traditionally rural social structures still intact. However, are there ways to work through cultural organizations to present the Time Bank idea and provide opportunities (both delivery and receipt of services)? The concept of service exchanges may have a different meaning in a cross-cultural context. The possibility that this idea could potentially have a negative impact upon recruiting from different cultural groups (e.g., certain immigrant groups viewing them as not reflecting their communal tradition) should be addressed as well.

Participant Tasks

Participant tasks in Time Banks are of two types. One is organizational, where an agency participates in the service exchange process. The other is the traditional volunteer model where an individual provides services and, in the Time Bank model, is eligible to receive them as well. Time Bank programs are increasingly collaborating with other agencies. For these organizations, Time Bank participation expands their service networks and involves their clients and even their staffs in community service. The traditional form of Time Bank participation is for community members to provide and receive services. As the system has evolved, the number of tasks performed has grown significantly.

The overall pattern for service provision is for a small percentage of activities to constitute the majority of tasks. Within these services areas, there is considerable variability in the hours of service produced. Given the concentration of service interest (for a service to be provided there must be a request for it), a recruiting question for Time Banks is the extent to which it should try and recruit participants with skills in these areas to meet the demand for services of this type.

Although some discussion appeared in the paper on the comparison between Time Bank services and those provided by conventional nonprofit agencies, this relationship could benefit from further analysis. The effectiveness of a participant-based system, such as Time Banks, It is an important question to understand from a program evaluation perspective. An important issue in program evaluation of services is the question of coverage and bias (Rossi & Freeman, 1989, pp. 182-184). Coverage refers to the extent that a target population participates at the level expected by a program. Bias is the degree to which subgroups of that population are differentially served.

The Time Banks programs examined in this research provided a wide variety of health-related services. These services were addressing the needs of the persons receiving them, but what is the degree of coverage provided by these services? What portion of the persons at-risk or at-need are actually benefiting? Is there bias against some subgroups? For example, could individuals with transportation might differentially benefit from a service because of their greater access to it.

Time Banks are not social service agencies in that they operate on a contract and fee basis with certain performance requirements so this question is not directly relevant to their functioning. In the United Kingdom, Time Banks do have contracts to work with government agencies to provide services to a specific target group, but such relationships represent a relatively small number of tasks performed by Time Bank participants. At the same time, if the Time Bank approach is to be effective in meeting community needs, coverage and bias are appropriate question to ask about the service delivery process. Assessments of Time Bank services that employs such concepts could serve to provide a more detailed understanding of its impacts and the ways in which in which it might be managed to increase the effectiveness of its volunteer (i.e., participant) system (see Clary, 1999).

Legal Liability

A particular liability problem posed by Time Banks is the large number of tasks that can be performed by volunteers. For example, during the year 2004, participants in New England Time Bank performed 148 service tasks. An interesting topic for legal research on volunteerism is how a system like Time Banks can respond to the liability issues attendant with its activities. The key issue is that the number of services, which are provided, can equal the number of participants. Where such a diverse set of activities exist, can it be assumed that the general state (United States) and U.K. statutes regarding volunteer immunity still apply, particularly where supervision of service provision, by design, are minimal. Time Bank programs are addressing this issue, but a more general legal treatment of the topic would extend understanding of the volunteer concept and its relationship to the law.

Management Information Systems

An MIS (TimeKeeper) is an important component of the ability of Time Banks to run their service exchange program. Without it, programs would have substantial administrative problems tracking participants, especially an accounting of credits and debits and matching community resources and needs.

The TimeKeeper system is a case study of where an information system has appeared to work quite effectively. Much of the literature on the organizations and their use of MIS is replete with examples of problems with implementation (see Riley, 1996). Time Banks provides an exception to these generalizations within the context of the nonprofit sector.

Quality Control

In a system such as Time Banks, where services are defined by the volunteers, quality control is an issue. Surveys are an obvious way to assess how services are provided through Time Banks. Programs have been experimenting with surveys as a form of service feedback, distributing them to both producers and consumers of services. Both groups are very satisfied with the service process and are willing to participate again. This willingness is the first step toward the development of reciprocity in the Fairshares system. If this process results in an ongoing community network, it is a form of social capital. Underscoring the link between Time Bank involvement and social capital creation is the attitude of providers and receivers to their involvement. Contributing to the community is a very important factor to them (stated by more than three-quarters of each group).

The measurement of quality control in service delivery through surveys always encounters problems of validity. The subjectivity of the persons making judgments about the services is a potential source of bias. Ideally, other methods of service assessment, such as gains in outcomes levels based on record or other sources of nonsurvey data should be employed (see Rossi & Freeman, 1989, pp. 244-247). Future thought should be given to how such measures can be developed. For Time Banks, where the number of services can be in the hundreds due to the nature of its volunteer system, it may be technically impossible to use service-specific measures. However, efforts could be made to target certain services, such as those related to health care for which there is a tradition of outcome measurement. Nevertheless, given the likely reliance that Time Banks will have upon surveys, it is important that thought be given by organizations to effective ways to disseminate, collect and analyze them. This problem is especially important for surveys targeted at service recipients. As this research indicated, they had a much lower response rate than providers of services.

Time Banks provide an interesting contrast to the process of volunteer management usually seen in the nonprofit sector. The participant (the volunteer in the usual organizational context) drives the process, not the requirements of the organization that utilizes them. If the Time Bank movement grows, as it has shown the capacity to do, the kind of questions it raises will become more important to the field of volunteer management.

SECTION II

THE CONTEXT OF VOLUNTEER MANAGEMENT

INTRODUCTION

Matthew Liao-Troth

In this second section of the book, we are addressing what are the unique contexts of volunteer management. For example, we know that 65.2% of the volunteer work performed in the 12 months leading up to March 1999 in the United States was within nonprofit organizations (Weitzman, Jalandoni, Lampkin, & Pollack, 2002, p. 80). But additional 9.8% was in the private, for-profit business sector, and another 20.2% was in the public sector. The unique characteristics of volunteers in these different sectors of the economy is rarely addressed (see Brudney, 1990a, for a notable exception), but it is anticipated that there with be more of these "emerging areas" of volunteering in the future (Brudney, 2005). For a manager of volunteers, it is important to know what is unique about the context of the volunteers when applying the generalizable knowledge that has been accumulated. For this reason we looked to some specific areas where the management practices of volunteers may be more idiosyncratic.

What is considered one of the best, if not the best, books on volunteer management in its exploration of context was Jeffrey Brudney's (1990a) book on volunteer management in the public sector. We learned that although the degree of formalization in a public agency may be high, and may be similar to the high level of formalization found in some nonprofit organizations, there are specific public sector concerns in terms of volunteer management that are not necessarily present in nonprofit organizations. The second section of our book addresses the context of volunteering due to such idiosyncratic issues as organization sector and national culture.

For example, we know that context impacts the demographic mix of the volunteers. Recent research on demographic issues can be found in

Richard Sundeen and Sally Raskoff's (2000) work that identified what makes the recruitment and management of teenage volunteers unique, and Rosemary Leonard, Jenny Onyx, and Helen Hayward-Brown's (2004) study that looked at the unique issues of all-women volunteer groups and the management styles that work and those that do not with these groups. Others have focused on the public policy implications of providing public services with volunteers (see Susan Chambré, 1989; and Jeffrey Brudney, 1990a). Smith and Lipsky (1993) addressed the greater concern of outsourcing public service. Jeffrey Brudney and Edward Kellough (2000) did an overview of volunteer use, and Sarah Jane Rehnborg (2005) looked at national public volunteering.

Organizational Models for Emerging Volunteers in State Government (Sarah Jane Rehnborg & Thomas McVey)

In this chapter Sarah Jane Rehnborg and Thomas McVey advance the contextual approach in its in-depth exploration how Texas came to understand the breadth of public volunteering in its state. Their chapter clearly demonstrates that public volunteering is not monolithic—volunteer management issues depend on the organization.

In this chapter, the authors find that existing models of volunteer management are not rich enough to cover the breadth of volunteer management systems used by Texas, such as the "adopt-a-highway" program and various iterations that was started in Texas and has flourished in many states. Rehnborg and McVey also find that within a state government system, there are competing benefits to a more structured system (retention of volunteers within the structure) and a less structured system (retention of volunteer programs across policy and budgetary cycles) that is not necessarily evident in other sectors.

Challenges of Volunteer Management in Kazakhstan (Tamara Nezhina, Jeffrey Brudney, & Aigerim Ibrayeva)

Volunteer Management in Polish NGOs: Challenges of Formalization (Angela Bies & Stephanie Curs)

When looking at national culture Jeremy Kendall, Melmut Anheier, and Martin Potůček (2000) argue that it is important to look at the issues of the third sector outside of the West for two reasons: the meaning of civil society and the nature of the third sector vary from country to country.

John Hailey and Rick James (2004) further elaborate that the managers of international nonprofits need to understand the contextual relevance of their leadership practices. Following in this same vein, Marvin Nowicki (2000) examines the variation in the legal underpinnings of the nonprofit sector.

Tamara Nezhina, Jeffrey Brudney, and Aigerim Ibrayeva's chapter on volunteer management in Kazakhstan is an extension of these calls for research in a non-Western setting. They examine the volunteer management practices found in Kazakhstan, similar to the contribution in the first chapter of this volume by Hager and Brudney, and demonstrate that what is common practice in Kazakhstan is not common practice in the United States. Their chapter is also relevant to additional work by Jeffrey Brudney and Tamara Nezhina (2005) in identifying *effective* volunteer management practices. The chapter in this volume serves as the linking pin among these various works.

With respect to central Europe, Angela Bies, and Stephanie Curs look at the challenges of volunteer management in Poland. In their chapter they bring us back to the earlier discussion of formalization. Instead of looking at it in the normative sense, or one culturally bound by U.S. research, they address formalization in terms of mediating the effectiveness of volunteer management in Poland. Their results enable us to extend and generalize earlier work and demonstrate how formalization manifests itself in different ways in different contexts. Their study supports Éva Kuti's (1999) supposition that countries with transitional economies are at different "crossroads," and Joanna Regulska's (1999) claim that nonprofit organizations and volunteerism are impacted by the state's political ideology. Bies and Curs' work can even be seen to support Wojciech Sokolowski's (2000) model of social proximity and occupational interests. In some ways, both contexts present similar histories: both were Soviet states that had radical economic and political change in the late 1980s and early 1990s. In both countries, nonprofit organizations and volunteerism were not cultural norms under the former systems. In their chapter on Kazakhstan, Nezhina, Brudney, and Ibrayeva present an overview of the management practices across many different types of organizations, and find some commonalities with respect to size, management training and focus of the non-governmental organizations that are not necessarily consistent with other national contexts.

Unlike most Soviet states, Poland had a thriving church and geographic proximity and history with other European countries that led to the quick formation of a nongovernmental organization sector. However volunteerism is more suspect than in the European context due to the "hazard of newness"—it is a new concept for those that grew up under the

Soviet system. Bies and Curs review how volunteer managers deal with this cultural challenge.

Fine Lines: Design and Implementation Challenges in Employee Volunteer Programs (Mary Tschirhart & Lyndia St. Claire)

While we have looked at the context of the public sector and international nonprofit sector, there are also advances to be made in the context of the business world. Mary Tschirhart (2005) has previously examined the issue of corporate volunteering from a macro perspective in terms of the general trends, but in this chapter she has co-authored with Lyndia St. Claire, both researchers explore the nuts and bolts of how corporate volunteering is actually done. Academics will enjoy the rich data presented in two case studies, and practitioners will find use in two models describing how corporate volunteer systems can work. Drawing from two case studies, the authors argue that fine lines exist in the areas of encouragement of employee participation, recognition of participants, use of the employee volunteer program to enhance organizational image, and flexibility in program activities. Employees express concerns about the appropriate level and type of policies and practices in each of these four areas. However, they may disagree or be unsure about where these lines should be drawn and how to avoid crossing them. This creates challenges in designing and managing employee volunteer programs to achieve desired benefits for employees, employers, and communities served.

Fraternal Involvement in Volunteering: The Membership Impact of Join Hands Day (Robert Christensen & James Perry)

Finally, an issue of context rarely addressed is the divide between service organizations and member organizations in the independent sector. In Meijs and Ten Hoorn's earlier chapter, we treated this topic as an organizational design issue. However legal requirements in the United States (e.g., IRS 501c versus 501d status of nonprofit organizations) also impact these organizations in different ways. Joan Wharf Higgins and Ashley Hodgins (forthcoming) looked at nonprofit organizations' use of social marketing tools to recruit recurring participants in volunteer activities to benefit the organization. To follow up on this work in this volume, Robert Christensen and James Perry's chapter offers an interesting case study of voluntary associations engaging in external volunteering to recruit members. The overlap of the human resources issues and social marketing issues in their study permits a fruitful discussion between these two disciplinary approaches to a similar problem.

This final chapter by Christensen and Perry also can be considered an extension of the Tschirhart and St. Claire chapter that addressed the implementation of an employee volunteer program. In this final chapter, the authors explore the impact that a volunteer program has on the organization. They look at the unique issue of membership-benefit organizations—a type of nonprofit in the United States—organizing volunteers for Join Hands Day. From a strategic viewpoint, such organizations would hope this type of endeavor would positively impact both retention and recruitment. The authors find some evidence to support this purpose.

The challenge in looking at volunteer management is recognizing where insights can be gleaned, from both the usual and unexpected. I hope that this volume accomplishes our objective of sharing insights that build upon prior works in the field, and advances us to the next level of understanding. Among the original quantitative research, case studies, and thoughts on the nature of volunteer management, these chapters reflect and build on the development of the field of volunteer management over the last two decades, and we hope it will become a new "foundation" for the future in its own right.

CHAPTER 6

ORGANIZATIONAL MODELS FOR ENGAGING VOLUNTEERS IN STATE GOVERNMENT

Sarah Jane Rehnborg and Tom McVey

INTRODUCTION

Voluntary citizen participation is a central characteristic of the nonprofit sector (Frumkin, 2004; Salamon, 1999). While the history of the United States is replete with tales of barn raising, and associational life celebrated by DeTocqueville's commentary of *Democracy in America*, the critical work of volunteers within the public sector receives little to no attention in texts of public administration. Nonetheless, public sector volunteer involvement is tracked to a certain extent. The International City/County Management Association tracks volunteer engagement as an alternative approach to service delivery. For more than 20 years the Arkansas Department of Human Services has been enumerating volunteer involvement in public schools as well as state and federal governmental agencies on a biannual basis, and a handful of researchers periodically examine the volunteer involvement in the public sector (Brown, 1999; Brudney, 1990a; Brudney & Kellogg, 2000; Musick, 2005; Rehnborg, Fallon, & Hinerfeld, 2002).

Challenges in Volunteer Management, pp. 129–150
Copyright © 2008 by Information Age Publishing
All rights of reproduction in any form reserved.

Leading political figures and organizations draw attention to volunteerism and public sector service as well. The call to service through the Peace Corps is a cornerstone of the Kennedy legacy just as AmeriCorps served as a signature of the Clinton years. George H. W. Bush spurred volunteerism with his Freedom Corps and the challenge that all Americans serve 2,000 hours over their lifetime. During the Bush administration, the Bureau of Labor Statistics initiated a supplemental census survey tracking volunteerism on a national scale. In addition, the United Nations celebrated the International Year of Volunteers in 2001. As the commemorative year drew to a close, the world body spoke of the need for governments to support service through solid legal frameworks and encouraged governmental bodies to develop strategies to promote and facilitate volunteer efforts (United Nations Volunteers, 2001).

Concurrent with the national and international attention afforded volunteerism was the growing attention given to the subject within Texas state government. In January 1993, John Sharp, then Texas Comptroller of Public Accounts, published a report within the Texas Performance Review calling for increased involvement of volunteers in Texas state government. The report stressed that volunteers offer a highly potent means to limit the size yet increase the effectiveness of state government. The report went on to call for state government action that would more effectively channel volunteer resources and citizen participation (Comptroller of Public Accounts, 1993). Eight months later, in September 1993, the Texas Senate Research Center (1993) conducted a study on the level and impact of volunteer involvement in select state agencies during the 1992 state fiscal year. One purpose of the report was to document the value and cost-effective service volunteers provide for the state. The report notes that, "The state would have to appropriate funds to provide at least some of these services if volunteers were not available" (p. v). The report continued by documenting specific examples of services provided by volunteers that are federally or court mandated and would result in an increased expense to the state if volunteers were not actively involved (Texas Senate Research Center, 1993).

Ten years later, in 2003, a modified parallel study examined volunteer involvement in Texas state government. This study, prepared for the Texas Commission on Volunteerism and Community Service by the RGK Center for Philanthropy and Community Service at the University of Texas, returned to the 22 state agencies and the one quasi-public/community agency surveyed in the 1993 Texas Senate Research Center (Rehnborg et al., 2002). Following telephone contact with each state agency, a survey instrument was sent to the staff contact identified as either managing a volunteer initiative or serving as a liaison to community efforts. In all, 39 separate 20-page survey instruments were sent to the contact points within the 21 state agencies and one community organization that receives a legislative appropriation. The research team received an extraordinary 91% return rate from the selected organizations and gathered data on 39 specific volunteer initiatives within Texas state agencies. For the purposes of this discussion, programs from 17 of the state agencies will be presented. (For a listing of the state agencies see Tables 6.1, 6.2, and 6.3.)

Noting that volunteer participation is indeed big business, the study found that more than 200,000 Texans serve the state through structured service opportunities. Their contributions in time, in-kind contributions, and donations exceed $35 million. This study concludes however, that volunteers should not be considered a no-cost resource. Instead, the report argues, an investment in volunteers significantly expands the reach of state government, leverages scarce financial resources, and actively engages citizens in the work of a democracy (Rehnborg et al., 2002).

Drawing on that analysis of volunteer programs within Texas state government, this chapter examines some of the organizational models associated with public sector volunteer engagement. The chapter highlights the diversity of tasks performed by volunteers and explores the impact of recent legislation on the infrastructure that facilitates community engagement. The chapter concludes with the identification of the key issues affecting public sector volunteerism.

ORGANIZATIONAL MODELS FOR VOLUNTEER INVOLVEMENT

In their analysis of volunteer engagement as one of several alternative approaches to local government service delivery Valente and Manchester (1984) identified four organizational models of volunteer program design: the ad hoc model; the outside agency recruitment/internal agency management model; the decentralized model; and the centralized model. Each model represents an identifiable management approach to volunteer involvement.

In the ad hoc volunteer program model, volunteer involvement is generally short term, and focuses on volunteer involvement on task forces, or study groups. These opportunities engage people who may not be available to assist with ongoing commitments or direct service delivery. The outside agency recruitment/internal government management model represents a modified form of outsourcing certain aspects of the volunteer initiative. Essentially a community partnership, the government agency may contract with a community organization such as the United Way or a volunteer center for volunteer recruitment, yet retains the responsibility to place volunteers and manage the program.

Table 6.1. Centralized Programs

Agency	Program/ Initiative	Number of Volunteers	Hours of Service	Valuation of Service	Description
Office of the Attorney General	Child Support Division	672	81,563	$1,402,068	Volunteers work in 65 child support offices providing staff assistance in processing caseloads, developing and enforcing child support orders, and locating absent parents.
Department of Criminal Justice	TDCJ Volunteer Program	24,682	513,744	$8,831,259	The majority of the volunteers work to support the chaplaincy's efforts help offenders transition back into society.
Mental Health and Mental Retardation	TDMHMR Community Relations	2,685	184,818	$3,177,021	The agency houses a network of 23 Volunteer Services Councils that support the agency's fund development activities and special projects. Volunteers work in state hospitals, schools, and centers across Texas.
Texas Youth Commission	Volunteerism and Community Involvement Program	2,037	120,500	$2,071,395	Volunteers in this agency work in four areas providing mentoring, tutoring, chaplaincy services, and serving with one of the community resource councils which support volunteer services at each institution across the state.
Totals		30,076	900,625	$15,481,544	

Table 6.2. Centralized Programs (Facility Specific)

Agency	Program/ Initiative	Number of Volunteers	Hours of Service	Valuation of Service	Description
Commission for the Blind	Criss Cole Rehabilitation Center	12	Unknown (not tracked)	Unknown	Criss Cole Rehabilitation Center is a comprehensive vocational rehabilitation training facility. Volunteers assist with office support, mentoring, classroom assistance, and client services.
State Preservation Board	Bob Bullock Texas History Museum	200	8,000	$137,520	Volunteers provide administrative support and serve as docents, visitor guides, and special event assistants at this Austin-based museum.
Texas School for the Blind and Visually Impaired	TSBVI Volunteer Program	132	Unknown (not tracked)	Unknown	Volunteers provide adaptive P. E. assistance, mentoring, tutoring, special event support, clerical assistance, help translating text into Braille, computer entry, and other support.
Totals		334	Incomplete	Incomplete	

In the decentralized model, one or more departmental units operate independent volunteer initiatives designed to meet specific concerns. Considerable variation may exist among decentralized programs within a single agency as each unit or program establishes its own policies and procedures without either the benefits or constrictions of central oversight and coordination. The fourth design is the centralized model. In this model salaried staff, or a designated management committee, oversees a highly centralized, jurisdiction-wide volunteer system. Often, the

Table 6.3. Decentralized Programs

Agency	Program/Initiative	Number of Volunteers	Hours of Service	Valuation of Service	Description
Parks and Wildlife	Education Program Instructors	3,500	53,000	$911,070	This project trains and certifies volunteers who provide the state's hunter, boater, and angler education programs.
	State Parks Volunteers	Unknown (not tracked)	451,560	$7,762,316	Volunteers help in park offices, assist with clean-up and construction work, adopt trails, and serve as park hosts among other jobs.
Department of Human Services	Adopt A Nursing Home	3,830	102,728	$1,765,894	This program promotes community volunteer involvement with Texas' long-term care facilities to enrich the lives of their residents.
	Family Pathfinders	1,118	29,616	$509,099	A community-based partnership of volunteer teams from faith-based organizations, civic groups, and businesses, helping families along the path to self-sufficiency.
	Volunteer and Community Services	110,375	823,502	$14,155,999	This program is made up of regionally operated programs across the state, engaging volunteers in activities that support programs across the agency.

Agency	Program	Volunteers	Hours	Value	Description
Department of Protective and Regulatory Services	Foster Friends	85	3,500	$60,165	Volunteers help provide support and meet the critical needs of abused and neglected children who are now in the Texas foster care system.
	Greater Texas Community Partners	5,344	42,387	$728,633	GTCP is a nonprofit organization that works through state and local collaborations to build partnerships with community volunteers and state and local governments to increase community awareness of child abuse and help children grow up to be healthy, productive adults.
	Students and Volunteer Efforts	36	6,587	$113,231	SAVE is a decentralized volunteer effort that is managed in collaboration between regional office staff and community partner groups.
Department on Aging	Benefits Counselors	221	Unknown (not tracked)	Unknown	Volunteer Benefit Counselors provide counseling services in 28 locations across the state.
	Volunteer Ombudsman Program	870	82,690	$1,421,441	A federally mandated initiative in which 870 volunteers are engaged in Ombudsman duties across 28 regional Area Agency on Aging offices.
Commission on Environmental Quality	Lake and River Clean Up	25,436	Unknown (not tracked)	Unknown	Large groups of volunteers are organized to conduct 'clean-up' events around the state.
	Source Water Protection Program	30	Unknown (not tracked)	Unknown	Designed to protect the safety and integrity of the water supply, this program trains volunteers to inventory potential water sources for contaminants.

Table 6.3. Decentralized Programs (Continued)

Agency	Program/ Initiative	Number of Volunteers	Hours of Service	Valuation of Service	Description
General Land Office	Adopt A Beach	8,966	Unknown (not tracked)	Unknown	Since 1986, nearly 300,000 volunteers have removed 5,200 tons of trash and debris from hundreds of miles of Texas coastlines.
	Adopt A Map	275	Unknown (not tracked)	Unknown	Through partnership with civic organizations, clubs, and companies, Adopt A Map volunteers raise funds to preserve historic maps and other documents.
Department of Health	Summer Youth Volunteer Program	53	Unknown (not tracked)	Unknown	Annually, 50-70 youth volunteer in agency offices for 8 weeks in the summer.
	Texas VISTA Health Corps	23	29,120	$500,573	AmeriCorps*VISTA volunteers work with Texas communities promoting public health services and supporting grassroots community development efforts.
	Texas Volunteer Health Corps	536	59,377	$1,020,691	Annually, 400-500 unpaid students and community volunteers support public health efforts statewide in agency offices and state hospitals.
	Volunteer Mailroom	188	5,951	$102,298	Volunteers from a wide-range of programs serving persons with disabilities provide administrative support that also serves as developmental opportunities for the volunteers.
Historical Commission	Archeological Stewards Network	108	15,374	$264,279	A group of highly skilled and carefully selected volunteer archaeologists work to preserve Texas' archaeological heritage.
	County Historical Commission	3,145	159,178	$2,736,270	Volunteers help link local communities and the historical commission by providing education, reviewing applications for historical markers, and preserving artifacts.
	Visionaries in Preservation	192	Unknown (not tracked)	Unknown	This program facilitates community-based strategic planning initiatives to help communities chart their future based in part on the roots of their historical traditions.
Totals		164,444	1,910.880	$32,748,027	

Table 6.3. Decentralized Programs (Continued)

Agency	Program/ Initiative	Number of Volunteers	Hours of Service	Valuation of service	Description
State Library and Archives Commission	Archives and Information Services	7	1,308	$22,484	This program identifies, collects, and makes available for research the permanently valuable official records of Texas government, as well as other significant historical resources.
	Friends of the Library and Archives Commission	10	Unknown (not tracked)	Unknown	This program is a nonprofit organization whose volunteers generates support for the State Library and Archives Commission statewide, through its local chapters.
	Talking Books Program	Unknown (not tracked)	39,869	$685,348	This program provides books and other printed materials in an audio format to Texans who are unable to read standard print material.
	Volunteer Recording Studio	96	5,133	$88,236	Volunteers produce approximately 150 new books a year. Volunteers record books, operate audio equipment, deliver products, provide administrative support., and help monitor and proofread recordings.

program leader is a member of the unit's management team. The program generally enjoys fairly strong staff and fiscal support.

The typology outlined by Valente and Manchester accurately captures the majority of volunteer initiatives found within Texas state agencies. Although described more fully in the next section of this chapter, most of the state's volunteer programs operate as centralized or decentralized service-delivery systems. Essentially a workplace model of management, the Valente and Manchester system regards volunteers as nonsalaried human resources engaged in the delivery of services or operating as administrative aides to the management functions of the parent organization. As such, each of their four schematics treats volunteers as unpaid employees subject to job descriptions, interview protocols, orientation, and training programs, and the other accoutrements of a personnel or human resources initiative.

This model is less effective however, in providing a framework for some of the more innovative community engagement systems identified in the study. For example, numerous "adopt-a-programs" emerged in the analysis. Adopt-a-programs recruit groups as manpower units, rather than specific individuals, to undertake and essentially self-manage defined pieces of work, such as cleaning-up a designated section of a state road, conducting social events at nursing homes, or caring for environmental resources such as wetlands, trails or beaches. Although structures exist to delineate the parameters of these efforts, the leadership and management of the projects largely exists within the adopting group rather than the sponsoring agency.

Likewise a number of state agencies benefit directly from the work of small, volunteer-lead, incorporated nonprofit organizations formed outside of, but under the aegis of the state agency. In the case of the Greater Texas Youth Commission or the Department of Mental Health and Mental Retardation, these volunteer-lead nonprofits are generally dedicated to fund development activities. Nonprofit groups such as the Greater Texas Community Partners (GTCP) organization, however, have a somewhat different relationship with state government. Although GTCP operates in close collaboration with the Texas Department of Protective and Regulatory Services (DPRS), the organization is a free standing nonprofit formed as an outgrowth of a successful Junior League initiative (Rehnborg et al., 2002). GTCP sponsors an "adopt-a-caseworker program" connecting DPRS social workers with community benefactors. In addition the organization sponsors a donated goods program. Both these programs provide material resources to DPRS caseworkers as they address the needs of fragile, low-income families accused of abuse or neglect. Although founded in the Dallas-Fort Worth section of Texas, GTCP works in collaboration with the DPRS to replicate their successful program in regions all over Texas.

Neither the GTCP Organization, nor the nonprofit organizations formed in support of the work of state agencies, are adequately captured by the service delivery models of volunteer management outlined by Valente and Manchester. Noting that "one size does not fill all" Rochester (1999) and others (see Meijs and Ten Hoorn's chapter in this volume for a more extensive treatment of this issue) offer alternative organizational systems to frame volunteer involvement. Based on extensive qualitative analysis of numerous voluntary groups Rochester distinguished four distinct models for volunteer engagement: the service delivery model; the support role model; the member/activist model; and the coworker model.

Rochester's (1999) service delivery model parallels the organizational models described by Valente and Manchester. In this scheme a clear distinction exists between volunteers and salaried staff. Salaried staff recruit community members for specific positions and then support volunteers through training, supervision, and recognition as they assume their front-line duties. Rochester's support role model is similar to his service delivery model. Here volunteers provide the back-up support to staff in the form of administrative tasks, bookkeepers, receptionists and other office support duties allowing staff to concentrate their work on the front-line duties. Rochester clarifies however, that agencies engaging volunteers in this support role model are generally small organizations lacking the capacity to undertake a full-scale volunteer effort. Without the time to fully engage a volunteer cohort, the support function is often performed by friends or relatives "lending a hand" when needed. The author goes on to note the motivation of volunteers in this scheme may differ from that of the service delivery model. Here volunteering may serve as a transition from work to retirement or conversely as a stepping-stone to employment. Likewise job descriptions for the volunteer helpers, if they exist, are generally more fluid and negotiated as the relationship between the helper and the organization evolves. Over time volunteers may extend or revise their relationship with the organization as they join committees or connect in other ways.

Member/activist volunteers are generally groups or associations of individuals banding together to support a common cause or pursue a shared purpose (Meijs & Karr, 2004; Rochester, 1999). Rather than volunteer/staff distinction, boundaries emerge between members and nonmembers, or between member/doers and leader/directors. Members acting in various capacities negotiate duties and perform all of the work of the organization. A variety of motivations propel the work of member/activist groups including a passionate belief about a cause or issue, the benefits that accrue to the member, or the public good generated by the activity.

The coworker model concludes this schematic (Rochester, 1999). Somewhat analogous to the support role model, the coworker model emerges when the work of the organization cannot be achieved solely by staff. The way in which duties and responsibilities are allocated, however, distinguishes these two complementary systems. Characterized by nonhierarchical teams or collectives often found in cause-oriented groups, the coworker model manages through nurturing and shared commitment rather than authoritarian directives or clear lines of roles and responsibilities. An ethos of solidarity frequently under girds the coworker model.

The goals of the organization, its size and purpose, along with the financial resources of the group and its cultural mores all contribute to the structural systems surrounding volunteer engagement. It is no wonder that state agencies, particularly human service organizations, operate their volunteer initiatives according to the service-delivery management schemes outlined by Valente and Manchester and noted by Rochester. Like salaried staff, volunteers within government programs generally perform client support duties or engage in administrative support functions. The management systems operated to support this type of volunteer involvement parallel staff personnel systems and include recruitment, interviewing, training, supervising, evaluation and recognition. Much of the U.S. literature in volunteer administration is predicated on this structural model (Ellis, 1996; McCurley & Lynch, 1996; Wilson, 1976).

The nonprofit organizations and the adopt-a-programs, however, depart from the standard service delivery model. Both of these endeavors essentially engage self-managing groups in support of the work of the state. Although the survey did not delve into the intricacies of either of these systems, they are likely more characteristic of member/activist management models than work-place management service delivery systems. The next section of this chapter examines the specific volunteer engagement models with Texas state agencies.

VOLUNTEER INITIATIVES WITHIN TEXAS STATE GOVERNMENT

Tutoring, mentoring, training guide dogs, leading 12-step programs, conducting boater, angler and hunter education, performing archeological digs, serving as translators, repairing cassette recorders, and monitoring streams are a few of the more than 100 different positions available to those wanting to assist state government (Rehnborg et al., 2002). Of the 17 agencies featured in this discussion, seven organized their volunteer service initiatives centrally within the agency while nine operated decentralized structures. One agency, the Texas Commission on the Arts, characterized its structure for volunteer involvement as more ad hoc in nature. Regardless of the dominant structural system facilitating service delivery, most of the state agencies also engaged the community through ancillary nonprofit organizations and adopt-a-programs. These group initiatives generally operate as self-managing units in the member/activist organizational model.

Centralized Volunteer Initiatives

In the centralized management model guidelines governing volunteer programs emanate from the agency's central office. The systems established by the central office apply uniformly to all regional volunteer initiatives governed by that agency. In most cases the agency employs management personnel at both the state and regional levels with the explicit task of overseeing the volunteer initiative. The agency's central office establishes uniform record keeping and tracking systems, develops policies and procedures governing volunteer involvement, frequently assists with the hiring of regional volunteer managers, and usually sponsors in-service and staff development opportunities. In addition, the state agency allocates a budget to support the volunteer initiative at both the regional and central office levels. On the regional level, staff are employed to manage volunteers and oversee general community relations duties. The regional staff provide periodic updates to the central office which in turn tracks volunteer involvement on a state-wide basis. For the purposes of this study, the central office staff completed one state-wide survey instrument that captured the volunteer work of all the agency's regional facilities.

This general management structure was most obvious in the Office of the Attorney General, the Texas Department of Mental Health and Mental Retardation, and the Texas Youth Commission. The Texas Department of Criminal Justice charged a centralized oversight committee with management responsibilities in lieu of a single staff person or office of volunteerism. As noted in Table 6.1, these four agencies, together with their multiple regional facilities, collectively engage more than 30,000 volunteers who contribute in excess of 900,000 hours of service valued at more than $15 million.

Three significantly smaller state agencies, each with one physical plant, noted a parallel structure. The Commission for the Blind reported a small volunteer initiative at the Criss Cole Rehabilitation Center. Likewise the Bob Bullock Texas History Museum operated by the State Preservation Board and the Texas School for the Blind and Visually Impaired engage volunteers in their work. Because these latter programs operate significantly smaller initiatives, and because each initiative is restricted to one physical plant that serves citizens across the state, these agencies are the focus of Table 6.2.

DECENTRALIZED MODEL

Variation and independence, the hallmarks of decentralized volunteer programs, accurately describes the volunteer and community service initiatives of the Texas Commission on Environmental Quality, Department of Aging, Department of Health, Department of Human Services, Department of Protective and Regulatory Services, Department of Parks and Wildlife, the General Land Office, the Historical Commission and the State Library and Archives Commission. In the decentralized program model, each volunteer project operates as a free-standing entity without standardized central agency oversight. Policies that may apply to a program in one division of an organization are often not known by, nor necessarily applicable to, a volunteer program in a different division of the same organization. Each of the volunteerism initiatives in the decentralized system completed their own survey instrument. In some cases an agency submitted as many as four different surveys.

Record-keeping systems vary on a project-by-project basis. For example, the Texas Department of Parks and Wildlife (DPW) keeps detailed accounts of the hours served by the state park volunteers yet neglects to capture, on a state-wide level, the number of volunteers engaged in this work. On the other hand, DPW's Education Program Instructors project, captures information about the number of volunteers serving in this capacity, but generally estimates service hours. Although both of these projects operate out of the Department of Parks and Wildlife, the two programs report to different people in different departments at the state headquarters and volunteer engagement data is rarely, if ever aggregated.

Similar differences existed among the other state agencies operating decentralized volunteer initiatives. The State Library and Archives Commission engages volunteers in four distinct and unrelated initiatives: Archives and Information Services; Friends of the Library and Archives Commission (a nonprofit organization); the Talking Books Program; and the Volunteer Recording Studio. When asked, each initiative offered a different perception of the liability coverage available for volunteers working within these projects and acknowledged little programmatic interaction within the agency. Data collection varied project by projects as well.

Data collection was problematic throughout the study, but especially so among the decentralized programs. Some projects tracked the number of volunteers, others tracked hours served while still others noted outputs of service. In other situations numbers were estimated based on program guidelines. For example, the Department of Human Services' Adopt-a-Nursing Home project requires that adopting groups have at least three members and that each group visit the "adopted" nursing home three to four times per year. These requirements combined with other information were used to estimate the number of volunteers and their service hours. Such inconsistencies make it virtually impossible to truly capture the service contribution of volunteers.

Economic valuation of service proved equally uneven and illusive. In some instances programs adopted national benchmarks for placing a monetary value on time, while others adopted federal standards emanating from federal grant guidelines, and still others used minimum wage as a universal assessment of volunteer time.

Finding decentralized programs was an equally arduous task. Decentralized programs, by their very nature, operate without central oversight. Finding these community engagement initiatives involved considerable investigative work. Most of the staff managing these projects operated from job descriptions that addressed responsibilities for the project, such as beach clean up, or library services, but may or may not have mentioned volunteers as the mechanism for the delivery of service. Some programs were also more politicized than others. Family Pathfinders, a project designed to assist welfare clients with life and job skills, operated through the Department of Human Services; however, the program had its beginning within another state agency as the signature initiative of an agency executive running for state-wide office. As noted in Table 6.3 no less than 150,000 people volunteer in these programs. A conservative estimate places the economic valuation of their service in excess of $27 million for over 1.5 million hours of service.

Ad Hoc Model

The Texas Commission on the Arts reports that it engages volunteers in an ad hoc fashion (see Table 6.4). When surveyed about their work with volunteers, the Commission staff specifically noted the importance of their commissioners' contribution of time as they reviewed grant applications, advocated with state legislators, and assisted with policy decisions. It should be noted that commissioners are appointed to their leadership position with the Commission on the Arts by the Governor. Although commissioners receive no monetary compensation for their time, the appointment carries considerable status and prestige. The agency went on to acknowledge the willingness of Texas celebrities to create public service announcements on a pro bono basis. At the time of the survey Willie

Table 6.4.   Ad Hoc Programs

Agency	Program/ Initiative	Number of Volunteers	Hours of Service	Valuation of Service	Description
Commission on the Arts	As needed —no formal program	74	1,383	$23,774	The Texas Commission on the Arts handles community engagement initiatives on a "project-by-project" basis. The agency recruits and works with volunteers as a project requires, but has no ongoing volunteer management structure in place.

Nelson was filming an advertisement on behalf of the Commission on a pro bono basis.

No specific employee at the Commission on the Arts is assigned the task of managing volunteers. Rather the agency assigns staff to volunteer initiatives on a project-by-project basis in order to meet specific objectives. Nonetheless, the arts organization reported that 74 volunteers contributed 1,383 hours of service. Not counting the pro bono contribution of celebrities to agency projects, the Commission valued the effort of its volunteers at $23,774.

Member/Activist Model

Initiated in 1987, Texas is credited with the nation's first Adopt-a-Highway program, an initiative now found in virtually every state (Texas Senate Research Center, 1993). Although road adoptions are structured undertakings, the management of each adopting entity falls to the group that agrees to remove litter from a certain section of public roadways on a regular and recurring basis. Since the inception of this novel program, the state has witnessed a significant increase in these group-oriented projects. Nine such programs now exist including the Adopt-a-Beach, Adopt-a-Caseworker, Adopt-a-Cemetery, Adopt-a-Highway, Adopt-a-Map, Adopt-a-(Historical) Marker, Adopt-a-Nursing Home, Adopt-a-Trail, and Adopt-a-Wetland. Patterned after the Adopt-a-Highway model, each "adoption" carries with it expectations for group-facilitated work, whether that work is fund raising to preserve historic maps, or maintenance work to sustain cemeteries, wetlands and trails. Although perhaps not fully in line with the activities witnessed by Rochester (1999) in his description of the member/activist model of volunteer involvement, those participating in the adoption self-organize the work and assure its completion.

Self-organizing and semi-independent generally characterizes the leadership behavior of the various nonprofits organized by community volunteers to support the work on state agencies. As noted in Table 6.5, seven state agencies enjoy the support of nonprofits.

In several cases a state-level nonprofit helps facilitate the work of regional nonprofits. For example, the DPW, like the Texas Youth Commission and the Department of Mental Health and Mental Retardation each have a state-level nonprofit entity as well as separately constituted nonprofit organizations each supporting a specific regional facility or park. The local nonprofits each look to the state nonprofit organization for guidance and in some cases organizational direction. For the most part these nonprofits exist to raise funds for the state agencies. Although the relationships between the nonprofits and the state agencies vary, the ties are generally close and supportive. The nonprofit organizations allow the local facilities and parks to enjoy programs and services not possible with limited or earmarked state funds.

Table 6.5.   Nonprofits Supporting the Work of Texas State Agencies

State Agency	Collaborating Nonprofit Organizations
Texas Commission on the Arts	Texas Cultural Trust Council, a nonprofit organized to solicit contributions for the Texas Cultural Trust, a funding mechanism established by the Texas Legislature in 1993.
Texas Historical Society	Friends of the Texas Historical Commission Friends of the Sam Rayburn House Museum
Texas State Library & Archives Commission	Friends of the Libraries & Archives of Texas Friends of the Volunteer Recording Studio
Texas Department of Mental Health and Mental Retardation	Volunteer Services State Council, Inc. – one state-level nonprofit with 22 local organizations
Texas Parks and Wildlife Department	Parks and Wildlife Foundation of Texas, Inc.—a state-level nonprofit. Sixty additional local nonprofits support specific parks.
Department of Protective and Regulatory Services	Greater Texas Community Partners—more than 90 regional groups work to support child protective services across Texas
Texas Youth Commission	State Volunteer Resources Council for Texas Youth—state-level organization with six chapters. Eighteen independently incorporated local nonprofit advisory councils to specific facilities, known as Local Community Resources Councils.

Although the role of the government funding of nonprofits is well known, less well known are the ways in which nonprofits come to the aid of state government. The Texas Telephone Pioneers, an affiliate of the Telephone Pioneers of America organizes retired electronic technicians to fix the talking book machines loaned out by the Texas State Library and Archives Commission Talking Book Program. The Source Water Protection Program of the Commission on Environmental Quality relies heavily on senior adults and noted specifically the powerful role of the Retired Senior Volunteer Program in meeting the programs manpower needs throughout the state. Other organizations noted as critical partners included local United Way agencies, Keep Texas Beautiful groups, Lions Clubs, and others.

Management of Volunteers Across State Agency Initiatives

The effective management of volunteers matters. When asked why people stopped volunteering, a 1998 United Parcel Foundation report found that "two out of five volunteers have stopped volunteering for an organization at some time because of one or more poor volunteer management practices" (p. 14). In order of importance 26% of volunteers left because the program was not well managed, 23% reported that the service opportunity was not a good use of their time, while 18% indicated that their skills were not being well utilized.

In order to address this important question among state agency volunteer programs, the survey instrument queried program managers about 18 different management practices. For the purpose of this chapter, we have divided those practices into two groups: the volunteer management practices that support the volunteer while serving; and the management practices that under gird the infrastructure that supports solid program management. The categories and practices are as follows:

Management Practices that Support Program Volunteers

1. Volunteers are interviewed and screened
2. References are checked
3. Criminal background checks are performed
4. Volunteers are oriented
5. Volunteers are trained
6. Volunteers skills / interests are matched to positions
7. Volunteers are provided with relevant continuing education
8. Volunteers are interviewed when they leave the program

9. Volunteers receive performance feedback
10. Volunteers are evaluated
11. Volunteers are recognized

Management Practices that Support Program Infrastructure

1. Volunteers are covered by liability insurance
2. Personnel files are maintained
3. The volunteer program itself is evaluated
4. Software tracking program is used in program administration
5. Agency has policies and procedures that govern volunteer involvement
6. Agency has mission/vision statement regarding volunteer involvement
7. Agency produces a volunteer services fiscal year end report and/or includes information about volunteer involvement in its fiscal year end report

As noted in Table 6.6, the most effectively managed volunteer initiatives are found among the agencies that centrally organize the programs and establish policies and protocols emanating from the central office. The data would clearly suggest that the role of the central office leadership team in staff development activities, and hiring assistance combined with a fiscal allocation to support volunteer initiatives leads to more effectively managed initiatives. A significant drop-off exists in the management practices of all of the other organizational models. Unfortunately it was beyond the scope of the survey to delve more deeply into the management practices of the member/activist adopt-a-programs and the ancillary nonprofits supporting the work of these agencies.

NEW DEVELOPMENTS

Not long after the completion of the 2002 survey of volunteer programs within Texas state agencies, the Texas Legislature found itself wrestling with an exceptionally tight budget and a political predisposition against tax increments of most any kind. It was within this climate in May 2003, that the 78th Texas Legislature passed House Bill 2292 (H.B. 2292) which set in motion the most significant state-level governmental reorganization in recent Texas history. House Bill 2292 mandated a transformation of health and human services in Texas by consolidating the roles and functions of 12 existing state agencies and entities. Of the 12 existing

Table 6.6.   Nonprofits Supporting the Work of Texas State Agencies

	Organizational Model			
	Centralized	Centralized Agency-Specific	Decentralized	Ad hoc
Management Practices				
Average number of management practices supporting program volunteers	86%	66%	58%	82%
Average number of practices supporting program infrastructure	93%	28%	61%	29%
Average Total number of quality management practices utilized in program:	90%	47%	60%	56%

agencies, 10 were abolished as a part of this legislation, creating a single system comprised of the Health and Human Services Commission and four new state agencies. The goal of this legislation was the creation of a consolidated and coordinated system of health and human services in Texas that is rationally organized, effectively managed, centered on client needs, and accountable for results. H.B. 2292 also set expectations for significant improvement in the cost effectiveness of health and human services agency operations in order to generate substantial, measurable, and sustainable savings (H.B. 2292, 1993). H.B. 2292 resulted in the transfer and reprioritization of a large number of functions, powers, duties, programs, and activities, including the established volunteer programs, of the former state agencies and entities.

Of the 12 health and human services agencies affected by the passage of H.B. 2292, 6 had formalized volunteer programs within their organizational structure; these agencies were the Texas Commission for the Blind, Texas Department on Aging, Texas Department of Health, Texas Department of Human Services, Texas Department of Mental Health and Mental Retardation, and Texas Department of Protective and Regulatory Services. Although HB 2292 passed in 2003, and took affect in 2004, the ramifications for the future of volunteer initiatives in Texas' health and human service agencies remains in transition at the time of the writing of this chapter. Some programs operate under an interim plan of action while awaiting decisions about the future direction of the new agency and its programs. Other volunteer programs are on an indefinite hiatus until further decisions are made.

One of the more recent outcomes of the HHSC consolidation is the mandate that all five of the health and human service agencies follow a common template when crafting their organizational chart. This template has a number of features that are designed to ensure a common framework across agencies. One reason for this similarity is that it will increase the alignment of the work, make coordination easier, and help ensure a common direction between the five agencies. An Office of Volunteer and Community Engagement (OVCE) that reports to the Deputy Commissioner is one of the required organizational elements for each of the state's health and human service agencies. At the time of this writing, each agency is in the process of determining the role and function that OVCE will play in their agency as well as the level of support it receives. The scope and support the OVCE plays in each agency will be an indicator of the degree to which volunteerism is seen as integral to the accomplishment of the agency's mission and the collective mission of the state's health and service agencies.

CONCLUSION

In examining the data on volunteer programs in Texas state agencies reported in this chapter and the policy trends that affect volunteerism is Texas government, we can draw three general conclusions.

First, the structurally more defined and organized volunteer initiatives within state government agencies appear to be simultaneously more productive in terms of volunteer outcomes as well as potentially more vulnerable to the political winds of change. The centralized programs demonstrated greater facility in the management of volunteers, in the outcomes associated with community engagement and were also the most vulnerable to legislative initiatives and general budget cuts. Decentralized programs on the other hand, while perhaps less sophisticated in terms of volunteer management, appear to fly "beneath the radar" of organizational re-structuring and fiscal actions.

Second, generally speaking, volunteer engagement in state agencies experienced the same challenges shared by the broader world of volunteerism. The engagement of volunteers is poorly understood, marginalized, and generally lacks the support of upper levels of management. Staff is expected to assume multiple responsibilities of which volunteer coordination is only one of numerous tasks assigned. Nonetheless, effective programs have much to show for their efforts. Not only are funds raised, but these programs accomplish many of their goals and provide meaningful service for the state's residents and the target populations served by their parent agencies.

Third, volunteer programs have been ingenious in responding to the available time commitment of citizen. One of the more notable examples of this is the wide spread use of "adopt-a-programs." Not only do these projects encapsulate the time commitment of volunteers to specific identifiable projects with generally clear outcomes, but they distribute program planning and management to staff throughout the organizations and share the burdens of management with the organizations engaged in the adoption.

In conclusion, effective volunteer involvement that provides meaningful and cost-effective services for state residents does exist within selected state agencies. Regardless of the organizational model applied or the location of programs within state government, the public sector has successfully captured the time and talents of hundreds of citizens. However, effective volunteer programs require the investment of fiscal as well as human resources and the support of senior management to maximize these benefits and ensure that they continue on an ongoing basis.

CHAPTER 7

CHALLENGES OF VOLUNTEER MANAGEMENT IN KAZAKHSTAN

**Tamara G. Nezhina, Jeffrey L. Brudney, and
Aigerim R. Ibrayeva**

INTRODUCTION

Everything is new in Kazakhstan—including the concepts of volunteering and volunteer management. Kazakhstan is a young nation, which became independent in 1991 after the disintegration of the Soviet Union. It has experienced substantial social, political and economic change, to which people are adapting with difficulty. "Numerous Soviet-era institutions which took care of many needs of the population have disappeared or been severely weakened, making the situation of vulnerable groups even more precarious" (United Nations Development Programme [UNDP], 2002). Under these conditions, the importance of the nonprofit sector, and especially the involvement of the population in socially valuable activities of nonprofit and nongovernmental organizations (NGOs), cannot be overestimated.

Among the problems that the nonprofit sector in Kazakhstan has encountered is the effective involvement and management of volunteers.

Challenges in Volunteer Management, pp. 151–171

Research on volunteerism in Kazakhstan is very limited. The first survey on nonprofit organizations in Kazakhstan was conducted by the Center of Public Development Accord to define relationships between the organizations and volunteers, and to learn about the motivations of volunteers. Another research project on volunteerism was conducted by the United Nations Volunteers program (Hansen, Askarbekova, & Yerofeeva, 2002), together with local Kazakhstan analysts. The main purpose of this research was "to raise awareness of the value and contribution of volunteerism to Kazakhstan's society and economy, to identify strengths and weaknesses of Kazakhstan's voluntary sector" (UNDP, 2002). Although both research projects did not focus on managerial issues, they identified poor management of volunteer work by nonprofit organizations as one of the major obstacles to the development of a strong volunteer base in Kazakhstan (Oliferov, Vinogradova, Birzhanova, & Chelidze, 2001; UNDP 2002). Underdeveloped volunteer management practices in nonprofit organizations are a common problem for many post-Soviet countries (Grigoryan, 2002).

The present research is the first conducted in Kazakhstan to address the issue of volunteer management directly. At a time when the nonprofit sector has become a reality in Kazakhstan, improving its performance, scope, and reach depends on sound volunteer management practices. The purpose of this research is to learn about existing practices of volunteer administration in Kazakhstan and their implementation. To carry out the research, we implemented a survey of nonprofit organizations in Almaty, the largest city in Kazakhstan. The first part of this paper describes the context for the development of civil society organizations in Kazakhstan. The research methodology is outlined in the second section. The third part presents findings. In our conclusion we discuss the implications of our analysis.

KAZAKHSTAN: ESSENTIAL BACKGROUND

The modern history of Kazakhstan begins in 1991, the year of independence from the Soviet Union. Therefore, we can speak of slightly more than a decade of independent development of the Republic of Kazakhstan and the nonprofit sector. Naturally, the present Kazakhstan political, social and economic institutions still bear a heavy legacy from the communist past. This brief explanation is based not only on the scant literature available, but also interviews with six leaders of nonprofit organizations and support organizations in Kazakhstan.

Political Realities

Democratization in Kazakhstan is developing from the top-down, rather than from the bottom-up. Kazakhstan leadership has declared democracy as its preferred course of development (Nazarbayev, 1999). The new constitution of Kazakhstan has legalized this choice. Yet, Kazakhstan is a presidential system with a very strong president and government and a comparatively weak Parliament. The Constitution of Kazakhstan affirms freedom of associations (Article 23), but at the same time limits the funding opportunity for public associations by prohibiting government financing (Article 5). The "Law on Public Associations" also prohibits the assignment of state agency functions to a public association or state funding of a public association (Article 4), thus raising a wall between the government and the nonprofit sector. However, the intensive awareness of international organizations to the development of civil society in Kazakhstan and the increasing visibility and popularity of some nonprofit organizations, have brought the emerging nonprofit sector to the attention of the President. This attention has induced the government to reconsider its relationships with the third sector. Currently, a new law, "On Social Partnership," is being drafted and will serve to define relationships between the government and nonprofit sector organizations (Shindaulletova, 2003). This draft law is motivated by the desire "that more should be done for non-governmental agents to engage in effective social service delivery" (Forrester, 2003). It also includes vague provisions that might be used to limit activities of political parties and religious organizations (Forrester, 2003). Most NGOs in Kazakhstan provide social services. According to the UNDP report, 66% of NGOs in Kazakhstan have a social orientation (UNDP, 2002).

Economic Realities

In its communist past, Kazakhstan was a centrally planned economy. Now, as an independent state, Kazakhstan is developing a market economy by introducing the appropriate laws and institutions. The process is slow because market relations and competition are still new notions for most of the population. The fact that market institutions are formally legalized does not guarantee smooth market operations. In addition, widespread corruption is a great inhibitor to further development of the economic market.

The break from the Soviet Union has resulted in a huge disruption of the formerly highly integrated economic system. In Kazakhstan, many industries were shut down and many people lost their jobs. However, rich deposits of oil have helped to ease the transition period and to solve some of the social and economic problems besetting the nation.

Social Realities

The economic transition period has introduced many problems into the social life of the Kazakhstan people. One of the current social problems is the division of society into two major groups, a small group of rich and a large group of poor, with an almost invisible middle class. At the expense of others, massive privatization programs have led to enrichment of powerful former party officials. As the tax base shrank, the budget has become incapable to finance the expansive social protection programs that existed before the break up (Cook, 2002; Olcott, 1998). Many hospitals, kindergartens, and schools were closed down. During the first years of independence, many poor and unemployed people did not receive any support from the government. The level of trust in formal institutions was low before the break, and it fell even further after independence (Sergeyenko, 2000). However, the level of interpersonal trust remained strong, thus creating informal links for helping each other. Research conducted by Rose (1997) in several former Soviet states found that although the level of trust of government and nongovernmental institutions in former Soviet countries was very low, the informal support network was common and well developed.

Volunteering

Helping friends and relatives is a long-standing tradition in Kazakhstan, which originated in times of nomadic life and strong kinship relations. Such informal volunteer assistance survived through the Soviet era but was never formalized. During the last years of Soviet rule in Kazakhstan, as in Russia and other Soviet republics, people developed low trust in formal "voluntary" organizations because of the close control of the communist party (Nowicki, 2000; Voicu & Voicu, 2004; Zlotnikov, 1997). As a result, organized volunteering is developing slowly in Kazakhstan, primarily due the low level of trust. In addition, the nontransparent finances of nonprofits also contribute to low trust. Another reason for the low level of volunteering, as compared to many western countries, is that the role of churches and religious organizations was extremely limited during the 70 years of communist power (Heap, Ibrayeva, Kabdiyeva, Sharipova, & Dissenova, 2003). As a result, religious motives to volunteer are not widespread.

Nevertheless, volunteering is gaining popularity, especially among the young. Survey results by the Center of Public Development Accord indicated that 50% of their convenience sample of 108 organizations in Kazakhstan involved mostly college and university students as volunteers. Although the sampling of these organizations was not random, the predominance of young volunteers is confirmed by the opinions of many experts. Young people have fewer responsibilities and more free time to assist nonprofit organizations. In 2001, Accord conducted a survey among young, educated people at higher educational institutions. The results of a survey indicated that 25% of the respondents were ready to volunteer immediately and another 40% were not sure. Many of the surveyed students had found volunteer work beneficial. About 20% of respondents stated the acquisition of useful skills and knowledge was the most motivating factor in their decision to volunteer, followed by the opportunity to find a good job (13.6%), and the chance for communication and socialization (13.2%) (Oliferov et al., 2001). Volunteering among adults would likely have been higher if people were able to devote time and energy to their favorite causes, instead of working at several jobs to support their families. As the UNDP report contended, in Kazakhstan many people's predominant motivation was to make more money, or simply to survive. "Working for free for the welfare of society was an extremely rare motivation" (UNDP, 2002).

Three Periods in the Development of the Nonprofit Sector

According to the opinion of the nonprofit experts, after the independence there were three periods in the development of the nonprofit sector, which were characterized by three distinctive motivations. The first period was from 1987 until 1993, immediately prior to the transition to the market economy began. As many veterans of the nonprofit sector in Kazakhstan recall, this period was characterized by the idealistic anticipation of freedom and democracy. Under President Gorbachev, the Soviet system started to show signs of collapse. During this time, the groups that advocated for human rights and a safe environment became most active in Kazakhstan. The leaders of the oldest nonprofit organizations maintained that this was a period of pure and massive volunteerism. People thought little about compensation for their work. Instead, they were inspired by the cause and by the mission and worked enthusiastically for it. At that time, the economic hardships did not yet strike the majority of the population of Kazakhstan and did not deter people from volunteering.

The second period started after 1994, when the privatization program in Kazakhstan brought major change in people's lives. Impoverished, jobless, and unprotected people started to band together in search of assistance. During this period, many self-help organizations were established, such as ones for single mothers that developed to help with childcare. Another example was the association of homeless people, which brought together families that moved to big cities in the search for jobs and who had to advocate for their right to build houses within the city limits.

During this period, major international nonprofit organizations arrived in Kazakhstan, such as the UNDP, the Soros Foundation, the United State Agency for International Development (USAID), the European Commission program for Technical Assistance to Commonwealth of Independent States and Mongolia (EC TACIS), Eurasia Foundation, The International NGO Training and Research Center (INTRAC) and others. The purpose of most of them was to facilitate democratic developments in an emerging economy, which included assistance to civil society organizations. Local experts maintained that these organizations have been the key actors in strengthening the third sector and helped to organize, support, and finance activities of many nonprofits in Kazakhstan. The flip side to the financial assistance from foreign groups was that many Kazakhstan nonprofits developed a dependency on these organizations' support. Some Kazakhstan organizations learned to "adjust" their agenda to the needs of donor organizations by stepping back from their original causes and missions (Luong, 1999).

The distinct feature of this second period was an influx of nonprofit organizations in Kazakhstan (Franz, Shvetsova, & Shamshildayeva, 2002).[1] Experts maintained that for many active people the third sector was a means to create jobs for themselves and others. Some organizations were specifically created to receive grants. This development explains the impressive number of registered nonprofit organizations at this period that were small in size (Luong, 1999).

At the same time, many Kazakhstan people were struck by disillusionment with the values of the market and even democracy; market values were understood as an integral part of democracy. In addition, people experienced severe economic hardships, which contributed to the overall decline of service ethics.

The third period, from 1999 onward, is characterized by the gradual withdrawal of international financial support, and as a consequence, the closure of many weaker nonprofit organizations. The lack of funds also induced many strong, popular, and productive nonprofits to engage in profit-making activities, such as education, consultancy, and research. Another distinguishing feature of this period is the decrease from high levels of volunteerism. According to the UNDP data, 68% of surveyed organizations said that they would like to involve more volunteers.

However, the UNDP report found that the need for volunteers exceeded the number of volunteers available (UNDP, 2002).

Nonprofit organizations in Kazakhstan are in this third phase of development. Training, provided by international organizations, has taught them the importance of management. Nonprofit organizations are more aware of the necessity to manage human resources, especially volunteers. Several factors, identified in reports by UNDP and INTRAC, challenge nonprofit leaders and volunteer coordinators in the management of volunteers: a limited supply of volunteers, scarce resources, and a lack of government support. These reports concerning the development of the nonprofit sector in Kazakhstan maintain that the status of volunteers is not yet defined or legalized by the legislature. Furthermore, a lack of professional and skilled managers in civil society Finally, "the public and the Government do not see volunteer activity as a strong, skilled resource, which is essential for the resolution of many socially significant problems and for getting people involved in civil society" (UNDP, 2002).

Many hurdles exist in developing a strong pool of volunteers in Kazakhstan. One challenge that the leaders of nonprofit organizations face is the effective management of those people who continue to give their time and knowledge to the organizational missions. A more professional approach could be necessary to raise the effectiveness of volunteer programs. In order to assess the state of volunteer management practice in Kazakhstan nonprofit organizations, we conducted a survey of nonprofits that enlist volunteers in their work. The following section describes the survey procedures and sample.

METHODOLOGY

The data for our research emanate from the city of Almaty, the former capital and the largest city in Kazakhstan (population—1.3 million people). This focus is justified by the number of nonprofit organizations registered in Almaty: one-third of all nonprofit organizations in Kazakhstan (32%) are based in this city, and most international organizations have offices there (Franz et al., 2001; UNDP 2002). Because many nonprofit organizations in Almaty interact with foreign nonprofit organizations, we would expect them to be more informed about volunteer management practices. Thus, if our survey finds limited knowledge and practice of volunteer management in Almaty, we can anticipate that nonprofit organizations in other regions of the country would, at best, attain the same level—or more likely, a lower level of managerial awareness.

Our sampling decisions for the study were guided by the fact that many nonprofit organizations in Kazakhstan do not have volunteers. Volunteering is still a developing concept in Kazakhstan (see introduction section), and only the largest, most visibly active organizations are able to attract many volunteers. As a result, with random sampling we risked including a considerable share of organizations that do not have volunteers. To avoid this problem, we sought expert opinions about the types of nonprofit organizations in Almaty that enlist volunteers through interviewing directors and managers of several nonprofit and government organizations. Based on this information, we decided to focus the research on the most visible areas of nonprofit activity which are the women, youth, and environmental sectors. Organizations in these three sectors were expected to involve volunteers regularly in their operations and programs.

Because data collection in Kazakhstan was a challenge in itself, we went through several stages to obtain a sampling frame for our survey. The first task was to locate a reliable list of nonprofits in Kazakhstan. We found, however, that such a list was nonexistent for several reasons. Although the Statistics Agency of the Republic of Kazakhstan keeps registration records of nonprofit organizations, accurate and timely information on the closing of nonprofits is not available. The closure procedure is cumbersome and costly, and many nonprofits do not bother to close down officially. The list of nonprofits that we obtained from the Statistics Agency and the list provided by the Almaty city government contained 2,014 public associations and foundations registered in Almaty since 1991. Even though the Statistics Agency routinely keeps track of "idle" organizations, the number of "active" organizations is grossly overstated.[2] We consulted the experts[3] on the number of organizations in Almaty; almost unanimously the experts indicated that the number of operating nonprofit organizations did not exceed 300.

Another reason for the absence of a comprehensive list of nonprofits in Kazakhstan is that no organization or association is committed to investing time and resources in compiling and maintaining such a list. Several organizations, at different times, have undertaken the compilation task, but they had no incentive to update the list.

We decided to obtain all existing lists from various organizations that had ones recently compiled (defined as after 2000). We discovered that these organizations maintained their lists for their own internal purposes. International organizations, such as the UNDP and the Soros Foundation, compiled the lists for programs that were on their agenda. The Central Asian Sustainable Development Information Network (CASDIN), a resource organization, maintained a list to offer their services. The USAID together with the Counterpart Consortium, a nonprofit development organization, have put the most resources into the systematic maintenance of a comprehensive list. However, their list was hopelessly outdated for our survey purpose:[4] on this list, only about one in nine organizations were active and accessible. The other organizations were either nonexistent or have changed their addresses and telephone numbers without giving notice.

In order to pursue our research, we decided to create our own list of nonprofits in Almaty based on lists provided by the above organizations. We compiled the lists that we had received from the various agencies and organizations and targeted our survey toward environmental, youth and women's organizations. These three types of organizations were expected to use volunteers more extensively than others and, hence, held the most promise for our study. As Table 7.1 shows, the compiled list that included only environmental, youth and women's organizations consisted of 130 organizations. To refine the list and to ensure that we were dealing with working organizations, We telephoned all of the organizations on the list. Some organizations were easily accessible, but others were out of reach for several reasons: address change, telephone number change, the "idle" phase, or closure. Those organizations that we defined as closed did not answer multiple telephone calls or answer e-mails and could not be found even with the help of a special telephone locator service.

As Table 7.1 indicates, these procedures revealed that of the 130 nonprofits on our list, 54 organizations were nonexistent. This left a total of 76 organizations that we proceeded to contact. Because our interest is in volunteer management practices, and 16 of the 76 organizations (21%) reported no volunteers, 60 organizations remained as our effective sample. We contacted and sent the questionnaires to all 60 of these organizations. We received responses from 45, for an excellent effective response rate of 75%.[5] Our respondents consisted of those individuals who said that they have responsibility for volunteers in their organizations.

FINDINGS

Volunteer Administrators in Kazakhstan

Description of Respondents

We received information from 45 respondents employed by the targeted nonprofit organizations. As Table 7.3 shows, 78% (35) of them held managerial positions, with 58% (26) in the highest rank such as executive directors, chairpersons, and presidents of nonprofit organizations. From this group of 26 top leaders in organizations, 89% (24) reported personal responsibility for managing volunteers. Twenty percent of the respondents held managerial positions, such as public relations managers, general

Table 7.1.   Sampling Frame

Respondents	Environmental Organizations	Youth Organizations	Womens Organizations	Total Organizations		
				N	Population	Sample
Initial sampling frame	48	52	30	130		
Contacted sampling frame	29	31	16	76	100%	
Reported no volunteers	13	3	0	16	21%	
Effective sample	16	28	16	60	79%	100%
Responses	11	23	11	45		75%
Refused	2	1	0	3		5%
No response	3	4	5	12		20%

managers, and editors. Only half of these managers reported responsibility for volunteers, which they combined with their other duties. Another 20% (9) were in clerical positions, with only one person being directly responsible for volunteers. Just one respondent in our sample claimed that she focused exclusively on volunteer management.[6] For convenience, we call "volunteer coordinators" those who combine their regular job with coordinating volunteers in Kazakhstan nonprofits, even though an explicit position rarely exists.

About 70% of the respondents worked full-time and received a salary. The average experience of the respondents in their positions was about 4 years (3.8). Forty-four percent of the volunteer coordinators had received training before they began working with volunteers in their organizations. While on the job, 47% went through volunteer management training, organized by either local or foreign nonprofit support organizations. Some respondents had received multiple trainings. In all, slightly over half of these officials had received training in volunteer management, either before or on-the-job (53%).

The average volunteer coordinator spent about 30% of her or his time on the job managing volunteers in the organization (mean); the median was smaller, 25%. The modal value indicated that the time most often listed for managing volunteers was just 10%. This variable had a wide range, from 1 to 100%. Based on hours per week, 36% of all volunteer

Table 7.2.   Respondents Job Classification

Positions	N	Percent	Number (Percent) of Respondents who Work With Volunteers
Top-rank officials	26	58%	24 (53%)
Managers	9	20%	5 (11%)
Clerical	9	20%	1 (2%)
Not indicated	1	2%	2 (4%)
All respondents	45	100%	30 (67%)

Table 7.3.   Demographics of Respondents

Demographic	N	Percent
Ethinicity		
Kazakhs	15	33%
Russians	15	33%
Turks	2	4.4%
Tatars	2	4.4%
Uygurs	1	2.2%
German	1	2.2%
Greek	1	2.2%
No indicated	8	17.8%
Sex	*N*	*Percent*
Female	33	73%
Male	11	24.4%
Not indicated	1	2.2%
Age	Average	37.7 years of age
Education	Average	16.5 years of formal education

coordinators devoted just 1 to 2 hours per week to volunteer management; about 9% (8.9) devoted 2 to 3 hours, 11% devoted 3 to 4 hours per week, 20% devoted 4 to 5 hours per week; and about 9% (8.9) devoted more than 15 hours per week to volunteer management.

In sum, most of the volunteer coordinators in the sample were simultaneously fulfilling the role as the top-rank leaders of their nonprofit organizations. About 60% of volunteer coordinators spent, on average, from 1 to 4 hours per week managing volunteers. They reported that they devote about 30% (29.7%) of their time to this job activity. Only half of these individuals had received training in volunteer administration.

Demographic Information

Kazakhstan is a multiethnic state. Various governmental and nongovernmental sources indicate that more than 100 ethnicities reside in Kazakhstan, with Kazakhs and Russians constituting the largest groups.[7] Our survey respondents' ethnicity closely reflected the demographics of the country. Table 7.2 shows that one-third of respondents were Kazakhs, one-third were Russians, and the remainder consisted of other ethnicities. The average age of respondents was 37.7 years, with the lowest age of 16 and the highest of 63. The age data were skewed toward younger respondents because in our sample, the most numerous group of organizations worked in the youth development sector.

The distribution of respondents by gender in these nonprofit organizations was comparable to many western societies. In our sample, women constituted 73%, and men about 24% (one respondent did not provide this information, 2%) (Brudney & Schmahl, 2001). The educational level of the respondents was high. The average number of years of formal education completed was 16.5, which suggests that the average volunteer coordinator has a university education.

To summarize, the typical volunteer coordinator in our sample of nonprofit organizations in Kazakhstan was a female of various ethnic backgrounds, 37-38 years old, with a university diploma. This coordinator was usually a full-time, salaried employee with between 4 and 5 years of service in the organization, and about 4 years (3.8) in her present position.[8] This volunteer coordinator spent, on average, about 30% of her time working with volunteers.

Volunteer Programs in Kazakhstan Nonprofit Organizations

General Tendencies

Given the general characteristics of our sample, the average nonprofit organization employed about 10 salaried workers, whereas the median was about 7 workers. These organizations were not large by Western standards. The organizations involved about 55 volunteers, on average, with a median of about 8 volunteers. This divergence was explained by the wide range in the numbers of volunteers involved—from 1 to 801 volunteers across the organizations in the sample.

Most of the organizations used volunteers in several ways. About 64% of the organizations used volunteers for direct service provision, such as services to their client groups. Sixty percent of organizations attracted volunteers for internal management functions, such as filing, bookkeeping, receiving telephone calls, and other clerical office tasks. About 37% of all organizations involved volunteers in external management operations, such as public relations and fundraising. Finally, 28% of the organizations used volunteers for indirect services, such as planting trees, cleaning streets, and maintaining grounds.[9]

A question in the survey regarding the budget for the volunteer program turned out to be difficult for some organizations and sensitive for others. This item resulted in the most missing and unreported cases. Of the 45 organizations in our sample, 38 did not provide any budget numbers. Among those organizations, 19 reported no budget for volunteer programs, and the other 19 organizations refused to answer the question. One possible explanation was that questions about budget size continue to raise the apprehensions of nonprofit, for-profit, and government organizations in Kazakhstan. The Soviet legacy of secrecy in financial and budget matters had left its mark on the behavior of many organizations in Kazakhstan: only seven organizations reported their volunteer program budgets. For 2003, the largest budget was a reported $34,600, and the smallest was just $215.

In all, the average nonprofit organization in the Kazakhstan sample was not large, with just 10 salaried employees. Each organization involved on average about 55 volunteers. Organizations used volunteers for various purposes, including direct, indirect, internal, and external functions. It is impossible to measure the size of volunteer programs by budgets because our respondents did not provide sufficient information.

Differences by Types of Organization

The information presented above describes the sample in general. In addition, important differences are evident across the types of organizations: youth, women's, and environmental. Our data showed that some differences do occur in volunteer programs and management practices depending on the policy domain of the nonprofit organizations.

As Table 7.4 shows, youth and women's organizations involved more volunteers in their activities than do environmental organizations. On average, in 2003, youth organizations involved 88 volunteers per organization. While women's organizations involved 21 volunteers per organization and environmental organizations involved only 12 volunteers per organization. The number of volunteers per youth organization confirmed conclusions made by previous researchers, and opinions of experts in Kazakhstan, that young people volunteer more readily there (Oliferov et al., 2001; UNDP 2002). In addition, the average volunteer in youth and women's organizations contributed more hours on an annual basis (132 and 146 hours, respectively) than the average volunteer in the environmental organizations (39 hours). From interviews with experts, we knew that youth and women's organizations often appealed to their target population to volunteer, while environmental organizations usually

Table 7.4.   Differences in volunteer programs

Program Description	Youth Organizations (23)	Womens Organizations (11)	Environmental Organizations (11)
Number of volunteers per organization	88	21	12
Contributed hours by an average volunteer	132	146	39
Average number of clients served by volunteers per organization	1,703	55	69
Organization has:			
Information on number of clients served	26%	45%	27%
Information on number of hours volunteered	53%	72%	63%
Paid staff	70%	90%	90%
Unsalaried, part-time volunteer coordinator	39%	9%	18%
Paid, full-time volunteer coordinator	61%	91%	81%

provided education, advocacy, and expertise services to external constituencies, both individuals and organizations.

Internal structure also differed across the three types of organizations. Youth organizations were less formal. The youth organizations had the largest percentage of unsalaried and part-time volunteer coordinators, 39%. Record keeping appeared to be loose and not performed by many youth organizations. About three-fourths of the organizations (74%) did not provide statistics on the number of clients served, and nearly half (47%) did not provide information on the number of hours that volunteers contributed to the organization. Volunteer coordinators in 7 youth organizations reported no paid staff (30%), which leads us to conclude that about 30% of youth organizations were volunteer-run organizations. Youth organizations may stay informal on purpose because this is more attractive to young people who want to be on equal footing with each other and with the leaders.

The women's organizations were more formal. Full-time and salaried volunteer coordinators constitute about 90% of respondents here. They had better record-keeping practices than the youth organizations: 45% of the women's organizations kept records of the number of clients served and 72% had records of hours contributed by volunteers. Only one women's organization was volunteer-run, and the rest had paid staff.

Environmental Organizations Were Also More Formal

Most of the organizations had full-time salaried volunteer coordinators (81%). These organizations did better keeping some records as compared to youth organizations, and were comparable to youth organizations in keeping other records. The information on the hours that volunteers contributed (63% provided the data) are recorded by most organizations, but the information on the number of clients served by organizations (73% did not provide the data) is incomplete. Ninety percent of respondents in environmental organizations reported having paid staff. As in the sample of women's organizations, only one environmental organization was volunteer-run.

To summarize, although many nonprofit organizations in Kazakhstan did not keep records of their volunteer management statistics, youth organizations were the least likely to keep or be cognizant of the information. Youth organizations were less formal than the two other types of organizations, as indicated by the number of nonsalaried and part-time workers, the number of volunteer-run organizations, and the more lax record keeping.

Adoption of Managerial Practices

The remainder of the analysis is concerned with how the differences by type of organization, youth, women's, and environmental, may translate into practices for managing volunteers. On the one hand, because of the greater number of volunteers, one might expect youth and women's organizations to have adopted more recommended practices for volunteer administration than environmental organizations (Table 7.4.) On the other hand, the youth organizations were more lax and less formal in record-keeping, paid supervision, and instituting rules and procedures and so may show lower rates of adoption. Table 7.5 lists eleven practices recommended in the literature of volunteer administration (Brudney, 1999). Table 7.5 displays the rates of reported implementation of these practices by the sample of organizations as a whole and as by the sub samples of youth, women's, and environmental organizations.

Table 7.5 shows that in the sample of nonprofit organizations, only twelve agencies (26%) reported having official rules governing the involvement of volunteers. Almost half of the women's organizations

Table 7.5.   Volunteer Management Practices Implemented by Types of Organizations

Practices Reported by Respondents	All Org-S (45)	Youth (23)	Womens (11)	Environmental (11)
Official rules for involvement of volunteers	26%	22%	46%	18%
Training for employees in working effectively with volunteers	18%	30%	9%	0%
Liability insurance for volunteers	2%	0%	2%	0%
Job descriptions for volunteers	38%	35%	54%	27%
Recognition for volunteers, such as award ceremonies, certificates	51%	61%	55%	27%
Participation of volunteers in luncheons	56%	61%	55%	46%
Reimbursement for the work-related expenses of volunteers	44%	48%	46%	36%
Formal record keeping for volunteer activities (hours contributed and work assignments)	11%	13%	9%	9%
Outreach efforts to recruit volunteers	20%	30%	9%	9%
Formal orientation for volunteers on how to do the job	62%	70%	64%	46%
Training and professional development opportunities for volunteers to assume greater responsibility	40%	57%	27%	18%

Source: Kazakhstan Nonprofit Survey (2004).

(46%) had such rules, the highest percentage across the three types of organizations.

Less than 40% of the sample (38%) developed job descriptions for their volunteers (17). Women's organizations were more likely to use this practice. More than half (54%) of these organizations had job descriptions, compared to slightly more than one-third (35%) of youth organizations and slightly less than one-third (27%) of the environmental organizations.

About half of the organizations in the sample used recognition for volunteers to enhance morale (51%). Youth and women's organizations used this practice at a considerably higher rate than did environmental organizations (61%, 55%, and 27%, respectively).

The most popular volunteer appreciation practice in these organizations was an invitation for luncheons. Fifty-six percent of all organizations used this practice. The three types of organizations regularly provided this reward to their volunteers.

In 44% of the sample (20), the organizations reimbursed volunteers for their work-related expenses. Almost half of youth (48%) and women's (46%) organizations reimbursed their volunteers, while only 36% of environmental organizations used such a practice.

Over 60% (62%) of the organizations had formal orientation for volunteers on how to do the job (28). Youth and women's organizations reported this practice more often than environmental organizations (70%, 64%, and 46%, respectively).

None of the remaining practices were widely implemented across the sample, although interesting differences occurred by organization types. Almost one-fifth (20%) of the organizations practiced outreach to recruit volunteers; the practice was much more common in the youth organizations (30%). Training for employees in working effectively with volunteers reveals a similar pattern, implemented by 18% of all organizations, and 30% of youth organizations. Eleven percent of organizations kept records of volunteer activities, such as hours and work assignments, with minimal differences by organization type. Finally, only one organization in the entire sample (a women's organization) had liability insurance for volunteers.

The results in the Table 7.5 suggest that two types of organizations— youth and women's—used particular practices, such as recognition ceremonies, reimbursement of expenses, orientation of volunteers and others, more often than do the environmental organizations. Youth organizations reported the highest level of implementation. Environmental organizations reported the lowest level. The number of volunteers and intensity of their work for youth and women's organizations (as indicated by Table 7.4) may partially explain the differences across the types of organization in applying some practices while ignoring others. Another explanation for the difference across types may be the numbers of volunteer coordinators that had received training in volunteer management; youth organizations had the highest level of volunteer coordinators who reported that they have received training.

DISCUSSION

In this section, we attempt to explain why the variations in adoption of volunteer management practices are found across the types of organizations. As mentioned above, although we observe some differences across the types of organization in terms of the level of formality (number of paid employees and record-keeping), these differences do not appear to translate into the adoption of managerial practices for volunteers. Environmental organizations are most formalized, yet have the lowest level of adoption. By contrast, other factors such as the number of volunteers involved, the hours that volunteers contribute, and the number of trained managers influence how organizations apply volunteer management practices. The size of the volunteer program and managerial competence may make the difference.

On average, youth organizations have far more volunteers (88 per organization), followed by women's organizations (21 per organization), and by environmental organizations (12 per organization). Respondents who had received volunteer management training were more likely to be found in youth organizations (61%) and the women's organizations (55%) than in the environmental organizations (36%). Table 5 shows that the youth organizations apply the recommended managerial techniques more often than do the other organization types, and that the environmental organizations do so least often.

Variations across the organizations in application of recommended practices may also stem from differences in the types of activities organized by the three groups of nonprofits. In general, youth organizations involve more volunteers because most activities of youth organizations require mass participation, such as sport events, cleaning the national parks, celebrations and youth forums. By their nature, such activities require high levels of coordination, orientation, and training. Table 7.5 demonstrates that youth organizations in most cases apply appropriate managerial techniques and outreach more often than do the other types.

Women's organizations involve fewer volunteers, but volunteer involvement occurs on a regular basis. In many cases, volunteers are also beneficiaries of their programs. This explains the fact that volunteers in these organizations contribute more hours than volunteers in environmental organizations. The work of volunteers in some women's organizations is bound by more regulations and rules because these organizations' clients are needy and abused women. A number of women's organizations work closely with international organizations, providing gender analysis of laws, consultancy and expertise. A close connection to international organizations may be one of the factors that influences how women's organizations manage their volunteers. Some women's organization leaders claimed that sponsoring organizations often closely control implementation of the programs to make sure that results are achieved.

The leaders of some environmental organizations explained that these organizations typically prefer experts in the field of environmental protection to work as their volunteers. They often limit involvement by untrained volunteers for this reason, and do not spend much time on training and education. Such experts require minimum supervision, training, rules and regulations. The high level of volunteers' competence in this domain may help to explain why environmental organizations seem to pay the least attention to volunteer management practices.

Our discussion suggests that the most important factors that may account for differences in application of volunteer management practices are the size of volunteer programs, competent staff trained in volunteer management, and the nature of activities performed in the various organizations. The larger the size of the volunteer program and the higher the incidence of trained volunteer coordinators, the more we can expect these organizations to apply the recommended practices for volunteer administration. The activities of these organizations may also affect the managerial techniques chosen. Activities involving greater number of volunteers may require more outreach efforts, coordination, and training.

CONCLUSION

The study of volunteer management in former countries of the Soviet Union is rare. In this paper, we have presented the first enquiry focused on the state of volunteer management in Kazakhstan. The study was conducted on a sample of 45 nonprofit organizations in Almaty, the largest city in the country. Because our interest is in volunteer management, the sample was targeted to three types of nonprofit organizations in which the involvement of volunteers was anticipated to be robust: youth, women's, and environmental. An exhaustive search to establish a listing of these types of nonprofit organizations in Almaty resulted in an effective sample of 76 active nonprofit organizations. Sixteen of them involved no volunteers, leaving an effective sample of 60 organizations that we contacted to participate in our survey. Of this group, 45 completed the survey for a high response rate of 75%.

The particular findings are summarized throughout the article. Here we close with some general results.

Kazakhstan has been an independent state for only a short time, and the nonprofit sector and the volunteer movement are relatively new to this developing nation. Perhaps as a result, the volunteer programs in our sample of nonprofit organizations are modest in size and on average, involve smaller number of volunteers compared to nonprofit organizations in western countries. As might have been expected, the volunteer coordinators in these nonprofit organizations do not seem to regularly apply the practices for volunteer management recommended in the Western literature (e.g., Ellis, 1996; McCurley & Lynch, 1996). Yet, our research findings show that the rate of implementation of the volunteer management practices varies according to the three types of organization, youth, women's, and environmental. These findings suggest that even at this early stage of development of Kazakhstan's third sector, the management of volunteers seems to have been adapted to organizational circumstances. Among the factors that we speculate might explain these differences in implementation are the size of the volunteer program, the level of managerial preparedness, and the nature of the activities performed by the different organizations. These findings and results merit further attention as we try to explain and understand the growth of volunteer management practices in former Soviet Union countries.

NOTES

1. Annual growth of nonprofit sector in Kazakhstan is described in publication of the Institute for Development Cooperation, the nonprofit research and support center. The Institute used the Statistics Agency registration data in order to follow the dynamics of the third sector development.

2. "Active" is defined by statistics Agency of Kazakhstan as those organizations that annually report their activities. "Idle" are those nonprofits that do not report their activities for two years. To give an example, in 2002 the number of registered organizations in the whole Kazakhstan was 6,796, while the number of "active" organizations was 3,836. However, the experts on the nonprofit sector of Kazakhstan maintained that in fact there were only 700 to 800 of actively working nonprofits in Kazakhstan. The trick is that "active" in the statistics agency sense is different from the "actively working" in the sense the experts who monitor the activities of these organizations imply. This distinction is important for our further discussion. Yet, having the full registration list from the statistics agency was useless for the purpose of this research because 90% of the organizations on the list were not actively working, according to the experts.

3. The nonprofit sector experts are the officers of nongovernmental, international, and local resource organizations that provide institutional, educational and financial support to grassroots in Kazakhstan. Such organizations are the UNDP, the Soros Foundation, the USAID, the Counterpart Consortium, and so on.

4. It may sound strange to people who live and work in Western societies that organizations change their location and contact information so often. But in the situation of general social and economic instability in Kazakhstan, nonprofits as well as small businesses come and go, and move quite often.

5. Three organizations (5%) refused to participate; two of the organization leaders said they did not believe in the usefulness of surveys, and one leader refused without explanation. The completion of 45 questionnaires required multiple follow-ups. We contacted some organizations four or five times to persuade their leaders or volunteer managers to respond to our survey. Some organizations participated only after seven to eight follow-ups. Despite our efforts, nonrespondents constituted 20% of our sample. We classified as nonrespondents those who initially promised to fill in the ques-

tionnaire and never did it regardless of our follow-up efforts. After analyzing the situation with nonrespondents we came to the conclusion that these organizations were in the "idle" phase of existence. Idle organizations try to keep their reputation as working organizations in the community of nonprofit and international donor organizations. The leaders of the "idles" participate in the conferences, training sessions, and forums organized by nonprofit support and donor organizations to maintain visibility. Often they have their office at home, where there is somebody to answer the phone. In reality, the leaders of these organizations work as consultants, or trainers while looking for the opportunity to receive a grant and to continue their regular nonprofit operations. Despite our efforts to contact them, they were not accessible. We have classified these organizations as "idle," that is, as existing but temporarily having suspended their operations. Other nonprofit leaders corroborated our assessment.

6. We are skeptical about the one subject in our sample who said that she was a director of volunteer programs and devoted 100% of her time to volunteer administration. She reported only three volunteers working for her organization in 2003.

7. Kazakhs—44%, Russian—36%, Ukrainians—5%, Germans—4%, Uzbeks—2.3%, Tatars—2%; Azerbaijanis, Uygurs, and Belarusians each represented 1%; and the remaining 4% included approximately 90 other nationalities (http://www.country-data.com/cgi-bin/query/r-7519.html)

8. Our interviews with leaders of nonprofit organizations have revealed that flexible volunteer management assignments existed in some organizations. When organizations worked on specific projects that involved volunteers, the leaders assigned a project manager to work as a volunteer coordinator for the duration of the project. As soon as the project was completed, the assignment was temporarily dismissed.

9. Because organizations reported using volunteers in several ways, the total number of organizations using volunteers for the four major tasks does not sum to 100%.

CHAPTER 8

VOLUNTEER MANAGEMENT IN POLISH NGOs

Challenges of Formalization

Angela L. Bies and Stephanie A. Curs

BACKGROUND AND PURPOSE

As the environments of public and nongovernmental organizations (NGOs) in the former Soviet states have become increasingly complex in recent years, concern for the development of institutions of civil society and new forms and delivery mechanisms of public services has intensified. These trends are of critical importance to NGO sectors in such contexts as nongovernmental actors are increasingly called on to respond to complex social needs, increasing performance demands, competing priorities, divergent stakeholder needs, and shifting financial, human resource and regulatory environments, as well as emergent institutional forms. With an increased scope of economic activity and sphere of influence, the activity of NGOs has come under heightened attention, with concern for managerial, governance, and operational practices of NGOs emerging as paramount for funders, policymakers, and NGO leaders. With this concern comes a

Challenges in Volunteer Management, pp. 173–204
Copyright © 2008 by Information Age Publishing

focus on human resource development, particularly as it relates to the participation of volunteers in NGOs, and more importantly, the management of such volunteers. The case of post-Soviet Poland is particularly valuable in illuminating challenges to and opportunities for volunteer management in the NGO sector.

Since independence in 1989, Poland has transformed itself from a centralized, state-controlled system to a market-driven, democracy that joined NATO in 1999 and the European Union in 2004. Poland has also experienced rapid and expansive transformation, not only in the private and governmental sectors, but also in the nongovernmental sector. Polish NGOs historically have played and will continue to play an integral role in building and maintaining democracy (Council of Europe, Parliamentary Assembly, 1995). Poland's NGO sector plays a vital role by contributing to the economy through employment and community development and by providing social service, arts, cultural, and educational programs (Phare Civic Dialogue Program, 1998). It is estimated that there are approximately 52,000 functioning organizations (United States Agency for International Development [USAID], 2004).

Study of volunteer management in the context of Poland is valuable, as the Polish NGO sector is often pointed to as an example of an emergent NGO sector with a relatively well-developed infrastructure, a historic context that includes traditions of philanthropy, charity and voluntarism, and relatively ample resources for NGO training, development, and capacity building (Phare Civic Dialogue Program, 1998). During the process of establishing and developing the post-Soviet NGO sector, Poland did not simply import or adopt philanthropic, educational, and institutional models from more established foreign NGO contexts, but rather the Polish NGO sector adapted various foreign models for local contexts, and even exported its own innovations to other established NGO settings in both the West (Council of Europe, Parliamentary Assembly, 1995, p. 95) and more emergent NGO contexts, such as those of Kosovo and Ukraine (Bies, 2003).

As this chapter will illustrate, the challenges facing Poland's NGO sector are in many ways similar to those encountered by organizations and institutions in older and/or more formalized NGO sectors. These challenges include resource constraints, the promotion of philanthropy and volunteerism, and the improvement of NGO management practices. The Polish NGO sector, however, faces heightened intensity and formalization challenges as it builds itself anew within a changing economic, social, and political context.

In recent years, discussion has increasingly turned to the issue of developing volunteers and volunteer management practices, including the establishment of a national network of regional volunteer management support centers. Such initiatives face formalization challenges at the societal level, in terms of fostering the idea of volunteering, and at the sectoral and organizational levels, in terms of helping NGOs develop and manage volunteer involvement in their mission and work. Thus, in this chapter, volunteer management in Poland is examined in three primary ways: (1) through a description and analysis of the current NGO landscape in Poland in relationship to volunteerism and volunteer management, (2) by a review of current facts and figures associated with voluntary action in Poland, and (3) through a description and analysis of current NGO organizational realities, and the related challenges and opportunities posed for volunteer management.

This chapter first introduces the methodology utilized in a recent national study of NGO management practices in Poland. The chapter then provides an overview of the Polish NGO landscape, a presentation of current voluntary action trends, and the presentation of themes related to organizational realities and formalization challenges for volunteer management in Polish NGOs. Implications and recommendations for practice are presented. The chapter finishes with insights for future comparative research.

METHODOLOGY AND DATA SOURCES

A mixed-method research design was utilized to gather in-depth qualitative and quantitative data necessary to describe and better understand issues of volunteer management in Poland's contemporary NGO sector. First, a thorough review of both the academic and practice literature in the domain of volunteerism and volunteer management was undertaken. Secondary data compiled by KLON-JAWOR,[1] an independent research center dedicated to documenting and supporting Polish NGOs, were utilized to describe the sector and to depict current volunteerism trends and volunteer management practices.

Primary data were derived from Bies' representative 2003 national study of 918 NGOs (representing a 52% response rate) in Poland, which included questions designed to obtain both quantitative and qualitative data. Participants responded to the following four areas of organizational-level activities: training activities, financial and human resources, organizational factors, and implementation of management practices. Data were also collected through in-depth interviews with representatives of 5 key institutional funders, 10 direct service NGOs, and 7 nongovernmental support organizations, including one regional volunteer center and several with explicit volunteerism goals. In general, chief executives and 2 to 3 other key personnel, including board members, were interviewed. In 2004-2006, interviews regarding employment and volunteer trends were also conducted with 15 advanced students of social and nongovernmental policy in Poland. Deductive and inductive processes of thematic, content analysis were used for analysis of qualitative data. Archival data from NGO support organizations, nonprofit organizations, and funders were also utilized.

Poland's NGO Sector

Since the mid-1980s, Poland's NGO sector has experienced exponential growth as a result of the increased presence of democratic principles and rights, as well as the triumph of the Solidarity movement. With the development of a more democratic system, Poland's NGO sector has changed dramatically in terms of the types and numbers, functionality, and management practices of NGOs, as well as current support structures and mechanisms in place for the NGO sector. As the entire NGO sector has experienced sweeping changes in terms of formalization so too has the notion of volunteer mobilization and management within organizations. It is the purpose of this introductory section to provide a holistic overview of Poland's NGO sector in light of recent history, relevant legislation, and current institutions and infrastructure. From this, a list of challenges, opportunities, and threats relating to volunteer management are summarized.

Historical Roots

A very simple snapshot of Poland's history might look something like this: a nation with more than 1,000 years of distinctive history, with a unique culture, language and heritage, alternatively rich and poor, alternatively an independent state and a dominated state, emerging triumphant in post-Soviet independence. The Solidarity movement, beginning in 1980, presented the people of Poland the freedom to act, volunteer, and congregate publicly in order to meet social demands (Kurczewski & Kurczewska, 2001). Yet even as Poland has developed its institutions of democracy and civil society, challenges relating to socialist ideological roots and processes of denationalization and decentralization remain (Imbrogno, 1990; Leś, 1996). Such challenges complicate the development of the NGO sector, as well.

This post-Soviet era is also characterized by rapid investment in and growth of Poland's institutions of democracy and civil society, including the establishment and formalization of NGOs, the number of individuals volunteering time or resources to social causes, and related infrastructure. It is natural that the free market democratization era that emerged after the nearly 40 years of Soviet repression captures most of the limited scholarship on Poland's NGO sector.

But the primacy of the role played by NGOs in the reform breakthroughs of 1989 often overshadows the rich history of voluntary association and social participation in Poland. It is important, therefore, to briefly highlight key points from Poland's arguably rich history of philanthropy, voluntarism, and NGO regulation. Three major periods of Polish history are influential to understanding the development and current state of affairs in Poland's NGO sector:[2] (1) early activities and formation of foundations and associations, (2) the intervening years between the World Wars, and (3) Poland under the Soviet Regime (Boczoń, Erene, & Gałęziak, 1996; Frysztacki, 1996; Leś, Nałecz, & Wygnaski, 2000; Phare Civic Dialogue Program, 1998).

Early Activities

Historical accounts of the development of philanthropy, civil society, citizen participation and action, and the NGO sector in Poland often refer to early feudal traditions, such as ancestralism and tribalism, as important points of origin. It is from these traditions that the notion of *caritas* (from Latin meaning loving kindness toward others, and taking form in the English language in the word charity) emerges and takes root in the form of Polish traditions of moral solidarity and responsibilities to one's neighbors. Similar to the role of the Catholic Church in Western Europe, the Roman Catholic Church in Poland, through its religious associations and monastic foundations of the fourteenth century, also played a critical role in shaping deeply embedded values related to education and charity (Leś, Nałecz, & Wygnaski, 2000).

Although closely affiliated with the Catholic Church, charitable brotherhoods, which were actually secular in nature, were formed to carry out charitable works. Other secular forms of civic association, participation, and philanthropy are associated with the fourteenth and fifteenth centuries, with a prominent example being the establishment of a formal organization of salt miners dedicated to improving working conditions (Leś, 1996).

The sixteenth and seventeenth centuries are associated with the first scholarly, dowry, and assistance foundations. Leś (1996) indicates that these foundations provided a framework for social initiative that eventually helped shape and form expectations for government. Such foundations and associations played critical roles during the late eighteenth and nineteenth centuries when Poland lost its sovereignty. "Lacking independence, being partitioned and ruled by foreign powers, Polish society started to build new forms of its own devising" (Frysztacki, 1996, p. 217).

Furthermore, Leś (1996) indicates that during the period of partitioning, social organizations took both unofficial and official forms to carry out functions normally provided for by the state. Coupled with the new societal role for such organizations is the increasing importance of citizen participation and volunteerism to execute such charitable deeds. It was also during this time that philanthropic and voluntary traditions gained prominence and were viewed as mechanisms for fostering an independent Poland.

Between the World Wars

The years immediately following World War I are defined primarily by the reestablishment of an independent, sovereign Polish state. In many ways, this era can be described as a period of relative normalcy, with the NGO sector working alongside a functioning public administration to provide for social services, education, and cultural activities. Also, because of a need to provide various services during this time frame, new opportunities for community and civic engagement were presented to Poles. Frysztacki (1996), however, also characterizes this period "by growing tensions and demands for social actions connected with such phenomena as stages of industrialization and growing complexity of urban life" (p. 217). Diverse NGO associations and forms of voluntary action emerged during this era including sports clubs, activist or political associations, labor associations, and, even tourism associations.

Poland also has a rich, and complicated, legacy of NGO regulation. Until 1919, Polish NGOs operated under the three legal systems associated with the partitions. In 1919-1933, the interim Decree on Associations served to begin to unify NGO regulation. The Law on Associations went into effect in 1933 and provided at least some unanimity and coherence to NGO law. The Law on Associations also provided guidance on what adequately constituted an association, provided for organizational foci on education, culture, sports, hobbies, and provision of care, and made firm the free right to associate. In 1939, 1,545 foundations were active in philanthropic and charitable work; more than 1,000 associations were documented to be active in a variety of youth, family and community activities (Leś, 1996).

Under the Soviet Regime

The communist era in Poland, during years 1945-1989, is typically viewed as being largely inhospitable to voluntary association and civic engagement. "In spite of constitutional guarantees, the freedom to associate and the freedom of expression, which constitute the mainstay for

NGOs, were systematically violated" (Leś, 1996, p. 11). Civic organizations could not be formed voluntarily; citizens were limited in their abilities to influence governmental policy and practice. Frysztacki (1996) emphasizes the "overwhelming presence of the state/communist party administrative and political apparatus; an apparatus trying to exercise power and control through broad process aimed at establishing or at least influencing different institutions and organizations" (p. 217).

To illustrate the systematic constraints placed on NGOs and general voluntary engagement, Leś (1996), points to the Decree of 1952, during which the assets of all foundations were acquired and the operations taken over by the state, as essentially limiting the potential form of civic initiative to a single type of organization, the association. In effect, however, legal regulations during this era largely limited any form of free association. Those associations that remained from previous eras or that were newly formed were largely controlled by or served as extensions of the state apparatus. Assets of associations, including physical plant assets such as school buildings and hospitals, were largely subsumed by the state. At the same time, the state facilitated various quasi-governmental organizations and social movements designed to carry out the objectives of the state and influence the masses. The vestiges of such quasi-governmental organization and compulsory civic participation remain in negative public perceptions, cynicism, and mistrust of NGOs and volunteering (Leś et al., 2000).

As the socialist welfare state established under the Communist regime began to fail in later years, grassroots social movements began to take hold, and the revival of the NGO sector was reignited:

> The society manifested its growing discontent with the communist system which failed to deliver on its promises: social justice and economic welfare. In the seventies and the eighties the disillusionment with the system gradually led to the emergence of the "alternative" or "parallel society," which manifested itself through spontaneous and informal civic initiatives in the social, economic, and political sphere. (Leś, 1996, p. 13)

Leś (1996), Leś et al. (2000), Frysztacki (1996), and Boczoń et al. (1996) all cite the role of civic and NGOs, the most emblematic example being that of the Solidarity trade union, as mechanisms for providing institutional, moral, and social bases for the relatively peaceful transition to a democratized Polish political system. Polish traditions of philanthropy, cultural preservation, civic association, voluntary action, and self-initiative all carried on in the rapid expansion of the NGO sector post-1989.

Thus, in the years leading up to and markedly in post-1989 Poland, the NGO sector played a pivotal role as an intermediary in the development and formalization of both the newly formed private and

public sectors, while shaping and forming new traditions, forms and institutions.

> The voluntary sector contributed to filling in the social area between formal
> sectors that belong to, as broadly understood, the state and the world of pri-
> vate patterns of life, in the private, family aspect and the aspect of economi-
> cal enterprises alike. (Frysztacki, 1996)

With the increased prominence of the NGO sector in Poland, sectoral and
organizational leaders began to focus on the importance of developing
volunteers, as well as the need for effective volunteer management in
order to successfully achieve the increasingly vital social and economic
expectations of NGOs.

Contemporary Trends

Poland is often cited as an excellent example of rapid post-Soviet
development and growth in the NGO sector, with 25% of NGOs being
less than 4 years old, and 80% being established and formalizing after the
collapse of communism in1989 (KLON, 2000). Poland is also strongly
identified as a state in which the NGO sector has been instrumental in
fostering institutions of civil society and democratization. For example, in
the NGO sustainability index that covers 28 countries of the former
Soviet block, Poland was ranked as second (USAID/Freedom House/
KLON-JAWOR, 2000). This section highlights key aspects of Poland's
NGO development, provides a general characterization and demographic overview of the Polish NGO sector, and discusses the current
funding, legal, and institutional environments of Polish NGOs, including
NGO support structures and mechanisms, as they relate to and have
implications for volunteer management.

Characterizing the Polish NGO Sector

The Polish translation and comprehension of the NGO sector is similar to that of the much of the rest of the world. Frysztacki's (1996) studies
indicate that, "descriptive and explanatory notions, like nonprofit,
interdependent and nongovernmental, charitable and philanthropic, and
voluntary sectors" are commonly utilized to illustrate the NGO sector
(p. 215).

The European Volunteer Center (2005, p. 4) notes that Poland's
conception of a nongovernmental organization is based primarily on the
past 15 years of NGO practice, and centers on five main criteria. Such
organizations must be: (1) institutionalized or formalized to some extent,

(2) must be independent from government and free to identify and pursue its own objectives, (3) must be self-governed, (4) must not redistribute profits to members or other involved entities, and (5) must have some measure of volunteer involvement. The Center's report notes that such criteria of independence and self-governance are "particularly relevant considering Communistic suppression of voluntary goals and activities" (p. 4). In addition, the volunteer involvement criterion is noteworthy, as

> the majority of NGOs do not have paid recruits and rely (at least partially) on voluntary contributions of people. Only state established foundations and private funded foundations have only paid staff positions and therefore they do not meet this criterion. (p. 4)

According to Wygnański (1996), many of the NGOs established in Poland today originally formed to institutionalize group activity and to address the "state policy regarding attempts at social self-organization" (p. 229). Additionally, after independence in 1989 and as governmental institutions became more open, democratic, and less authoritarian, the NGO sector witnessed a drastic influx in the number of organizations represented in Poland (Wygnański, 1996). This is not to insinuate, however, that traditions of civic participation do not have deep historical and cultural roots; on the contrary, and as illustrated in the discussion of the history of Poland's NGO sector, Poland draws on its cultural, religious, political, and legal conceptualizations of civic participation, and overcomes some lingering constraints on such participation associated with the Soviet era.

A mounting number of contemporary civic organizations contribute considerably to the modernization and amplified impact of social services afforded to citizens in Poland (Anheier & Salamon, 1999). Furthermore, as the NGO sector becomes more clearly defined, formalized and recognized by the Polish government and population, future success within the sector will depend profoundly on state and NGO cooperation, European integration, and ongoing investment in Poland's NGO sector by private and public sector donors.

Definition of the NGO Sector

In 2003, the Polish government adopted the new law on Public Benefit Activity and Volunteer Work Act, also known as the third-sector constitution or PBA Act. The law defines NGOs as

> legal entities or entities with no legal personality created on the basis of provisions of laws, including foundations and associations. NGOs are not bodies of the sector of public finances in the understanding of regulations

governing public finances, and operate on a not-for-profit basis.[3] (Government of Poland, Law on Benefit Activity and Voluntarism, 2002)

Government and socially recognized organizations typically fall under one of two types: associations or foundations. An association, by Polish law, is, "a self-governing, lasting (membership) organization, formed of free will and with a nonprofit motive ... no one can be forced to join or prevented from freely withdrawing from an association" (United States International Grantmaking, 2008). A foundation, on the other hand, is much more difficult to define. A generally accepted definition of a foundation is, "a non-membership organization, established by a founder (who provides the foundation with the initial endowment) that pursues 'economically and socially beneficial objectives' " (USIG, 2004). Associations and foundations differ on public benefit status, tax exemption, and funding bases. Both types indicate Poland's strides in formalizing and recognizing the NGO sector.

Legal Frameworks

In addition to providing the contemporary legal definition of an NGO, the April 23, 2003 Public Benefit Activity and Volunteer Work Act, or PBA Act, also

> addresses key issues important from the perspective of the Third sector. It defines the criteria for public benefit status of Polish NGOs; provides a procedural framework for NGO cooperation with public authorities; introduces a version of the '1% law,' which means that every citizen has a right to donate 1% of its income tax to a selected NGO. (European Volunteer Center, 2005, p. 6)

Once the PBA Act was adopted into law, the Polish Ministry of Social Policy's Department of Benefit Activity became the governmental entity responsible for supporting and promoting the development and formalization of the NGO sector, which includes encouraging volunteerism on a national level (European Volunteer Center, 2005, p. 10).

Initially, some critics expressed concern that the PBA Act did not adequately address cross-sector cooperation issues; however, it is now nationally recognized that the "PBA Act did provide clarification on a number of issues that had been previously omitted in legislation, and gave NGOs an opportunity to build their awareness about laws governing the sector" (USAID, 2004, p. 197). The PBA Act set forth new protections for volunteers, which include: regulations to reimburse volunteers for expenses incurred while they are volunteering; mandatory health checks and insurance provided for volunteers; a signed agreement between the volunteer and the organization to formalize the relationship; and new opportunities for training within organizations and for leaders (European Volunteer Center, 2005). Each of these has greatly influenced the number of Poles who are volunteering in organizations and have fostered a formalization process within organizations and the NGO sector as a whole.

Furthermore, the Law on Public Benefit and Activity and Volunteerism contains numerous provisions intended to provide greater incentives to domestic donors and to strengthen monetary support of foundations and association in Polish tax laws (United States International Grantmaking, 2008). Volunteer mobilization has been made simpler in the past 2 years due to the implementation of explicit rights granted to volunteers under the Law of Public Benefit Activity and Volunteerism. The recently supported volunteer rights under the Law include: safe and hygienic work conditions; comprehensive information on potential risks involved with the services to be provided; volunteers' travel expenses while providing services incurred by the organization; per diem provided for volunteers for subsistence costs; training costs for volunteers; and general health care coverage for volunteers automatically provided for volunteers (Association of Voluntary Service Organizations [AVSO], 2003). Combined these encourage volunteerism, help to establish standards for volunteer management, and provide mechanisms for managers to protect and reward volunteers.

Demographics of Poland's NGO Sector

Depending on the source, the number and typology of established organizations vary significantly. In any analysis, rapid development post-1989 and the ongoing growth of the NGO sector thereafter are apparent. The European Volunteer Centre (2005) estimates that 91% of the registered NGOs were founded after 1989, with 30% being less than 3 years old. Similarly, USAID (2004) reports that the number of recognized organizations comprising the NGO sector grew from a very few in 1989 to nearly 35,000 in 1999. Though conflicting approximations exist, today it is estimated that there are approximately 52,000 functioning organizations (41,000 associations and 11,000 foundations in 2004, up from 36,500 associations and 5,000 foundations in 2002), consisting of an average size of 15 to 150 members (Kurczewski & Kurczewska, 2001; USAID, 2004).

KLON-JAWOR classifies organizations into 20 areas of organizational activity. These are listed from most common to least common in Table 8.1 below.

Of Poland's registered NGOs, almost half are located in Warsaw, the nation's capital city and economic center (KLON-JAWOR, 2000). KLON-JAWOR estimates that approximately two-thirds of the registered NGOs are active. NGOs in Poland are primarily engaged in the following

Table 8.1. KLON-JAWOR NGO Activity Areas (Rank Ordered)

1. Education	8. Regional and local development	15. Religion
2. Social aid	9. Science	16. State, law, and politics
3. Family, children, youth	10. Hobby	17. Agriculture
4. Healthcare	11. Human rights	18. Housing, transportation, and construction
5. Sports	12. Mass media	19. Communication
6. Art, culture	13. Professional interests	20. Public safety
7. Ecology	14. Economy	

Sources: Wygnański (1996); Kurczewski and Kurczewska (2001).

activities: work in health care and rehabilitation, 20.6%; social assistance and charity work, 17%; educational activity, 16%, and arts, culture, historical, and cultural preservation, 11% (KLON-JAWOR, 2000; Phare Civic Dialogue Program, 1998).

In Poland, the NGO sector comprises approximately 2% of nonagricultural employment (Leś, et al., 2000) with some 100,000 people serving in paid posts with NGOs (compared to 0.6% in Romania and 12.6% in Holland) (KLON-JAWOR, 2000). Because nearly half of all Polish NGOs employ no paid staff and more than 85% utilize volunteers to carry out their missions, the contributions of volunteers are significant, although not easily monetized. 24% of adult Poles reported working or volunteering in at least one NGO in their spare time (KLON-JAWOR, 2000).

Financial and Funding Trends

The financial resources of NGOs are cited as an often incompletely or inaccurately discussed topic in relationship to Poland's NGO sector (Phare Civic Dialogue Program, 1998; Wygnański, 1996). Wygnański indicates that such discussion on NGO financial resources "too often feeds on illusions, misunderstandings.... One of the principal illusions is the conviction that non-governmental organizations are sponsored exclusively from public money and, moreover, this process is highly criticized" (p. 239). He argues that such falsehoods are based, in part, on assumptions and convictions about the role and relationships between the public and nongovernmental sectors in Poland. In Poland, a tension exists between those who believe the government should fully support social services, and by extension the work of the NGO sector, versus those who believe that NGOs should be separate and independent from the sector and who associate heavy government funding with a lack of NGO independence (Boczoń et al., 1995; Wygnański, 1996).

In actuality, most Polish NGOs are relatively small in terms of annual budgets, with 43% of the NGOs having annual budgets that do not exceed PLN 10,000 (approximately 2,400 U.S. dollars). Although most do not rely heavily on governmental funds, 30% of the total combined revenue of all NGOs in Poland does come from public sector funds (largely from local, regional, and European Union funds) (European Volunteer Center, 2005). The financial resource trends in Poland's NGO sector are as follows:

1. The most frequent source of revenue is membership fees (with 69% of NGOs reporting utilizing this source).
2. The second most frequent funding source is philanthropic support (46.5%), primarily through grants or donations, from private individuals and firms.
3. The third most frequent source of financial resources is local government support (29%), followed closely by support from the central (national) budget (23.7%).
4. The fourth most frequent source of funding is grants from other NGOs (18%), which sometimes serve as intermediary distribution channels for foreign and domestic funders. The frequency of such funding is approximately parallel to that of direct funding from domestic and foreign donor agencies (23%).
5. The fifth most frequent source of funding relates to commercial activities and capital income gains of individual NGOs. This type of internally generated funding is increasing in its scope, representing 14.5% of funding sources in 1998, a 27.8% increase in prevalence over 1993 figures.
6. Approximately 14% of NGOs report practically doing without any actual financial resources (KLON-JAWOR, 2001; Phare Civic Dialogue Program, 1998).

Fostering the development of private, voluntary philanthropy is seen as critical to the future stability and vitality of Poland's NGO sector (Frysztacki, 1996) and as a necessity as Poland's NGO sector matures and becomes less reliant on foreign sources of funding (Phare Civic Dialogue Program, 1998). A recent study on philanthropic activities carried out by KLON-JAWOR (2001) provides baseline data for future comparison.

1. During fiscal year 2000, 18% of small- and medium-sized corporations gave donations for various activities, with 57% of their sup-

port being directed at "charity-related work." On average, the companies devoted 5% of their gross income to charities.

2. In 2000, 57% of Poles reported making a contribution in some manner to an NGO. Over 20% made formal donations to NGOs, but only 10% of these donors utilized the related charitable tax deduction for which they qualified. Over 65% of respondents indicated that they would consider giving 1% of their income tax to NGOs (KLON-JAWOR, 2000).

Moreover, though it is evident that Polish NGOs rely heavily upon volunteers and citizen participation, volunteer time is often not considered in the funding schemes for NGOs. Research indicates that Poles are more likely to volunteer money and goods as opposed to time, which, again, is primarily a result of former, totalitarian regimes (Regulska, 2001). Organizations within the voluntary sector, coupled with preconceived notions of older regimes, may lack sufficient the capacity and skills to recruit necessary personnel to provide services within organizations.

Nongovernmental Support Structures and Mechanisms

The term nongovernmental support organizations (NSOs) refers to organizations that contribute to the knowledge development, policy advocacy or political lobbying, and research efforts in the field of NGO management. NSOs (also referred to as nonprofit management support organizations, in the literature) are focused on the provision of management resources to NGOs with the goal of improving organizational operations (Connor, Kadel-Taras, & Vinokur-Kaplan, 2003). The largest component of this mission involves training and educating managers. This definition is similar to the definition utilized by the Phare Program (1998) of the European Union, which labels such organizations as "nonprofit infrastructure organizations" and is extended to also include the term "community support organizations" (Conner et al., 2003, p. 135), which operate on a more grass roots level.

Poland has a well-developed and well-functioning network of NSOs. Primary NSOs in Poland include: (1) Working Community of Associations of Social NGOs in Poland (WRZOS), the national association with regional organizations and international exchange programs; (2) The Network of Information and Support Centers for NGOs (SPLOT), the national association of management support organizations with sixteen regional organizations; (3) KLON/JAWOR, the national NGO databank which conducts research and evaluation activities related to the Polish NGO sector; (4) The Association for the Forum of NGO Initiatives (FIP), with a mission of advancing the role of the third sector in civil society, to create a common identity with the sector, to advance relationships among citizens, NGOs, government and the private sector, and to advocate for a legal environment favorable toward NGOs, and (5) the network of 16 regional Volunteer Centers, including the National Volunteer Center, the first of its kind when it began in 1993 (European Volunteer Center, 2005).

Organizational Environment

In addition to the need to develop private philanthropy, concern also focuses on the development and strengthening of individual NGOs. A survey conducted by KLON-JAWOR in 1997 reveals the following training needs of NGOs: (1) over 70% of NGOs reported a need for training on fundraising, (2) 47% are interested in training related to expanding their activities, including the involvement of more volunteers, (3) 41% are interested in training on financial management and accounting, (4) 40% would like training related to grant proposal writing and project management, (5) 38% are interested in training on cooperation with local government, and (6) 30% are interested in training related to evaluation or NGO regulation.

The authors of the Phare report (1998) indicate concern over the "very low indexes applicable to training needs with respect to internal mechanisms of self-organisation ... with only every fifth organization interested in improving the difficult abilities of evaluating its own actions" (p. 72). The Phare authors cite the low attractiveness of training concerning the "method of work inside organizations" as disturbing and called for efforts to increase interest and responsiveness to such training initiatives. These authors also state that low interest in such self- evaluation topics indicates

> a dangerous lack of self-criticism among those working in the organizations. Everyone who really has contacts with NGOs knows that unfortunately, it is often not the lack of funds but the lack of management skills that are the basic problem in the functioning of organizations. (p. 73)

Related to imperatives for training are additional perceived problems facing NGOs. In a 2000 survey, KLON-JAWOR identified the following trends: (1) 90% of NGOs report difficulty with fund-raising for their operations, (2) 76% consider a lack of NGO advocacy and representation to be a problem, (3) 57% view inadequate legislation as a barrier, (4) 44% feel there is a lack of cooperation with governmental entities and public administrators, and (5) 34% mentioned a lack of public support and public trust. These trends are fundamentally critical to the formalization and growth of NGOs, which must be recognized by governmental and societal leaders, as well as by organizational leaders and managers. These formalizations and management concerns relate closely to and have implications for volunteer management practices. Such concerns will be explored in the following sections.

Volunteer Management in Poland

It is first necessary to understand how volunteerism is conceptualized and to examine current trends in volunteerism before considering complications for volunteer management in Poland. In the sections that follow, data are presented from national two studies conducted by KLON/ JAWOR (2002, 2004), a summary report compiled by the European Volunteer Center[4] (2005), and the Bies (2003) study. This presentation of volunteerism and voluntary action trends in Poland sheds light on issues of NGO formalization and related challenges for volunteer management.

Conceptualizing Volunteerism in Poland

Although the common understanding of volunteerism in Poland is becoming more widely and socially understood and accepted, framing volunteerism in Poland in positive terms has proved to be challenging due to negative and preconceived notions of compulsory volunteering reminiscent of the Soviet era. Under the former totalitarian regimes, volunteerism was imposed top-down by the government for over 40 years, thus explaining the hesitance of the population to volunteer their services (Regulska, 2001). Furthermore, Poles are more reluctant to associate with organizations established prior to the Solidarity movement because of party politics and concerns related to corruption. The perception of volunteerism in Poland is, however, evolving in positive directions due to the changing public sector structures and capacity. Numerous studies also note that younger generations are more willing to volunteer than the older population (European Volunteer Center, 2005).

According to the Circle Network (Cultural Information and Research Centres Liaison in Europe [Circle Network], 2001), a commonly accepted contemporary definition, is,

> unpaid voluntary activities undertaken within the framework of any cultural institution, event or organization. Volunteering may mean both individual services given freely to professional organizations or the running of entire cultural organizations as volunteer-led entities. (1. Definition, para. 1)

Moreover, 2004 KLON-JAWOR data reveals that 44.4% of NGOs included in their study were utilized volunteers in both day-to-day operations and in more specific programmatic and activity-focused functions (European Volunteer Center, 2005).

The Bies (2003) study reveals similar conceptualizations of volunteering, but indicates variation in terms of the functional aspects of volunteering and formality or professionalism of volunteers. Although there was general agreement about what a volunteer is as well as the unpaid and uncoerced or independent nature of volunteer participation, only those organizations that were comparatively professional in their operations articulated a detailed definition of specific functions undertaken by volunteers in their agencies. Despite the fact that the respondents in the Bies study were associated with NGOs with primarily voluntary staffing, the notion of volunteer management, as a specific functional domain of management was rarely mentioned. This presents a challenge, and an opportunity for nonprofit and volunteer support organizations, especially those working with young organizations or those just beginning to initiate more formal or intentional systems for utilizing volunteers.

Participation Levels of Volunteers in NGOs

Anheier and Salamon (1999) report that at least 20.5% of the Central and Eastern European population is volunteering in some capacity (p. 58). The European Volunteer Center (2005) reports, according to the 2004 KLON-JAWOR study, that "in 2004, around 5.4 million Poles, which is 18.3% of the population, engaged in a voluntary activity" (p. 7). This estimate represents an 8.3% increase in Polish voluntary participation in NGOs since 2001, which suggests a changing perception of the NGO and voluntary sectors throughout the country. One explanation for the rise in the number of volunteers in Poland can be attributed to the Polish Volunteer Centers, which promote voluntary sector involvement and assist organizations in recruiting volunteers.

An additional contributing factor to this influx in number of volunteers, among other factors, is likely the increasing popularity of "corporate voluntarism," or "voluntary work stimulated and to some extent organized by an employer" (European Volunteer Center, 2005, p. 9). Corporate voluntarism, also referred to as corporate social responsibility in many Western nations, is a trend becoming of increased importance within the corporate arena of many, possibly most, developed nations. The support of volunteerism within corporations holds promise for increasing the flow of volunteers assisting the NGO sector.

Furthermore, approximately 87% of Polish organizations identified that they work with volunteers; however, 60% of organizations report that they do not employ any paid staff, thus placing a large responsibility of services provided to citizens on the shoulders of volunteers within the organizations (AVSO, 2003). Referencing data collected in 2004 by KLON-JAWOR, The European Volunteer Center (2005) reports, that the majority of volunteers dedicate 1 to 5 hours per year of their time to assisting organizations. The number of individuals volunteering 1 to 5 hours per year fell from 29.2% in 2003 to 17.7% in 2005; however, the number of individuals volunteering 151 hours to 500 hours per year rose from 1.1% in 2003 to 10.2% in 2004 (p. 17). These trends suggest that organization leaders and managers are presented with a unique opportunity to capitalize on the continued willingness of Poles who currently volunteer. NGO and volunteer support organizations will also need to consider ways to stimulate an important role in recruiting new volunteers and helping constituent NGOs foster increasing levels of commitment by such volunteers.

Volunteer Management Support Structures

As the number of volunteers in Poland continues to rise, the need and demand for volunteer resources will continue to rise as well. To respond to this need, Poland established a network of 16 volunteer centers strategically located throughout the countryside. The primary purpose of the volunteer centers is to provide a resource hub for and to provide linkages between volunteers and NGO managers. The volunteer centers provide training programs for organizations and advertise volunteer opportunities for Poles.

Primary Volunteer Functions

The 2002 KLON-JAWOR study revealed the primary tasks within organizations executed by volunteers, as reported by both volunteers and organization managers. These include: general organizational activities (planning meetings, office assistance, campaigns, etc.) (78.8%); organization advertising and marketing (50.4%); direct customer/client relations (46.4%); physical office maintenance and janitorial services (41.9%); office administrative functions (35.9%); consulting services and training (25.3%); collecting funds (17.0%); and participation on executive councils and organization committees (14.0%) (European Volunteer Center, 2005, p. 16).

Profile of Volunteers

As the acceptance and promotion of volunteerism in Poland levitates, it is important for organization managers and leaders to comprehend the general defining characteristics of the average volunteer. The following information was revealed in the from data collected by KLON-JAWOR in 2004:

- The average age of volunteers ranges from 18 to 35 years. Within this group falls over 40% of all volunteers. In 2001, however, slightly less than 16% of volunteers fell within this age range.

- The percentage of volunteers from each gender remains relatively the same.
- The more educated a person is, the more likely they are to volunteer. Of the responses, over 45% had either a medium or higher education.
- Volunteers are relatively equally distributed throughout the regions of Poland.
- The majority of volunteers (60.6%) are currently employed in another establishment. Approximately 27.5% of retired individuals surveyed volunteer and 9.1% of volunteers are unemployed (European Volunteer Center, 2005, pp. 14-16).

As Poland's NGO sector strengthens and expands, these numbers are expected to drastically increase. This information is helpful to current NGO leaders and managers as the need to understand, recruit, and retain volunteers is of paramount importance. Understanding volunteer demographics such as these and interpreting such information also sheds light on specific groups that have not been, but could be, targeted as future volunteers, such as volunteers or unemployed persons looking to gain new skills or affiliations.

Motivations for Volunteering

In Poland, similar to other nations, three of the motivating factors for volunteerism are: "altruistic, instrumental, and obligatory" (Anheier & Salamon, 1999, p. 56). The European Volunteer Center 2005 research more specifically indicates that the majority of the 2004 KLON-JAWOR survey respondents volunteer for "moral, religious, and political" purposes (89.4%), which is followed 76.1% volunteering for the sake of volunteering (p. 15). Another motivation for student and young professional volunteers is the increased marketability and employability due to volunteerism. Organization leaders, managers, and marketers should capitalize on these motivating factors in order to increase the number of volunteers for their respective organizations.

Time and Economic Value of Volunteers

Volunteers in the NGO sector provide considerable time and economic value to Polish organizations, as can be deduced by the number of hours per year Poles are volunteering in such organizations. As Poles as a society better understand the importance of volunteers and as the government continues to provide clearer legislation relating to NGOs and volunteers, the role volunteers play as an economic stimulus is expected to rise. The 2004 KLON-JAWOR study indicates that the "percentage of Poles volunteering more than 151 hours a year has almost doubled since 2001," which indicates that volunteering may be beginning to take greater hold in Poland (European Volunteer Center, 2005, p. 17). In simple economic terms, volunteers save organizations significant amounts of funds per year. The Johns Hopkins Comparative Nonprofit Sector (Salamon, Sololowski, & Associates, 2004) project estimates the annual value in Poland to exceed 150.8 million USD.

Voluntary Board Participation

Data collected in 2003 by Bies provides insight into board participation, and represents one of the only data sources on voluntary board involvement and governance in Poland's NGO sector. Board development and governance are often viewed as being beyond the scope of volunteer management functions with the responsibilities of such activities resting with executives and boards themselves. The data collected by Bies reveals that in Poland boards are conceived of as being within the purview of volunteer development and management. Furthermore, NGO leaders often play both general management and volunteer management roles simultaneously. For these reasons, as well as the important voluntary contribution played by boards, it is useful to examine voluntary board participation issues in the context of this chapter's more general examination of volunteer management challenges.

The number of board members utilized in Polish NGOs was measured by an item on the questionnaire that instructed respondents to indicate, "As of today, how many of the following people are involved with the work of your organization? Please indicate the number of people serving on the board of directors." It is useful to compare this with a similar item, which asked respondents, "As of today, how many of the following people are involved with the work of your organization? Please indicate the number of persons involved with the organization on a day-to-day basis." Construction of this item provided for measurement consistent with the KLON-JAWOR measure for total number of personnel and refers to involvement by both paid and volunteer personnel.

Table 8.2 presents the descriptive data about number of board members and number of personnel. Although comparison data do not exist with KLON-JAWOR data for the number of board members, it is useful to compare this study's sample for the variable number of personnel with that of KLON-JAWOR. A comparison of median and mode scores is useful: the study sample's median (*Mdn* = 10) and mode (*Mode* = 10) scores are very similar to those of the KLON-JAWOR sample (*Mdn* = 13; *Mode* = 10). Although the number of board members and number of personnel vary across organizations in the sample, the median and mode scores suggest that most organizations in the sample have five or so board members

Table 8.2.   Number of Personnel, Number of Board Members

Statistic	Number of Board Members Study Sample	Number of Personnel Study Sample	Number of Personnel KLON-JAWOR
Valid *n*	894	813	1,346
Missing *n*	22	103	582
M	10.15	59.00	77.36
Mdn	5.00	10.00	13.00
Mode	5.00	10.00	10.00
Skewness	12.867	11.949	21.406
SE	0.082	0.086	0.067
Kurtosis	185.322	147.665	526.841
SE	0.163	0.171	0.133

and ten or so persons involved with the organization on a day-to-day basis.

Arguably, board participation is an important form of volunteer participation in Polish NGOs. Yet board participation rates alone, however, are not sufficient to illuminate some of the aspects of board governance that relate to volunteer management challenges. It is useful, especially in light of the legal and conceptual criteria of voluntary participation, independence, and self-governance in Polish NGOs, to consider aspects of "good governance," that relate to such things as voluntary board participation, meeting regularly to conduct business, and adherence to conflict of interest policies. Findings in these three areas have implications for the deployment of volunteer management practices.

In terms of voluntary participation, respondents were asked, "Do the members of your board of directors receive payment for their work on the board?" The vast majority of respondent organizations (91.3%) indicated that their boards served voluntarily. A ratio of paid staff serving on the board of directors is also insightful to determine levels of voluntary involvement. The concept of percentage of paid staff serving on a board of directors relates to the perceived independence of the board to carry out its governance and fiduciary responsibilities. The interpretation of such standards is generally that a larger percentage of paid staff accompanies a greater the concern related to a board's independence. Although variation within the sample is large, 50% or more of NGOs in this sample report that board are all voluntary with no paid staff members serving on the board of directors. More than three-quarters of the sample report that 80% or more of their board members serve without pay.

In terms of the number of board meetings annually, the sample distribution is bi-modal with a large part of the distribution holding board meetings defined by cycles of the year: 121 NGOs reported having quarterly board meetings, and 118 NGOs reported having monthly board meetings. The remainder of the sample can be characterized as holding a certain number of board meetings per year, almost normally distributed. Although various standards exist in practice to provide guidance on minimal or appropriate numbers of board meetings annually, there is no standard rule. In general, the vast majority of NGOs in this sample hold one or more board meetings annually. More than 75% hold board meetings at least quarterly. A relatively small percentage holds no meetings annually. From this, one can conclude that a focus beyond the simple question of whether board governance is occurring should shift to a question of how board governance is being conducted.

Less than half of the respondent organizations (41.5%) indicated that organizations had a conflict of interest policy. When asked, "How many times did you invoke the policy during the year 2000?" more than three-quarters of the sampled indicated never. The range for this variable is zero to six invocations. Of the 104 respondents who added narrative comments to this question, 44 (44.3%) indicated that they simply had no conflicts. Some of these respondents added that the absence of conflict results from familiar relationships among a small board and transparent operations. Conversely, 23 (22.1%) indicated that formal mechanisms, such as a Peer's Jury Commission, an independent advisory board, or an oversight committee that is part of the board of directors, were utilized to interpret conflict of interest policies and settle conflicts of interest. These narrative responses suggest that there is variation in how conflict of interest policies are interpreted and applied.

In terms of the perceived influence of boards over management practices within NGOs, Board chairpersons ranked highest, with 65.9% of the sample reporting this to be the most influential role. Boards as a whole collectively ranked second, with CEO/executive director third at 10.2% and founders fourth at 3.6%. Because volunteer boards appear to play such an influential role, board development and training may be an area in which improvement in volunteer management practices is warranted. This is particularly important in consideration of the fact that more than 50% of the sample reported receiving no general management training, which was defined as including training on working with and recruiting volunteers. In addition, more than 75% of the sample reported receiving no training on topics relating to ethics, evaluation, reporting, and accountability. These topics, too, have aspects that overlap with both governance and general volunteer involvement.

CHALLENGES FOR VOLUNTEER MANAGEMENT

In this section, we present an analysis of the Bies (2003) data set, which includes the narrative responses to several open-ended questions on the national survey ($n = 918$) and the in-depth interview responses. The sections signify the six primary themes that resulted from the process of thematic content analysis, which explored relationships among answers from a single respondent and among responses across the interviews and survey responses. At times themes emerge solely from within one of the three types of respondent groups, NGO leaders, NGO support organization leaders, or funders; in most instances, a cross-case analysis emerges from across the three types of respondents. In addition, respondents fluidly shifted points of view between matters internal to their organizations and matters pertaining to the NGO sector.

This combination of ideas and vantage points was explored through a systematic, process of data coding and synthesis that involved both a deductive approach, centering on issues we anticipated from the literature on volunteer management practices, and an inductive approach that allowed for the identification of emergent themes. This combined approach resulted in the following themes, which highlight challenges for volunteer management in Poland.

Perceptions of Volunteerism

Similar to the literature and as identified in the European Volunteer Center's study (2005), Polish NGO and nonprofit support organizational leaders report that negative perceptions persist regarding what it means to be a volunteer and what volunteering involves. A respondent NSO leader reported that despite a decade of work on this issue and many positive changes in terms of participation levels, "the first challenge remains for us to articulate what it means to be a volunteer, not just in our day to day work, but to try and promote the idea of volunteering more broadly."

Even after more than 15 years of post-Soviet development in Poland's NGO sector, it is apparent that the idea that volunteering relates to government coercion is still well rooted. One head of a women's organization reported that the term volunteer is still associated with Soviet era of compulsory volunteering.

> Even now, people will still associate volunteering with those school days when we were obliged to dig potatoes. Yet the idea of helping improve one's lot or one's family or even one's neighbor can be appealing. And people also do not always trust the idea of NGOs, thinking of them as personal or

political tools rather than helping tools.... It just takes time and patience to
cultivate and animate a new idea of being involved.

Such mistrust is also extended to understanding the role of neutral or
independent NGOs, as well.

Such perceptions cause practical problems for NGO leaders who wish
to recruit and involve people in their agency's work as volunteers.

> When I try to invite people to be involved in our work, the first response is
> to either to try make a distance between us or to respond with some ambi-
> guity or hollow interest. There is a fear that I will overwhelm them with
> requests, or that when I say the word 'volunteer' I will come again and again
> with unreasonable requests. There is a certain lack of trust or pessimism
> that I must overcome.

Although 2004 research by KLON-JAWOR indicates that volunteerism
is being seen in a more positive light in the general population, for NSOs,
the challenging, yet very basic, role of moderating broadly-held negative
stereotypes about volunteering remains essential to ongoing well-being of
Poland's NGO sector and is a necessary, ongoing early step in the process
of establishing volunteer management practices. In addition to the work
of promoting the concept of volunteers in the general population, NSOs,
also play an important role in helping teach and support individual
NGOs to combat negative stereotypes and erroneous assumptions about
volunteers and volunteerism in their day to day work and with their own
local constituents. One respondent suggested that only after such view-
points are moderated, can NSOs continue to expand their work to help
individual NGOs learn how to manage volunteers. "It's a matter of
urgency. One must have some faith in volunteering and some access to
volunteers before it seems logical to discuss how to manage volunteers
within organizations."

Hazard of Newness

NGOs in Poland are experiencing a shift in leadership and management roles, which coincides with emerging NGO institutional practices.
The majority of organizations in Poland is less than 10 years old and
relies extensively on largely all-voluntary human resources (Bies, 2003;
KLON-JAWOR, 2000). With these relatively new or young organizations
come relatively new or young organizational leaders, many of whom initially served on a voluntary basis. One NSO leader described this process
as being evolutionary in nature,

> It is natural we have young organizations. Organizations begin as ideas or
> projects with one or two animators, and then they evolve and become more

formal. Yet it takes a change of consciousness to consider volunteers objectively, because so many of the NGO innovators were simultaneously heavily involved and working on a project or contract basis or essentially as volunteers themselves.

Respondents reported important and dynamic shifts that occurring as organizations formalize and begin to, in turn, formalize and professionalize leadership structures with paid executive personnel. Such personnel are challenged to make the shift to paid managerial positions, while developing other primary organizational personnel, many of whom continue to serve on a voluntary basis. As one NGO respondent indicates,

> It has been exciting and challenging to change into a professional organization. We now have three of us with our full attention on our work, and we have to now learn how to engage others in meaningful ways. It is a shift of mentality to think about expanding and the related organizational needs. Yet we see we must do this with intention.

At the same time, organizational leaders are challenged to allocate direct staff assignments to volunteer management and to engage in and develop effective volunteer management practices.

Constraints and Formalization

In response to an open-ended question relating to problems facing NGOs, financial and resource constraints were expressed as being of primary concern to NGO leaders. Such concerns were articulated as a continuum of formalization, "You start to do well. You attract some attention, some funders, and you begin to be effective. But then the challenges begin, how to account for your work, how to get more organized. You need more people, and you need more funds, yet you are overwhelmed." An experienced leader of a regional NSO describes the phenomenon similarly,

> They need help, and sometimes they even want more involvement, yet they are too overwrought to know how to effectively incorporate people in their work. On the other end, we are beginning to see a few very well-developed volunteer programs in some established agencies.

In the initial formalization stages NGO leaders, who are often times volunteers themselves, are primarily concerned with immediate survival needs. Respondents described the following process and related constraints for volunteer management. As organizations evolve and begin to formalize, they begin to be able to consider incorporating additional human and financial resources, but face operational constraints associated with expansion, not the least of which is the question of how to properly manage volunteers. The formalization of volunteer management practices is closely tied to this more general organizational process. A respondent funder sums up this formalization process in the following discussion.

> It is not that all-voluntary organizations are unsophisticated. Quite the contrary. They have produced, and undoubtedly will continue to produce some of the most important changes in the social and political arenas. But I do observe in organizational terms that organizations and their leaders have to be at certain maturity, a kind of ripeness, to begin to be able to plan and integrate new voices, new people, and new structures into their work. Part of this is being able to dedicate time and resources to this integration and development. Part of it involves a new vision or sense of organizational possibility. And then to work, it involves a series of professional moves to be able to effectively incorporate voluntary inputs.

It is important for NSOs and volunteer centers to try to understand such organizational development processes as they approach their assistance roles.

Formalizing volunteer management practices, such as the establishment of volunteer policies, recruitment practices, retention studies, and volunteer training and evaluation, must be considered in light of day-to-day operational preoccupations. Individual approaches may need to be designed for specific NGOs and their specific stages of formalization and constraints.

Individual Motivation and Role Issues

Although there is limited research related to motivations for volunteering in the Polish NGO sectoral context, the European Volunteer Center (2005) indicates that ethical and moral motivations are a primary driver. Qualitative results also suggest that younger Poles volunteer to gain practical work experience; others volunteer simply in the absence of opportunities for paid work. In interviews with advanced social policy students, it was revealed that volunteer motivations center on a both desire for social change or action and a desire to gain practical or professional experience, particularly in light of current unemployment trends in Poland.

In addition, in the absence of adequate paid employment and as a vehicle for social change or action, some NGO volunteers revealed their motivations to be entrepreneurial in nature. One student who at the time of the interview was involved in a local self-governance project indicates,

> I can design a project and seek some sponsorship. This is a practical approach, and I can build on my current volunteer project work at the local

level. This is one way to make opportunities for myself, but to also help realize some expectations for local integration.

Yet tensions related to the experience of volunteering emerged in relationship to professional and volunteer roles and identity.

For some of us, we are combining together several projects, the sum of which does not necessarily equate to a sufficient salary. Yet at the same time our identity is deeply associated with the tasks and focus of these projects. It is a dilemma then to consider how to engage others in this work. When there are so few opportunities for payment, how do you promise or predict the future for others? And yet you want others with a heart for the work, too.

Another respondent described this phenomenon similarly, but in more stark terms,

Listen, to be dramatic: I do need to eat. Yet we all wish to have meaningful lives. So we carry on, but we must try to think more strategically about building something rather than just hovering with a sustenance model, or a subsistence model for NGOs.

Better understanding and more rigorous measurement of volunteer motivations, attitudes, experiences, and preferences are warranted. Such study is important to understanding processes of formalization and improving volunteer management in Poland.

Mission and Advocacy Perspectives

Interviews and extensive sight visits with several NGOs that provide direct services revealed an important role for advocacy as a volunteer management function. Having a clear sense of mission and commitment to this mission was identified as being central to effective advocacy and volunteer engagement. The case of an NGO serving children with disabilities is instructive. This agency started out as a self-help group of a small number of parents of children with disabilities who, in the absence of adequate public services, self-organized to create rehabilitative and occupational therapies and social support networks. The leader of this organization indicates the following:

I started out simply determined to make life better for my son, and for other children....When we first started, it was our challenge to engage other parents. But as we designed our work and became more advanced in our therapeutic approach, we became more and more committed to engaging others in our work. Educating the public about disabilities became part of our therapeutic mission. To advocate for our children, and our clients, we had to advocate beyond the boundaries of our offices and school. We had to show people and expose them. Then we could engage them, to donate, to spend time with us, to accept our children in normal life, and, even to join us in our work. *Respondent NGO*

Other respondents echoed the challenge to engage people who did not have a direct connection with the work of the agency. One respondent discussed overcoming this challenge in the following way,

I am always curious about why people volunteer with us, and I talk to them about this. Many times it is not a direct link to our cause, but some encounter that led to a higher consciousness about our work. Understanding this has helped us to be less insular in our work, and to seek ways to collaborate and to share about our cause.

Thus, advocacy for one's mission becomes a strategy for volunteer recruitment.

In terms of policy advocacy or legal forms of advocacy, the NGO sector has been relatively successful in promoting legislation that provides a set of provisions regarding the relationship between NGOs and beneficiaries, and that, as discussed in a previous, hold promise for improving volunteer management practices. Yet, as discussed below, challenges and opportunities exist in terms of public advocacy and cooperation with public sector entities to promote volunteerism.

Public Sector Cooperation

The importance of NGO involvement in the democratization of new member states to the European Union was pointed to repeatedly by funders and NSO respondents as being simultaneously a remarkable leadership opportunity and a challenge for the NGO sector. One respondent NSO indicated,

European integration and local self-governance are on all minds. Yet close cooperation with public entities involves patience and trust. It is a learning process for both sides, and in many instances, it is local NGO innovators driving this process, teaching and prodding such relationships.

Increasingly, the credibility of the NGO sector depends on its ability to employ appropriate volunteer management practices within individual NGOs and to model such practices in their partnerships with the public sector, particularly at the local government level. To create an environment for its nongovernmental sector supportive of NGO, volunteerism, and philanthropic development and more closely aligned with prevailing standards of EU member nations, a number of accession states have initiated programs of NGO development reform and capacity building, funded in large part by private foundations and the EU Phare Program (Lange, 2003; Phare Civic Dialogue Program, 1998). Support of Poland's network of regional volunteer Centers is one such example, with funding from the European Union's Phare program, the European Commission, and local governments. The public sector funding partnerships, combined with initiatives designed to stimulate civic participation, including volunteerism, at the local level, makes the formalization of effective volunteer management practices of strategic importance.

But as the 2003 Civil Society for Trust in Central and Eastern Europe indicates, relationships between local NGOs and local public agencies can challenge NGO independence when NGOs are dependent on local governmental actors for funding and the use of office space. In addition, the CEE Trust research reveals that NGOs often lack legal knowledge and financial capacity. These shortcomings jeopardize healthy cross-sectoral collaborations, and put NGOs at a disadvantage. Overcoming resource constraints and providing opportunities for NGOs to learn about public policy, pertinent legislation and legal rights is an important volunteer management role of NSOs and volunteer centers, and one that should be expanded.

RECOMMENDATIONS FOR PRACTICE

This chapter provides nongovernmental practitioners, nonprofit support organizations, voluntary centers, and policymakers with a detailed snapshot of current facts and figures on voluntary action in Poland. It includes detailed information regarding issues of volunteer management practices, needs, and challenges. The results from this study also provide insight into sectoral and organizational formalization processes that have particular implications for volunteer management in Poland.

From this, the following recommendations emerge as relevant to volunteer management challenges in the Poland.

1. *Strengthen Support Structures.* Although Poland's NGO support structures are sophisticated and well-developed, continuing financial support and ongoing development of such entities is necessary. And despite the fact that NSOs and volunteer centers are in many instances entrepreneurial in their efforts to obtain financial support, ongoing donor support is critical because of the nascent nature of private and individual philanthropy in Poland and the limited ability of client NGOs to provide a large share of NSO funding. In addition, NSOs and volunteer centers also need to attend to their own internal professional development and

organizational capacity needs. The intermediary role of NSOs and volunteer centers needs to be reinforced, as well, as such structures have an important role to play in terms of policy advocacy and promotion of cross-sector collaboration.

2. *Reinforce Volunteer Management, Including the Dedication of Staff Resources.* More formalized organizations tend to dedicate staff time and expertise to the volunteer management function. Such allocations, with either paid staff or volunteer staff assigned to oversee the volunteer management function, should be encouraged in less formalized organizations. In addition, adherence to the volunteer rights established under the Law of Public Benefit Activity and Volunteerism, which promote aspects of volunteer management practices related to risk management, training, contracts and formalized understanding of duties, and remuneration for expenses by volunteers, should be encourage. Implementation trends should be monitored and reported on by local NSOs or regional volunteer centers. High levels of implementation should be celebrated.

3. *Enhance Management Training and Expand Audiences.* The Bies (2003) study revealed that the vast majority of Polish NGOs do not receive high levels of training of any type. This is especially true for smaller, newer, and more rural organizations. In addition to expanding training opportunities, matters of content also need attention. Volunteer management topics should be tied to general management training. This will encourage more widespread consideration of volunteer management practices and may help to normalize and formalize volunteer management practices. Because of the important role and significant voluntary contributions of voluntary boards of directors, an expanded focus to include training on voluntary board governance is also recommended.

4. *Create Self-assessment Tools.* The research reported on in this chapter indicates that one-size-fits-all approaches are not effective in light the interrelatedness of organizational formalization and the formalization of volunteer management practices. At the same time, NSOs and volunteer centers need to be strategic and efficient in their deployment of resources. Self-assessment tools related to "best" volunteer management practices, legal expectations, and volunteer personnel needs would help NGOs plan for the expansion of their volunteer management programs in consideration of their organizational constraints and organizational development needs.

5. *Promote Policy Approaches and Advocacy for Volunteer Management.* Individual NGOs, NSOs, and volunteer centers must continue to play public advocacy roles at a number of levels including: the promotion of volunteerism and efforts to continue to positively influence public perceptions of NGOs and volunteerism; consciousness raising and the promotion of effective, proactive, yet independent relationships with local government officials; education on the legal rights of volunteers and the related obligations of NGOs and public entities; education on effective ways for individual NGOs to frame and promote their mission to attract potential volunteers; and the creation of networks of NGOs to continue to push for legislation favorable to promotion of volunteerism and sound volunteer management practices

6. *Enhance Volunteer Management Through Experiential Approaches.* This chapter revealed that there are exciting volunteer management practices underway in Poland. NGOs should be brought together to document and exchange good ideas and to discuss potential experiments and solutions to current challenges. NSOs, volunteer centers, funders, and other NGO subfield networks are well placed to promote such dialogue and learning.

7. *Enhance Volunteer Management Through Research-Based Approaches.* With any new field of study, definitional, conceptual and measurement challenges exist. This is exacerbated when comparative analyses are undertaken. Poland's sector is well-served by the KLON-JAWOR database and related research. Poland also has several scholars dedicated to the study of NGOs. It would be useful to support ongoing refinement of measures by KLON-JAWOR, especially in continued cooperation with Polish scholars, experienced NSO and NGO leaders, with other similar databanks in Europe, and with the Johns Hopkins nonprofit comparative study. KLON-JAWOR is in an excellent position to help refine volunteer management terminology, develop rigorous and more standard measures, and to engage in systematic, longitudinal study of volunteer management practices. Such study combined with ongoing case and qualitative research can serve practice, policy, and theoretical development, in Poland, and in other parts of the world.

CONCLUSION

Despite the importance of voluntary human resource contributions and the significance of voluntary action in Poland's civil society, conceptualizations and research on volunteer management is still relatively young.

In Poland and elsewhere, there is much to be learned about the possibilities for understanding alternative and potentially competing conceptualizations of terms such as volunteer, volunteerism, and volunteer management, as well as the measurement of specific elements and competing approaches to volunteer management. Similarly, there is much to be learned about sectoral and organizational formalization processes, especially in relationship to volunteer management. This holds true for NGOs themselves, and those policymakers, funders, and NGO support organizations charged with developing volunteerism and improvement volunteer management practices.

As discussed in the chapter's introduction, a goal of this research was to contribute to the growing interest in improving voluntary participation and enhancing voluntary management practices. Poland does, indeed, serve as an important and interesting context for understanding issues of volunteer management in a successful and rapidly changing NGO context. This research is not only relevant to those interested in Poland's volunteer management practices and challenges, but to the examination of volunteer management practices in other expanding or changing national NGO settings. Future comparative study, especially through studies with replicable designs, would further enhance our understanding of how context and processes of formalization matter to volunteer management practices.

NOTES

1. The primary source of contemporary data on Poland's NGO sector is the KLON-JAWOR database. Summary data on volunteer trends provided in this chapter are derived either directly from KLON-JAWOR, in its public reports, or from studies utilizing data collected and maintained by KLON-JAWOR, including studies on Poland carried out under the auspices of the Johns Hopkins Comparative Nonprofit Sector Project and the semi-annual reports produced by Phare, an NGO development program funded by the European Commission.

2. For a thorough introduction to historical background of Poland's NGO sector and to contemporary definitions and conceptualizations of the Polish NGO sector, please see the work of Leś et al. (2000), which is part of the Johns Hopkins Comparative Nonprofit Sector Project.

3. Available online at http://www.usig.org/countryinfo/laws/Poland /Poland%20PBA.pdf

4. The European Volunteer Centre recently used this KLON-JAWOR data to complete a comprehensive study on voluntary action in Poland, available at http://www.cev.be/Documents/FactsFiguresPoland.pdf. The study provides an overview of attitudes toward volunteering, recent developments of volunteerism, information on the infrastructure for volunteering, and general data on volunteering.

CHAPTER 9

FINE LINES

Design and Implementation Challenges in Employee Volunteer Programs

Mary Tschirhart and Lynda St. Clair

Many employers are setting up employee volunteer programs to address community needs and employee interest in helping their communities through their workplace. An employee volunteer program consists of the formal and informal policies and practices that employers use to encourage and help employees to perform community service activities. A better name for these programs may be "community service programs" given that some employees may not feel that they are volunteers in the pure sense of the term. Still, these programs often call their participants "volunteers" so throughout the paper we will refer to the programs as "employee volunteer programs."

Empirical research on employee volunteer programs is limited. In a review of studies, Tschirhart (2005) found that anywhere from 40% to 95% of the organizations in the study samples had some form of support for employee volunteering. Studies of trends in employee volunteering do not show a clear and consistent pattern. To cite the main studies, Witter (2003) found a drop in loaned executives and volunteer incentive

---

Challenges in Volunteer Management, pp. 205–225

programs in 2002 from 2001 and 2000. Xu, Haydon, O'Malley, and Bridgeforth (2002) show a drop from 1998 to 2002 in individuals reporting that their employer encourages volunteerism. They also found that the number of respondents with employers sponsoring volunteer programs was about the same but the number of individuals participating in employee volunteer programs increased. A 2002 Conference Board Report suggests a growth in employee volunteer programs (Muirhead, Bennett, Berenbeim, Kao, & David, 2002). A Canadian study found that, from 1997 to 2000, employers were increasingly accommodating volunteering through normal work hours and recognizing employees for their volunteer efforts (Hall, McKeown, & Roberts, 2001). Despite the difficulty in establishing exactly how many individuals are volunteering through their workplaces and how many employee volunteer programs are in existence, it is clear that these programs are part of the fabric of community service and deserve examination.

Organizations sponsoring employee volunteer programs can benefit by enhancing their image in the community and the morale of their employees. Employees who participate in these programs can develop leadership and other skills, enhance their visibility with supervisors, and ultimately increase their productivity and satisfaction. Communities gain valuable resources to address real needs. At least that is what much of the rhetoric surrounding these programs claims (Tschirhart, 2005; Tschirhart & St. Clair, 2005). Empirical data on the outcomes of employee volunteer programs are limited, many studies lack rigor, and findings are often based on anecdotal evidence (Cihlar, 2004). The studies that go beyond simple counts of programs and participants tend to have a strong normative tone and rarely include identification of challenges in the implementation and design of programs. Identifying these challenges is complicated by the fact that these programs are not one size fits all; they vary widely in their policies and practices (Business Volunteers Unlimited, 2003; Canadian Center for Philanthropy, 2004; Guthrie, 2004; Hall, McKeown, & Roberts, 2001; Thomas & Christoffer, 1999; VeraWorks, Inc., 2002; Witter, 2003; Xu, Haydon, O'Malley, & Bridgeforth, 2002). We could find little discussion in the literature on the pros and cons of various strategies, practices, and policies. In addition, empirical studies tend to focus on programs in large for-profit companies and focus on the views of top executives.

To address the gaps in the research literature on employee volunteer programs, we conducted in-depth case studies of the employee volunteer programs in two nonprofit insurance companies. One company, which we call NE, is located in the northeast and had, at that time, about 1,050 employees. The other company, called SW, is located in the southwest and had, at that time, about 480 employees. In late 2003 and early 2004, we distributed written surveys to all employees. Our response rates for the surveys were 71% for NE (68% of participants and 32% of nonparticipants in the program) and 30% for SW (96% of participants and 4% of nonparticipants in the program). In June and July of 2004, we interviewed a sample of employees of the two organizations. We interviewed 46 individuals at NE and 27 at SW; all but one of these individuals participated in their company's community service activities. The interview subjects represent the range of levels and departments in the organizations and the top executives. The findings from the interviews are consistent with the findings from the surveys and better represent the views of program participants than nonparticipants.

This paper identifies four major areas in which our respondents believe their companies have crossed the line or are close to crossing the line of appropriateness: encouragement of participation, recognition of participants, use of program to promote the company image, and flexibility in choice of program activities. These areas of concern emerged in both the survey and interview data. It is clear from our data that employees differ in their views on when or if a line has been inappropriately crossed. Our goal is not to identify where these lines should be drawn, but rather to inform the decision making of program designers and implementers by identifying the nature of the lines that employees perceive to be important. As Zerabavel (1991) argues, clear lines often should not be drawn despite our often strong psychological needs to do so. We found in our study that while some employees have difficulty articulating their specific concerns with a program or practice, they often feel comfortable stating that something is right or wrong. Exploring the lines that at least some employees draw may help in the development of deeper research agendas to further delve into areas that seem worthy of sensitivity and balance.

Based on our case studies, the four areas in which program designers and implementers face a fine line are: encouragement of participation, recognition of participation, company image-enhancement, and flexibility in choice of program activities. Underlying each of these areas is a choice about the purpose(s) of the program, for example, how much the public relations value of the program has priority over its value to community agencies receiving services. While these outcomes are unlikely to be mutually exclusive, perception of an employer's prioritization of them seems to influence employees' cynicism and sense of the appropriateness of the employee volunteer program. Our paper explores the four areas and connects them to fundamental views on the nature of volunteering and employer roles in helping communities.

BRIEF DESCRIPTIONS OF THE TWO INSURANCE INDUSTRY NONPROFIT ORGANIZATIONS STUDIED

NE

NE began business in 1939 and today has the majority of the market share in its service area. The vision of the company focuses on improving the lives of customers, with the idea that this strategy should lead to reduced costs due to fewer insurance claims filed. The focus dovetails with the company's community service activities, which are mostly health oriented, such as walks to raise money for health-related causes, children's health fairs and fitness events, blood drives, and food programs. One notable exception is a house rebuilding program. As a general rule, sponsored activities are selected by the program director to fit with the company's focus on improving health, but employees can suggest projects for the program to coordinate and financially support.

The current version of the company's community service program began in 2000 when the company consolidated all NE community service activities into a single program. The history of community service by employees is substantially older than this formal program. For example, one of the 2003 winners of an employee volunteer award was identified as having volunteered in company service events during her entire 16-year career with the company. Prior to 2000, community service activities were on an ad hoc basis. The employees' association organized some activities; other activities were the result of someone's (usually a vice president's) interest in a particular issue; still others originated from the Human Resources department. The decision to centralize community service activities in 2000 was made by NE's former CEO. This decision was part of a broader organizational change that resulted in the creation of the community relations function. The former CEO, who initiated the program, felt very strongly that giving back to the community was a corporate obligation.

NE has an active community outreach program that includes not only community service activities but also community giving and grants programs, and partnerships with nonprofit agencies. Although the current CEO told us that he does not consider community service to be a key part of the company's strategy, community service is mentioned in the company's 5-year strategic planning document. NE's community service activities are coordinated through the office of community relations. The director of community relations has operational responsibility for the company's community service program and reports to the vice president of community relations who reports directly to the CEO. In developing the program, the vice president of community relations looked to organizations, such as The Points of Light Foundation and the volunteer center for the state, for insights and examples. The choice of a veteran employee with over 20 years of experience as the director of the program helps to ensure that it reflects the priorities of the organization and fits within the corporate culture.

The NE program does not officially provide any hours for employees to participate in community service activities. Managers use their discretion when deciding whether or not an employee can participate in community service activities during business hours and whether or not that time has to be made up by the employee. A monthly newsletter is used to keep all employees informed about the community service activities in which NE employees participate. In addition to the staff in corporate relations, the community service program is promoted by a group of employees who serve as program representatives. The company's Web page highlights community service opportunities and past activities. For 2003, NE reports that over 780 employees donated 45,000 hours of service to the community.

To recognize community service participants, the monthly newsletters typically contain photos of employees along with brief reports of different activities. At an annual recognition day celebration, the CEO thanks the employee volunteers for their community service efforts. The volunteers can also qualify for grants of $250 donated to the volunteers' chosen charity. Outstanding volunteers are recognized on an annual basis. In addition to these formal recognition events, many employees commented that they had received notes of thanks or phone calls after participating in an event. Often these messages came from the director of community relations, who, along with the vice president of community relations, appears to be extremely well respected and liked by employees at all levels of the organization.

SW

Like NE, SW has a long history in its region. Originally created in 1925 as a branch of a larger organization, SW became a separate self-supporting organization in 1969. Today it is the clear leader in market share in its state. The company's mission is to be the lowest cost provider of its insurance products. Unlike NE, SW does not have all of its employees in a single location; branch offices are located throughout the state. The main office is located in a major city; the largest branch is about 120 miles away and has approximately 50 employees. The other branches are considerably smaller. The employee volunteer program, coordinated through the main office, tries to involve all employees at all sites in service activities.

The employee volunteer program officially kicked off in March of 2002 as part of the vision of the CEO. Community service activities are coordinated through a charitable giving committee under the leadership of the customer education coordinator within the training and development unit of the human resources department. The customer education coordinator, who is ultimately responsible for SW's community service program, is an enthusiastic role model for employees and actively communicates community service opportunities. She created the program and has organized it since its inception. For her role as program creator and organizer, she won a company award for significant contributions to the company's goals. Team liaisons (charitable giving coordinators) help disseminate information about community service activities to their teams and meet as a group to discuss and plan activities. This is consistent with the company's recent focus on improving teamwork within the organization. There are liaisons throughout the company, in both the main office and the branches. The program coordinator regularly convenes the liaisons to share information and brainstorm ideas for encouraging participation and enhancing the community service experience. These meetings also are an opportunity for the liaisons to share concerns and ask for advice from other liaisons and the program coordinator.

Employees at SW have 12 paid hours a year for participating in community service activities. Employees are encouraged to report not only their 12 paid hours of community service through the company, but also any additional volunteering that they do. Hours are reported quarterly on a tracking form that includes space for company community service and for volunteering that is done outside of the company's community service program. Some employees choose not to report their hours. The company also matches employee donations to 501(c) 3 organizations and to the state employees charitable campaign, and provides direct support to community charitable activities and events. Charities that have or will use employees as volunteers are given special consideration for company sponsorships.

SW sponsors a broad range of community service activities and sees giving back to the community by employee participation in community service as an integral aspect of the culture. Some activities, such as preparing backpacks for children in disadvantaged schools, are designed so they can be done on-site to simplify employee participation. The estimated participation for 2003 was 30% of employees. Activities include blood drives, bake sales, rebuilding projects, sorting and serving food, and so forth. As at NE, although the current formal community service program at SW is relatively new, during interviews employees mentioned that they had been participating in more informal community service activities through the company for many years.

Internally, the company produces a monthly newsletter with information on community service opportunities and activities. E-mail is a frequently used medium for letting people know about activities. A volunteer fair is also used to introduce employees to community service opportunities. Presently, SW does not mention its community service program or report the donation of community service hours on its Web page but the program has been prominently featured in the company's annual reports.

Participants in community service activities may be recognized and/or receive rewards at an annual company event for recognizing superior teams and individuals. Small incentives and tokens are also used at each event to encourage participation. The program coordinator is generous in her praise of liaisons and other volunteers and finds opportunities to recognize special efforts at meetings. The company newsletter also regularly features stories about and photographs of employees who serve the community through activities coordinated through the company or on their own.

FOUR AREAS OF EMPLOYEE CONCERN

Encouragement of Participation

The literature on employee volunteer programs suggests that for some employees there may be an expectation by their employer, particularly for higher-level employees, that they will participate in certain employee volunteer program events and serve in volunteer positions in the community. To further business interests, many CEOs serve on nonprofit boards and encourage their top executives to do the same. Some employees believe volunteering as a representative of their employer is mandatory, and certain programs expect volunteering from some employees (Hall, McKeown, & Roberts, 2001; Walker & Pharoah, 2000; Witter, 2003). Participation and performance in volunteer projects is sometimes included in formal performance appraisal systems (Business Volunteers Unlimited, 2003; Meijs & van der Voort, 2004; Witter, 2003).

Pressure to participate in employee volunteer programs, and performance of volunteer work on company time, calls into question the extent to which some employee volunteer programs are involving only "volunteers" in service activities. This emerged as an issue of great sensitivity in both of our case studies. In both NE and SW, most employees indicate that participation is not mandated and many indicate that requiring participation or putting too much pressure on employees to participate is inappropriate. But what is too much pressure and does this fine line appear in the same spot for employees at all levels of the organization?

Most of the senior level executives accept that participation is part of their job description and that their performance evaluation will, rightly, be affected by their degree of participation in the formal volunteer program activities and in their participation on governance boards of nonprofit organizations in the community. However, we did find some resistance among top executives. For example, one senior executive at SW reported that she was being pressured to serve on boards but preferred to perform community service privately, not through board membership, and without informing the company. She recognized that this was not consistent with the CEOs desires and planned to pursue the issue with him and the other top executives. She stated:

> I guess he has a right to ask his executive team to do that for certain reasons, but we need to just talk as an executive team. I think it's just a really personal decision and I just don't. Unless there is some part of our strategy that really includes us being on boards and that's going to affect our business, well, then maybe it's just going to have to be part of my job to sit on a board. But, I still, I really want to do the other stuff.

There was strong resistance by the majority of employees in both organizations to the idea that lower level employees be expected to participate in the employee volunteer program and some of the interviewees were concerned that their company was getting too close to a line in its encouragement of volunteering. One assistant vice president at NE complained:

> I think employees feel like it's an obligation to volunteer, and I think it's an imposition for a lot of our employees here. Personally in my department, I have a lot of single moms and, you know, it's like they don't have time to give up, you know what I mean, they're working all the time. And they want to spend time with their kids. And Saturday is the only time. And, the timing of these events, sometimes you can have one right after the other, it's like enough.... I've actually gotten people, e-mails apologizing and saying why they can't go. Nobody should have to do that.

What made many employees nervous was the idea that volunteering was part of performance appraisals. As one NE employee put it, "That is another touchy, touchy spot there. I don't know if anyone has mentioned that, but a lot of people feel as though it should not affect the performance appraisal at all." One comment made by the CEO at NE has had lasting repercussions for employees' perceptions of the employee volunteer program. The NE Program director explained,

Before I was involved in the program, the CEO at an all-employee meeting made a comment about the fact that volunteerism is part of your job and that you are expected to do it. I have worked for three years to try and say that is not how we operate and that's not what he meant. Employees had a totally negative reaction to it.

Still, it is unclear how much sanctioning does occur of nonparticipants. The CEO at NE clearly expressed his view that employees should feel pressured to participate. In explaining to us how he encourages participation in an activity, he stated:

I would tell the people that report to me that I'm not interested in doing this by myself. They will have more involvement and they will see to it that their people have more involvement. Because some of this, the first time you do this, I don't say you force people to do it, but if you put a little pressure on to do it they may just find that they really like it.... We're after that middle group that might [participate]. Sometimes you've got to give them a push. So you know, I think the message is number one, sure, we can do some good things for the community and that is part of our job to the extent that you're more involved in that, people see you're more involved in that, quite frankly it's going to impact your evaluation. But two, you're going to be a better person for it. You're going to bond with employees. You know, you're going to make friends. You know when you're helping plant flowers, kneeling in the mud with somebody else and talking with them, you connect in a different way than you do in a work setting.

The CEO at SW is also committed to creating a culture where employees do community service and, like at NE, some employees are concerned about the company crossing the line. One SW employee who works closely with the CEO stated:

I think there's a fine line here and I'm very intimately associated with my boss's philosophy. I have a great deal of respect for him and I totally understand what he is trying to do. And I agree with it to a point. I guess it's that fine line of, sure its important that if we're going to establish an image to the public that we're here to serve the business community and that we also serve a public need. We're here for other people. We also contribute. We give back to the community. I think that's an important message, very important. I know there are companies out there that will not hire a person unless they commit to doing charitable work. And, I'm not certain that I agree with that philosophy.

Part of the resistance to the idea that participation be expected is due to employees' conceptions of what it means to be a volunteer. One NE employer stated, "I mean volunteerism is volunteerism. I don't think you can just make people do it. Otherwise it's not volunteering." Another concern is that the pressure to participate creates an atmosphere in which people who do not participate will be thought of negatively. One of the SW employees who expressed this view stated, "Some people say, if I don't want to do it why should I be made to feel like I'm not a great person if I don't volunteer." A further concern is privacy issues. At SW, the company tracks volunteer hours. One SW senior executive explained that collecting information on top executives' community service activities as part of their appraisals was acceptable, but she was concerned about doing the same for lower level employees for privacy reasons. She stated:

> Some people want to involve themselves with their church and they do that outside of work and they're not comfortable sharing that at work. And I don't think people should be pressured around their performance to do this. Anybody who is a leadership position in the organization, we are look- ing at requiring them to be networked and be a part of associations, to be involved in charity work as it pertains to [the company]. I think that piece does belong in performance because they're representatives of the company at that point.... So at a leadership level yes. At an individual level, I would say no, because I don't want people to feel pressured or to have to disclose any kind of thing that they are working on that they're not comfortable sharing. You now, sometimes parents will want to participate in the Leuke- mia Foundation because they've got a child who has got leukemia. They may not want to share that at work. It may be so personal. And I feel like we've got to give people that opportunity for privacy.

Our survey asked employees about their reasons for participating in their employee volunteer program. Their top reason was to help others (mean of 4.5 on a scale of 1 to 5, with 5 being a very important reason for partic- ipating). Few employees reported that important reasons to participate were because they were asked by their employer to participate, because it is part of their job to participate, and for their career development within the company (items had a mean of 2.2 or less). In our interviews, many employees stated that they volunteered for personal reasons though some felt that it was good to be able to help the image of their employer. Some called for clear direction on whether or not program participation was expected and evaluated and were uncomfortable with employees "volun- teering" for activities to meet a standard. One NE employee voiced his objection as follows,

> It's the insinuation that can be taken that, gee, if I don't go to this one, I've only got two, and now it's November, I need to get one more in, and that's what's unfair I think. To quantify what your participation should be in any way.

Thus, employee volunteer programs are faced with the challenge of creating opportunities for participation while keeping the sense that participation is voluntary. The messages conveyed to encourage participation may create a sense of pressure or coercion that is either planned or unplanned. Some employees charged with promoting the volunteer program respond to this challenge by simply conveying facts about upcoming events without actually asking for participants. Others are much more comfortable asking for participation, even asking employees to stretch themselves beyond their initial commitments. Finding the proper balance for encouraging participation can be difficult. For example, when we asked an employee at SW about encouraging people to participate, she said, "I try to leave the people that I know are just not interested alone because I don't want to alienate them." Decisions not to encourage other people, however, may be misinterpreted. Another SW employee indicated that although he sometimes became frustrated that there were so many different activities, he did not want to be thought of as someone who did not care, an assessment that he felt was being implied when some employees were asked to participate but others were not asked to participate. In some cases, actions taken to create enthusiasm and encourage participation actually may dampen it for some employees. As one example, when the SW executive team decided to match the number of school backpacks donated by employees up to 600, some employees felt this put undue pressure on them to increase the number of backpacks that their team was planning to contribute. Offering appropriate levels of encouragement to not undermine the spirit of volunteerism and negatively affect morale is just one of the fine lines we found in our study. It is connected to our second fine line, the issue of recognition.

Extent and Nature of Recognition

Our survey and interview data indicate that employees who participate in the community service programs at NE and SW have a positive view of those programs and believe that they should exist for the primary purpose of giving back to the community. Not all employees, however, are confident that all participants are committed to that purpose. Some employees are uncomfortable with the idea that other employees may be participating for recognition and rewards. Some employees feel that there is too much emphasis on recognition; others feel that there is not enough recognition. This raises the first aspect of our second fine line for review, what are appropriate recognition and rewards for participants. An additional concern raised relates to the credit that the companies take for their employees' volunteer activities. In other words, to what extent is it okay for companies to publicize what their employees are doing in their voluntary service to communities. Some employees who volunteer outside the company feel that they and their company should get credit for this service, others feel that outside volunteering is private and the company should not ask about it, try to track it, or tell the public about it.

We heard from a variety of employees about their discomfort with using the employee volunteer program for personal gain. The most common personal benefit cited was recognition in the company. One NE employee critiqued, "The upper management makes some activities their personal quest to receive corporate recognition." Another NE employee stated that she avoided the program because of how others were using it to gain visibility with their bosses. The employee stated, "I don't really do a whole lot, because a lot of times I get the feeling that the people do things here just for publicity of self, throwing their face out in front of the VP's or things like that." Some employees are very firm in their belief that recognition for their community service activities is something they do not desire and some believe recognition and rewards are inappropriate. The following two quotes illustrate this point.

> I think, in terms of getting rewards, material types of awards, I think it takes away from the whole purpose of volunteering. I'm doing it because of what I'm going to get out of it personally, not for what I'm expecting to get from it. I think too much recognition and you end up having people that are there just for the recognition and not to truly help out. Anonymous volunteering is the most rewarding. (NE employee)

> Charity is about coming from your heart, wanting and being able to help just because. Not because you want a prize. Not because you want your picture in the paper, or not because you want to be honored at a ceremony. (SW employee)

Few employees objected to small tokens of appreciation that both companies offered to participants. We heard more objections to the more substantial rewards like competitive awards, special parking spots, free tickets, raffles available only to participants, vacation days, and for some, even time off from work to volunteer. Rejection of these rewards came from employees' conception of what it means to be a volunteer. The notion of sacrifice was important to this view of volunteering, and to use the words of some employees, giving rewards "undermined," "degraded," or "defeated" the spirit of volunteerism. As one NE employee explained:

> You're doing it because there's a call for a need and you're able to help out and fulfill that need. So whether they gave out t-shirts, or hats, or aprons, or didn't, it would not matter. I'm still going to go. Some people will say, why

don't they give us a vacation day. Well, if you're only doing it to get something out of it then you're not truly understanding the spirit of being a volunteer. Because a volunteer to me means you're willing to make a personal sacrifice. And the only thing you're going to get out of it is self-satisfaction and gratification, and the gratification of the people that you're assisting of course.

Awards for volunteers raised special concerns, especially given the understanding that some employees refused to report the full extent of their volunteer activity to the company and that some types of volunteering do not count in calculations for awards, such as volunteering for churches. In addition, there is resentment that some types of employees have more freedom to volunteer during work hours than others. Also, some employees question how much work is getting done by the "super" volunteers. One SW employee stated "Most recently somebody got an award for so many hours of volunteering. Well, yeah, you do the math, and was she doing anything else but working on volunteering? Well, then the question comes up, well is she even working?" At SW, some employees expressed concern that if they didn't qualify for the basic service award by going above the 12 hours provided for service by the company then you would be considered to be a bad employee. One SW employee expressed his cynicism by sharing a conversation he had with another employee at a company award ceremony. He stated:

> I sat down with somebody and they told me "you watch [name of person] is going to get [a major company service award] because they spent the entire year on charitable giving events." I said, really? And they said, that's right. And the comment to me was, "I'd love to have a job where I could just go around and just do all these feel good things all year, Do nothing that supports the company goals or interact with policy holders or heaven forbid write a policy and then at the end of the year get [name] Award and bonus for it."

Some employees do feel personally motivated when their community service efforts are recognized. One NE employee, talking about the CEO, said,

> There have been events where I have volunteered and he has taken the time to personally recognize me just through a phone call or through an e-mail, thanking me for my participation, and I think that's it's very helpful and it really lets you know that you are appreciated and that the time that you have devoted to this activity is appreciated.

The majority of employees that we interviewed appreciated being recognized and seeing their colleagues recognized for their community service activities. As one NE employee explained,

When you volunteer your time on the company's behalf, really you are doing it in the name of the company. It sort of helps to have a little bit of a morale booster or a little bit more thanks instead of just that you are expected. You know, a "we'll see you there next year attitude."

Use of Program to Enhance Company Image

It is not just recognition of participants that requires sensitivity to not crossing a line. Using the employee volunteer program to gain goodwill and promote a positive image for the company is, using an employee's words, a "sticky issue" for many employees. On the other hand, a minority of employees are comfortable with having the company ask for community service that can then be used to promote the company's image. One NE employee told us,

The employees are treated very well here and the benefits are very good. And you know, if you are being given things and the company wants you to give back to the community because they get some mileage from that, well, whatever, then I think that is fair.

Many employees at both SE and NW stressed the point that companies should not be involved in employee volunteer programs in order to help the company, though this is a nice side benefit. Like for employee participants, the motivation should be to help the community. One SW employee stated,

The opportunity to give money or time should be supported--not forced. I feel my personal rights have been infringed on. Never does [the company] want to participate in charity unless there is some sort of recognition. How is that charity? It isn't.

An employee from NE clearly stated this position:

If you're doing it to try to boost your image, try to make yourself look good, again you're missing the total spirit of volunteering. If, as part of you encouraging volunteerism, getting out there in the community and doing volunteer activities, if the end result is an improvement to your company image then that's all fine and well. But if you solely want to do it just because you want to make yourself look good because right now you're not too shiny, then that's wrong. That to me is immoral.

Even in their own minds, some employees struggle with the tension between a desire for the company to get credit for what the company has given back to the community and a feeling that looking for recognition undermines the value of the service effort. This tension is reflected in the following quote from an employee at NE:

> I don't know that the company gets as much goodwill from our volunteer efforts as maybe we could because I think we do give a lot back to the community; and that's okay to a point, and I was one of the people in the survey who responded that I didn't think it was right for the company to expect a photo op at every volunteer event that we did. I didn't think that was in keeping with the spirit of volunteerism.

Both SW and NE struggled with issues related to tracking volunteer hours for publicity purposes. Overall, employees we interviewed at SW seem more concerned about tracking hours and the impact of not participating in community service than employees at NE. Some NE employees even want the company to track outside hours. SW employees seem to feel comfortable reporting how they use the 12 paid hours on company time for community service, but are less comfortable tracking outside hours. As one SW employee who did volunteer outside of work and chose not to report her hours commented, "It's not a game I'm going to play." SW still uses a form that asks how much time was spent volunteering on company-organized events and how much on outside events, how much time was taken during work hours and how much time outside work hours. Faced with employee resistance, SW does not mandate the completion of the form. NE tried to survey employees to collect the same type of information that SW collects on its form. Employees complained about the survey and it was withdrawn and never repeated. At least three NE employees still remember this survey. One of them told us:

> This place came up with some such survey at one point in time asking you to write down or put down the amount of hours you volunteer, and the question was posed, suppose you do something outside of NE, and the answer was, "Don't put it down, only things that you do through NE." I think that turned off a lot of people right off the bat, and I've heard that comment made to me a number of times, especially after it was made initially. You mean to tell me that just because I don't wave the NE banner that what I'm doing isn't important? I mean, what are we volunteering for? We've volunteering to help less fortunate people in situations to improve their lives.

This employee went on to give advice to his company, "Know what the person does. Just because the person doesn't do it under the cloak of [company name] does not make it an evil situation that you shouldn't be aware of and know about."

However, other employees believe what they do as volunteers should not be presented by the company in its publicity material. Even a top executive at SW was uncomfortable with the CEO using the employee volunteer program to help in branding the organization. Many of the executives are aware of differing views about the use of the employee volunteer program to help the company. One NE executive explained the challenge of making employees comfortable with the company's desire to get goodwill from its employees' volunteer efforts:

> And people very rightly say, hey look I volunteer. Whether I work for you or whether I work for United, or whether I work for hospital XYZ, I would choose to be a volunteer. Therefore, I think in some cases there is resentment when somebody says, hey I'm a volunteer and there goes [the company] taking credit for it. Therein lies the importance of doing a better job of internal marketing. Of letting people know that we're not standing up to take credit for what you do, but what you do helps the security of the organization, the security of the job. There needs to be a stronger relationship or a stronger awareness built that we are not just trying to hog the credit for the fact that you are a volunteer or would be one way or another, but the fact that you're a volunteer and the fact that you work here. How do I make you, as an employee, see the value of saying, I'm from [name of the company]? Not gees, I'd volunteer anyways regardless. The issue becomes, hey I'm from [the company] and I am volunteering for you.

This executive's view is in sharp contrast to that of another executive at NE who believes that volunteering through the company should be sharply distinguished from volunteering outside the company. This executive stated:

> If I on my own am out teaching illiterate adults how to read it has nothing to do with [the company]. I'm not there with [company] shirt on and I don't think it is appropriate for the company to say, "and our employees teach adults to read" because I am not there as an employee, I'm there as an individual. If it's a corporate-sponsored activity, then yes. I think it's fair game for the corporation to be able to say "we are a good corporate citizen, let me show you some of the things that we do and here are our employees with their [company] shirts on marching for the American Cancer Society."

Program designers and implementers should be sensitive to differing opinions on how to promote the company through its employees' volunteer activities. It was unanimous among those we interviewed that the first priority of a company for its employee volunteer program should not be self-promotion, but rather helping the community. There was less agreement on how to appropriately show the public the good works of employees and what counts as fair game for use in promoting the image of the company. For some, anything that indicates that employees are being encouraged to volunteer to enhance the company image is wrong.

Flexibility in Program Activities

Employers vary in how much diversity they have in their employee volunteer activities. Organizations, such as NE, largely limit encouragement and support of employee volunteer activities to those matching specific causes or organizations connected to the organization's mission. Some scholars suggest that many organizations are using employee volunteer programs strategically to promote specific business objectives and leverage core competencies (Austin, 1997; Dutton & Pratt, 1997; Hess, Rogovsky, & Dunfee, 2002; Muirhead et al., 2002). Activities may also be chosen for their public relations value, to avoid controversy, and for their appeal to employees and company leaders. The rationale for what is included and excluded in an employee volunteer program is not always apparent to employees.

Many of the recommendations we received during our interviews had to do with expanding or restricting the types of activities that counted in the tracking of volunteer hours. As one SW employee noted, limiting the scope of the community service program might help the company "make more of a visible difference in the community instead of spreading ourselves so thin." Some employees at NE suggested that a broader array of service opportunities be offered and that this might increase volunteering and making employees happy which should be important to the program. For example, one NE employee commented,

> I would like to see the company take more of an interest in our campus, if you will. I think, I think that would be nice if we had some effort, even if it's just to pick up trash or to clean up graffiti or something like that, where we work and live, downtown here. I think that would, from my perspective, make our work lives even a little more enjoyable.

At least for most NE executives, the need to keep community service activities connected to company goals is very important, despite employee interest in broadening the activities. This was conveyed well by one NE executive:

> I think the activities we participate in are completely appropriate. The reason I say that is, from a management perspective, because you may get some employees who feel otherwise. And the reason I say that is an employee may have a specific interest, let's say with the SPCA, so they might come to the company and say 'would the company volunteer to clean up the kennel and do something with pets?' My answer to that would be no. And the reason I would say no is because, while we want to be a good corporate citizen and while we do want to participate in the community to the benefit of the com-

munity, we also want to make sure that the activities we are engaged in help to support the company's business goals.

One NE employee labeled other employees who did not believe the company should use the employees' volunteer activities to promote the company mission as "non-management, smaller thinkers." She told us,

> I was frank when I explained this to someone. Unfortunately we're not doing this just for charity, it's not just charity for charity's sake, it's charity toward the corporate goal. Politely I tried to get them to grow up in their view of it.

When employees critiqued the type of activities sponsored in relation to the tracking of volunteer hours, it was clear that we had found another sensitive line that some believed had been crossed. SW tracks not only community service though the company but also outside volunteering, so long as it meets certain requirements (typically volunteering has to be done at recognized 501(c)3 organizations). However, employees did not agree on what could/should and could not/should not be counted. Opinions were sometimes quite strong as demonstrated by a comment from a SW employee on the written survey, "Our [community service group leader] advised that our company is only interested in 501(c)(3) nonprofit organizations and we should not consider our volunteering though a church as volunteering! Volunteering is volunteering!!!" NE is focused on tracking community service through the company, much to the dismay of some employees who believes this is too restrictive. Some believe that if the company is going to do tracking, then a broader range of activities should be counted, even informal volunteering like helping a neighbor carry groceries or helping with snack time at your child's school.

Fund-raising events make up a large portion of community service events at both NE and SW. Some employees feel that the number of requests for fund raising are excessive and inappropriate, particularly when donations are solicited publicly. Employees report that not everyone can afford to contribute to everything and public collections can make people feel pressured to contribute to avoid looking as though they are unsupportive. Said one NE employee:

> I think we need to have a "no solicitation" policy that's enforced. We probably have one, and we certainly don't enforce it. I give every week to either somebody's going away party, or the United Way, or the Cancer Society, or somebody says I'm walking, I only charge a quarter a mile, or $2.00 per mile next week for the Cancer Society. In other words, I open my pocket every single week, and it's way overboard. I mean some of us can afford it

and some of us can't. So, people feel obligated and then they get a bitter taste in their mouth.

Issues were raised in both organizations on inconsistencies in how participating in community service activities during business hours is treated for different individuals. There is a perception that some employees are receiving more favorable treatment than others. Employees with flex time and who are paid on a salary basis have the most opportunity to volunteer during regular work hours. However, some of the employees who are given the leeway to take work time for volunteer activities do not think their increasing workloads permit this. This is amplified at NE where no paid time off is provided for community service. In some NE departments, managers require that any time spent on community service during business hours be made up by the employee. In other departments, managers use their discretion to allow employees to participate in community service activities during business hours without specifically making up the time. This decision is based on the belief by these managers that so long as the employees are getting their work done, it is not necessary to require that they work a specific number of hours. Not all employees with managerial responsibility believe that they have the authority and ability to offer employees flexibility to participate in community service activities during business hours. As one SW employee explained,

> With the structure of my department, the work flow would not allow us to miss work to volunteer. There are not enough people in the company that would be able to cover our department if we as a department want to volunteer together.

Not everyone agrees that employees should be allowed to participate in community service activities during business hours. Some people are concerned that employees would abuse such as system. Other employees regret the fact that senior management do not have enough confidence in employees to trust them not to take advantage of opportunities to participate in community service activities during business hours. As one NE employee said about trust:

> It's just not the culture here. And I would like to see it, I really would like to see the organization move a little bit more in that direction. It's not about 9-5. It's more about people will get their job done whether its 7 o'clock at night, but that they have an opportunity, and they feel that they have an opportunity to be able to go to their child's third grade class or first grade, and read a story or participate in a bake sale, or whatever. That, you know, people are coming and going in the organization, doing these things, in addition to, as well as doing all their work.

Some interviewees expressed the view that if companies were going to get public relations value from their volunteer service then the employees deserved to be supported by getting flexibility and time off from work. In discussing her push to get employees paid time off, a NE employee told us the typical response from her boss, "It's not volunteerism if it's not on your time. But it doesn't seem totally fair to me that the company takes the benefit without kicking in a little." Another NE employee agrees, stating,

> I think that's where I would draw the line and say that it's not fair for the company to springboard off of the good nature and will of its people when they didn't give them the time on company time to organize and participate.

A few areas stand out as sensitive when we think about the degree of flexibility an employee volunteer program should offer in its program activities. One is what should the activities be, with the sub-area of who should decide what the areas will be. Another area is how does request for donations appropriately fit into an employee volunteer program. How these requests should be conducted, if at all, is also a concern. A third area is how much flexibility should be allowed to perform the activities during company time.

CONCLUSIONS

Our case studies highlight a variety of sensitive issues for employee volunteer programs. While we chose to focus on nonprofit organizations in the insurance industry, it is likely that these issues are relevant for any employer who wishes to engage employees in community service. We grouped these issues under four general headings: encouragement, recognition, company image-enhancement, and flexibility. We found no hard and fast lines. Employee judgments of appropriateness seem dependent on how employees see the nature of volunteering and the link of employee volunteer programs to company objectives.

Our objective is not to make normative claims regarding what are right and wrong levels of encouragement, recognition, company image-enhancement, and flexibility. Rather, we wish to highlight the nature of the fine lines that need to be recognized and addressed by employee volunteer program designers and implementers. Our case studies show that all four of these issues are interrelated. Recognition tools such as tracking forms, for example, influence perceptions of what is required and the flexibility of the program to allow for individual choice of service venues. How much an organization seems to be using employee volunteer programs to benefit its image influences perceptions of what the company should offer employees in return. It also influences whether employees see these activities as volunteerism in its pure sense or community service as part of a job requirement.

Future research can help build our knowledge of the pros and cons of various policies and practices in use in employee volunteer programs, and how those policies and practices may reinforce or undermine program objectives. More work is needed to move beyond the positive rhetoric typically found in writings on employee volunteerism. By identifying concrete areas of concern, we can begin to offer balanced information on possible consequences of particular policies and practices for employee volunteer programs.

We have primarily focused in this chapter on the views of employee volunteer program participants, revealing a picture of lines in four areas that some employees believe should not be crossed. Employee opinions about exactly where those lines should be drawn, however, frequently differed. To complement this picture, additional research is needed to identify lines that service recipients believe should not be crossed. It is generally taken for granted that employee volunteer programs provide valuable service to communities. A more nuanced picture of the fine lines perceived by all the key stakeholders affected by employee volunteer programs may help to increase, or at least consciously balance, the benefits of these programs to the community, employees, and employers.

CHAPTER 10

FRATERNAL INVOLVEMENT IN VOLUNTEERING

The Membership Impact of Join Hands Day

Robert K. Christensen and James L. Perry

Corporate settings constitute important contexts and unique challenges for volunteering. Benefits of corporate philanthropy, including volunteer programs, span sector boundaries (e.g., Dunn, 2004, on corporate donation programs); indeed, corporations can be agents of public good. Although corporate volunteer programs may produce public benefits, they must first pass muster by satisfying a business case. Corporations are unlikely to pursue volunteer programs without first justifying them in terms of their business model. Despite a need for some form of business justification, corporations may have more flexibility in their involvements in volunteering; they have more latitude in how they can deploy resources for volunteering and are not subject to the same legal restrictions on ghost employment and other constraints that government organizations confront.

Despite the social desirability of volunteering, in many nations, particularly developing nations, corporate volunteering is rarer than other

Challenges in Volunteer Management, pp. 227–238
Copyright © 2008 by Information Age Publishing
All rights of reproduction in any form reserved.

forms of corporate philanthropy ("Enhancing Business-Community Relations," 2001). International and domestic research on the prevalence of corporate/employee volunteer programs yield widely varied results (for a review of the research see, Cihlar, 2004; Tschirhart, 2005). For example, research from Great Britain based on a Home Office Citizen Survey (Attwood, Singh, Prime, & Creasey, 2003) suggests that during 2001, "18 percent of employees (excluding self-employed people) worked for employers which supported schemes for volunteering, and seven percent of employees (4% of people overall) volunteered at least once through these schemes." One Canadian study (Hall, McKeown, & Roberts, 2000) suggests that

> employer support for volunteering may be increasing. In 2000, more than one-quarter of employed volunteers (27%) reported receiving approval from their employer to modify their hours of work in order to volunteer (compared with 22% in 1997), and 22 percent reported receiving recognition from their employer for their volunteer work (compared with 14% in 1997).

Whether the United States is following the same trend is difficult to surmise, because systematic data on corporate volunteer programs is limited (Alperson & Board, 1995; Cihlar, 2004; Wild, 1993). As Brudney and Gazley (2006) observe, these

> limitations include a reliance on anecdotal evidence and research reports that lack defined methodological techniques, including the potential for non-response bias in samples with small response rates. As a consequence, few academically rigorous studies have made their way into social science journals or other public forums. (p. 267)

A recent survey of MBA graduates observed that 70% of respondents were working for a firm with an employee volunteer program (Peterson, 2004a). On the other hand, a recent review (Cihlar, 2004) of the literature suggests a disconnect between the perceived benefits of corporate volunteer programs and the frequency with which they occur. Extrapolating from the British experience, where corporate volunteering has been more systematically studied, Cihlar hypothesizes that if United Kingdom and U.S. levels of employee volunteering are comparable, then less than one-quarter of Americans work for employers that support employee volunteering.

We found that understanding the prevalence of corporate volunteering is but one challenge to understanding corporate voluntarism. Equally contested is the link between corporate volunteerism and particular benefits. For example, some studies claim that corporate volunteering is catching on domestically (Hess, Rogovsky, & Dunfree, 2002), citing such benefits as improved employee teamwork, creation of healthier corporate/community environments, and improved perceptions of the corporation's image (*Corporate Volunteer Programs*, 1999).

This chapter addresses corporate volunteering at two levels: conceptual and empirical. Conceptually, we explore some of the instrumental relationships between corporate volunteering and outcomes of that involvement. In other words, we address why corporations might care to get involved in volunteer programs. Empirically, we focus on several strands of these outcomes and apply the conceptual analysis to discover what difference corporate volunteering makes in a specific setting. The empirical study we conducted focuses on Join Hands Day (JHD), a national day of service sponsored by America's Fraternal Benefit Societies and Points of Light. JHD is unique because it seeks to use volunteering in strategic ways to improve both short-term and long-term corporate results.

CORPORATE VOLUNTEERING: CONCEPTUAL MAP

Recent syntheses of research on volunteer programs suggest that empirical findings on the benefits of corporate volunteering are not conclusive, and rarely reach beyond the anecdotal. For example, Tschirhart (2005) observed that "there is a dearth of studies using theoretical models to explain or predict the adoption, type, and outcomes of employee volunteer programs and the attitudes and behaviors of individuals who participate and do not participate in these programs." In addition to more systematic and generalizable research on outcomes, Perry and Imperial (2001) and Cihlar (2004) prescribe investigations that would evaluate *why* volunteer efforts succeed or fail, not just *what* they achieve.

Research that has focused on what corporate volunteer programs achieve (Peterson, 2004b) reveals that corporate or employee volunteer programs are associated with benefits relative to employees, employers, and beneficiaries. We adapt Cihlar's survey of these benefits below (see Table 10.1), noting that many of the benefits flowing to employees also flow to employers. Similar surveys (Peterson, 2004b; Rochlin & Christoffer, 2000; Thomas & Christoffer, 1999; Weiser & Zadek, 2000) affirm these benefits. Although there are promising exploratory studies that seek to unpack the complexity of volunteer program outcomes (Peterson, 2004a, 2004b), much research still needs to be done.

We turn now to our empirical study. The research focuses on the effects of episodic service (via JHD) on a particular type of organization (fraternal benefit societies). Because the study provides direct evidence about

Table 10.1.   The Benefits of Volunteering

Outcomes for Volunteer Recipients	Outcomes for Employees	Outcomes for Employers
• support for beneficiary missions • access to more and better-organized volunteers than otherwise might be available • often the volunteer relationship leads to strengthening of philanthropic donations through employer match programs • because corporations frequently seek to promote their philanthropic work, volunteer beneficiaries can receive significant publicity that, in turn, has the effect of bringing in more volunteers and donations • community improvement	• building personal self-confidence • meeting new people and making friends • a feeling of satisfaction or self worth for making a difference	• heightened employee engagement with the sponsoring company • innovation provided by professional development • an improved public image • improved relationships with the communities in which they operate • increased ability to attract and retain high-quality employees • improved morale and sense of team spirit among employees • healthier economic and community environment

Outcomes For Employees and Employers

• organizational and time management skills
• people skills (caring, negotiating and listening)
• accountability and assessment reporting
• planning skills
• leadership development
• budgeting skills
• survival skills—stress management, prioritization

Adapted from Chris Cihlar from the Points of Light Foundation (2004). The State of Knowledge Surrounding Employee Volunteering in the United States. Report located at: http://www.pointsoflight.org/downloads/pdf/resources/research/StateOfKnowledge.pdf

outcomes from a corporate volunteering initiative, we hope the research moves us a little closer to understanding the challenges inherent in corporate volunteerism.

CORPORATE VOLUNTEERING: AN EMPIRICAL ASSESSMENT

JHD is a national day of service that seeks to bring youth and adults together through meaningful volunteer activity. JHD began in 2000 to address some of the challenges of an age-segregated society by encouraging youth and adults to join in an annual day of service. JHD is a collaboration among JOIN HANDS DAY, Inc., a 501 (c) 3 established by America's fraternal benefit societies, the Points of Lights Foundation, and the Volunteer Center National Network.

The rationale for initiating JHD rests with two different sets of circumstances. The first set of circumstances involves the perceived estrangement between young people and adults. Although generational differences are an accepted rite of passage, the perceived gulf between generations appears to have grown. Schneider and Stevenson (1999) report that American teenagers, on average, spend 20% of their waking time—3½ hours—alone each day. This is more time alone than with family and friends. Furthermore, the amount of time teenagers spend alone increases as they progress from middle to high school. Schneider and Stevenson attribute the large amount of time teenagers spend alone to major demographic changes like declining family size and increasing divorce rates. Robert Putnam (2000) goes as far as to suggest that increasing suicide and depression among young people is a product of the social isolation that Schneider and Stevenson document.

A second set of circumstances involves declines in membership in America's fraternal benefit societies. These societies, which were founded in the late nineteenth and early twentieth centuries, have been at the core of America's social capital for the last century. However, as Putnam (2000), Skocpol (2003), and others have shown, the membership in these societies has been growing older and gradually declining since the 1960s.

These circumstances brought the leadership of the National Fraternal Congress of America, the 120-year-old trade association for fraternal benefit societies that include organizations such as Modern Woodmen of America, Foresters, and Knights of Columbus, to create the JHD organization in 1998. The new 501(c)3 joined with the Points of Light Foundation and Volunteer Center National Network to initiate a national day of service in 2000.

Goals and Logic Models

JHD's founders articulated several goals for which logic models were created to support evaluation of JHD. The JHD Steering Committee identified the following long-term goals, which include several of the outcomes addressed in Table 10.1:

- Make a contribution to solving the problem of America being an age-segregated society;

- Address problem conditions in local neighborhoods;
- Increase the visibility and public awareness of fraternal benefit societies;
- Reenergize local lodges by increasing membership and participation in local chapters or lodges, particularly among young people.

The logic models created for each goal included the background factors, program activities, and immediate and intermediate outcomes. The models have guided JHD's development, specifying criteria to gauge success.

This study presents the results of research aimed at understanding the potential corporate impact of JHD. The key evaluation questions are:

- Are participating fraternal benefit societies better able to attract youth than nonparticipating societies?
- Are participating societies better able to retain youthful policyholders?
- Do participating chapters achieve better "results" than nonparticipating chapters?

The remainder of this chapter looks at the effect of JHD on one fraternal benefit society: Aid Association for Lutherans (AAL). Data were based on the annual branch activity reports of approximately 10,000 units, as well as yearly membership data. Data used for the analysis were collected prior to the 2002 merger of AAL and Lutheran Brotherhood to create Thrivent Financial for Lutherans, which, as a not-for-profit Fortune 500 financial services organization serving 2.8 million members, is now the largest fraternal benefit society.

The analysis consists of two parts. The first compares those AAL branches that sponsored a JHD activity with those branches that did not. The second component looks specifically at differentiating among those branches that sponsored a JHD activity in order to determine whether certain JHD practices were more/less successful from a business perspective.

Data Description

The data set consists of AAL data from 1999-2002. In 1999, only two measurements were available: total members and total new members. From 2000-2002, many more measures were available. These included the numbers of association, benefit, and youth members, and information about JHD attendance. The variables used for this analysis are described in Table 10.2. Table 10.2 also includes descriptive statistics that were used

Table 10.2.   Description of AAL Data and Variable Names (1999-2002)

Variable Name	Description	Descriptive Statistic
TMBR99	Total Members 1999	1,747,151
TMBR00	Total Members 2000	1,790,118
TMBR01	Total Members 2001	1,853,190
TMBR02	Total Members 2002	1,869,641
TNEW99	Total New Members 1999	67,045
TNEW00	Total New Members 2000	90,740
TNEW01	Total New Members 2001	99,470
TNEW02	Total New Members 2002	59,399
TNRAT99	Total New Members to Total Members (proxy for growth), 1999	0.038
TNRAT00	Total New Members to Total Members (proxy for growth), 2000	0.051
TNRAT01	Total New Members to Total Members (proxy for growth), 2001	0.054
TNRAT02	Total New Members to Total Members (proxy for growth), 2002	0.032
AMBR00	Association Members 2000	130,823
AMBR01	Association Members 2001	174,849
AMBR02	Association Members 2002	163,125
BMBR00	Benefit Members 2000	1,390,765
BMBR01	Benefit Members 2001	1,404,176
BMBR02	Benefit Members 2002	1,438,584
YMBR00	Youth Members 2000	268,530
YMBR01	Youth Members 2001	274,165
YMBR02	Youth Members 2002	267,789
HHCT00	Household Count 2000	1,023,178
HHCT01	Household Count 2001	1,051,468
HHCT02	Household Count 2002	1,062,575
MATT00	Members attending a Join Hands Day Activity 2000	12,420
MATT01	Members attending a Join Hands Day Activity 2001	15,323
MATT02	Members attending a Join Hands Day Activity 2002	16,115
ATT00	Nonmembers attending a Join Hands Day Activity 2000	29,855
NATT01	Nonmembers attending a Join Hands Day Activity 2001	31,446
NATT02	Nonmembers attending a Join Hands Day Activity 2002	30,417
TVHR00	Total volunteer hours 2000	79,597
TVHR01	Total volunteer hours 2001	100,703
TVHR02	Total volunteer hours 2002	98,595
JHDD00	Whether a unit hosted a Join Hands Day Activity 2000	908
JHDD01	Whether a unit hosted a Join Hands Day Activity 2001	1,124
JHDD02	Whether a unit hosted a Join Hands Day Activity 2002	1,008

to calculate general data trends, depicted more clearly in Figures 10.1 and 10.2. Note that in naming the variables, the last two characters of the variable name indicate the year from which the data were drawn, for example, "00" for 2000, "01" for 2001, and "02" for 2002.

Fraternal units were matched across the four years of reporting to facilitate tracking the impact of JHD on a particular unit over time. Figure 10.1 shows the membership trends for all of AAL's reporting units (aggregated), regardless of their participation in JHD. Year 2001 marks a peak in new, youth, and association members (see Figure 10.1).

Among those units that participated in JHD, 2001 was also a peak year for the number of projects, nonmembers attending, and total hours volunteered (see Figure 10.2). However, member attendance peaked in 2002, possibly indicating a trend of increasing buy-in from fraternal members (see Figure 10.2).

Participation Versus Nonparticipation

In comparing those units participating in JHD (participating units) with those units that did not participate, the analysis indicates that JHD

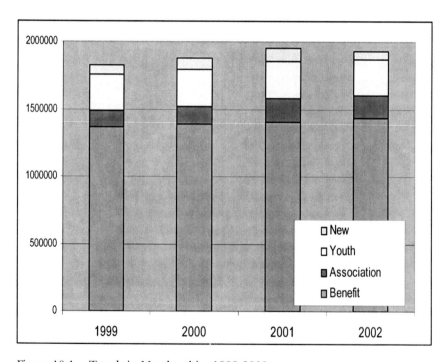

Figure 10.1.   Trends in Membership, 1999-2000.

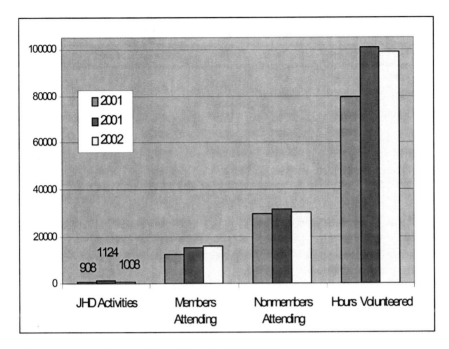

Figure 10.2.   Join Hands Day Trends, 2000-2002.

contributes to increased viability of participating units. The analysis was performed on the impact of JHD on an annual basis. An effort was made to account for the "spillover" effect that, for example, JHD 2000 might have on JHD 2001. It should also be noted that because branch activity reports are not due until the end of each calendar year, the effect of JHD is often not detectable within the year in which a branch participates.

Correlation Analyses

A simple correlation analysis served as the first step in this inquiry (see Table 10.3). Although the correlation statistics are inconclusive with respect to the impact of JHD on a fraternal unit's ability to acquire new members, they do suggest a positive relationship. For example, participation in JHD (JHD00, JHD01, JHD02) is positively correlated with new membership (TNEW00, TNEW01, TNEW02) in every year (see Table 10.3).

Pearson correlation statistics were also calculated to detect any linear relationship between new members and participation in JHD. A second statistic was calculated to reflect a standardization of new members (the ratio of new members to total members). Though neither was statistically

**Table 10.3.   Correlation Analysis—
Participation's Effect on New Membership**

	TNEW00	TNEW01	TNEW02	JHDD00	JHDD01	JHDD02
TNEW00	1.000					
TNEW01	0.545	1.000				
TNEW02	0.478	0.593	1.000			
JHDD00	0.069	0.027	0.026	1.000		
JHDD01	0.089	0.049	0.030	0.281	1.000	
JHDD02	0.067	0.063	0.044	0.198	0.309	1.000

significant, it is noteworthy that the JHD correlation statistics are as high as they are (between 0.05 and 0.06) considering the myriad of volunteer and other activities in which each branch participates (i.e., alternative explanations for size and growth).

Regression Analyses

Regression models were calculated for each year since JHD's inception. The models analyze the impact of participating in JHD on a unit's report of new members, a proxy for growth and vitality. With the exception of 2000, this is done by looking at the impact of JHD on the next year's report of new members. For 2000, because JHD did not exist in 1999, participation in JHD 2000 was used. To isolate JHD's effect, the models control for two of the most intuitively influential factors on growth—the unit's size (total members) and number of new members from the previous year. This variable, TNRAT, is the ratio of new members to total members (see Table 10.1), and serves to standardize this information to make it more statistically comparable across AAL units.

The models confirm that total and new members have a significant explanatory effect upon the report of new members for the next year. Notably, the models also confirm that JHD has a positive predictive relationship--although, as expected, on a much smaller scale than past membership—and that these relationships are statistically significant for participation in JHD in 2000 and 2002, and marginally significant for 2001.[1]

While these parsimonious regression models only explain a small portion of the variance in the data reporting new members (between 0.01 and 0.04), they do provide evidence that, in just three years, JHD is having a noticeable impact on fraternal growth.

As another measure of growth, regression models were developed that analyze the impact of JHD on the numbers of youth members. Again, although the predictive value of JHD is small compared to the control variable (total members in the preceding year), participation in JHD has positive, statistically significant predictive value upon fraternal vitality as expressed in numbers of youth members.[2]

Focusing on Units Participating in JHD

Looking only at the data from units participating in at least one JHD during 2000-2002, the following analysis explores whether "best practices" can be distinguished among participating units. In other words, do some JHD practices encourage growth more than others?

Correlation statistics show only small, not significant relationships between the types of JHD activity and a branch's ability to attract new or youth members the next year. For example, whether the project was dedicated to local service, Habitat for Humanity (fund raising or work project), or Partners in Service seems to have scant relationship with the growth of the unit.

In contrast, correlation analysis reveals that total volunteer hours from a project are positively related (.23) to the number of attendees who are not fraternal members. The number of youth members in a unit is also positively, but not significantly, correlated (.08) with the total number hours volunteered at a JHD event. This might suggest that projects involving youth can yield more hours than similar projects lacking youth. It may also suggest that bigger projects attract youth. But neither conclusion is supported from this data—further study would be necessary.

CONCLUSION

This study looked at corporate volunteering from both conceptual and empirical perspectives. We took stock of the range of views about the desirability of corporate volunteering and the outcomes that are typically linked to corporate volunteer programs. Although the literature identifies a range of benefits for employees, beneficiaries, and a corporation's image and bottom line, we noted that the extent of corporate volunteering falls short of the expected benefits.

The empirical analysis represented an attempt to assess the corporate impact of JHD, a national day of service sponsored by fraternal benefit societies. We addressed three general questions related to the impact of JHD:

- Are participating chapters better able to attract youth than nonparticipating chapters?
- Are participating chapters better able to retain youthful policyholders?
- Do participating chapters achieve better "results" than nonparticipating chapters?

By studying one fraternal organization in depth, we were able to confirm some of the outcomes that JHD was designed to achieved when it was created in 1998. While correlation statistics do not, on their own, provide causal evidence, they support the claim that JHD has encouraged growth both in new members and in youth members.

Our analysis confirms that volunteer programs can have positive effects on important outcomes for corporations. More importantly, the study and its findings provide a model for how corporations could approach the assessment of their volunteer initiatives. The literature indicates that perhaps the biggest challenge facing corporate volunteer programs—as reflected in their modest diffusion across the corporate world—is their ability to justify and sustain themselves in the absence of hard evidence that they make a difference in producing the results that executives and shareholders prize.

NOTES

1. Regression coefficients were 2.94* for 2000, 1.10† for 2001, and 0.67* for 2002.* indicates significance at the 0.05 level, and † indicates marginal significance at the 0.10 level.
2. Regression coefficients were 1.43* for 2000, 0.86† for 2001, and 0.63† for 2002.* indicates significance at the 0.05 level, and † indicates marginal significance at the 0.10 level. (Full regression results on file with authors.)

CONCLUSION

So What? And What's Next?

Victor Murray

In the foreword to this book, our editor succinctly summed up its focus as "a discussion of the challenges of volunteer management targeted to those who could most use the information" (p. vii). This has indeed what has been provided to us. The purpose of this short wrap-up chapter is simply to remind us how the elements of the journey we have taken hang together and outline where the path ahead might take us. More specifically, we will look at these three questions:

1. How are the papers in this volume linked conceptually?
2. What are some of the highlights of their contributions to understanding volunteer management?
3. Where might the field of volunteer management research go from here?

Challenges in Volunteer Management, pp. 239–246
Copyright © 2008 by Information Age Publishing

A CONCEPTUAL FRAMEWORK FOR VOLUNTEER MANAGEMENT

Volunteer management is all about means for achieving certain ends. The ends being sought are simple: From the point of view of the organization for which volunteers work, it wants:

- An optimal supply of suitable volunteers
- Volunteers who are suitably prepared (i.e., have adequate skills and knowledge for the work).
- Volunteers who will remain as long as they are needed.

In addition, from the point of view of volunteers, because volunteering is so much more than a simple "businesslike" contract for work in exchange for compensation, they must obtain adequate levels of satisfaction from their contributions.

Figure 1 presents a simple conceptual framework that outlines the ends sought in volunteering, the means that volunteer managers adopt to try to influence the extent to which these ends are achieved and the broad categories of factors that, in turn, shape the volunteer management practices used *and* the probability that these practices will produce the desired ends. Let's review how this framework operates.

In the box labeled "Key decisions related to volunteering" we see that the outcomes we seek only occur when enough potential volunteers make certain decisions, namely the decisions to: (a) undertake any kind of volunteer work at all; (b) choose a particular organization in which to do this; (c) seek or accept a particular assignment; (d) put forth a real effort to do the job well; and (e) stick with it as long as they are needed. So the next question becomes: What influences these decisions?

In the box labeled "Volunteer management structures, policies and practices," we are reminded that there may be (and experts would say *should* be) a number of things that volunteer managers can do to promote the outcomes they seek. For example, there may be formal statements outlining the goals of volunteering and the values that underpin the organization's view of the volunteer. But perhaps more important than these formal statements there is the actual culture of volunteering—the often unspoken, nonofficial beliefs, values, attitudes, and perceptions held by those who interact with volunteers that are communicated by everyday actions and words.

We also see in this box the major areas of focus that make up the typical components of volunteer management which are well summarized by Hagar and Brudney as well as others in this volume. And we also cannot neglect the "infrastructure" of the volunteer management program that creates specific positions in this area, provides training for those in it (or not) and sets up vital information and communications systems for its operation.

However, as the articles in this volume so frequently point out, there is no guarantee that the adoption of a particular set of volunteer management practices will automatically lead to the key decisions that produce successful outcomes. As well, there remains the question of what shapes the probability that such management practices will be adopted in the first place. This leads us to the remaining boxes in Figure 1. Looking at the box labeled "Characteristics of the Organization," for example, it is difficult for keen, knowledgeable volunteer managers to make headway with their visions for the perfect volunteer program unless there is sufficient support and complementary structures and policies in the larger organization of which the program is a part. The potential for these to exist may vary depending on such things as the organization's size, its stage of development, mission, and, of course, the size and stability of its budget.

Similarly, we can see in the box labeled "Characteristics of actual and potential volunteers" that even the most brilliantly conceived and executed recruitment, motivation and retention practices may fail to pay off if the potential pool of volunteers contains high percentages of people whose backgrounds and personalities are antithetical to the idea of volunteering or whose lives change as they get or lose employment, have families or experience health problems.

Finally, one can ask the even bigger question: What, in turn, influences the characteristics of the organization and the pool of potential volunteers? To answer that, we must look beyond the borders of the organization itself or the individual volunteers to the larger society in which they both exist. In that society there are widely shared values that represent its culture, many of which directly impact decisions related to volunteering. There are also political systems and changing governing parties that can radically alter the context of volunteering through their policy choices. And, in a global economy, world events can create periods of economic growth or recession that quickly affect the supply of, and demand for, volunteers (not to mention volunteer managers). Finally, related to these forces, there are the impacts of changing demographics, such as the aging baby boom and subsequent "baby bust" in most Western countries. And one cannot ignore the often unpredictable changes wrought by new technologies and even larger forces such a climate change and pollution.

Of course, these larger environmental influences do not usually impact volunteering directly. For the most part they are mediated through the actions of the organization's key stakeholders—those individuals, groups and other organizations that have an interest in one's own organization, have their own agendas and many possess enough power to exert influ-

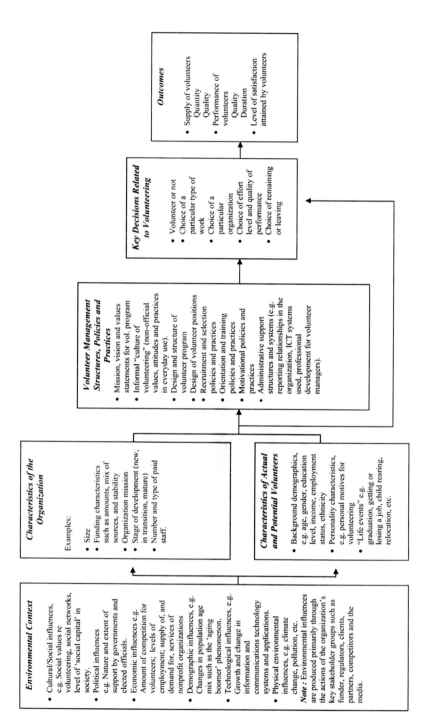

Figure 1. A framework for understanding the determinants and impact of volunteer management.

Environmental Context

• Cultural/Social influences, e.g. Social values re volunteering, social networks, level of 'social capital' in society.
• Political influences e.g. Nature and extent of support by governments and elected officials.
• Economic influences e.g. Amount of competition for volunteers; levels of employment; supply of, and demand for, services of nonprofit organizations
• Demographic influences, e.g. Changes in population age mix such as the 'aging boomer' phenomenon.
• Technological influences, e.g. Growth and change in information and communications technology systems and applications.
• Physical environmental influences, e.g. climate change, pollution, etc.

Note : Environmental influences are produced primarily through the actions of the organization's key stakeholder groups such as funder, regulators, clients, partners, competitors and the media.

Characteristics of the Organization

Examples:

• Size
• Funding characteristics such as amounts, mix of sources, and stability
• Organization mission
• Stage of development (new, in transition, mature)
• Number and type of paid staff.

Characteristics of Actual and Potential Volunteers

• Background demographics, e.g. age, gender, education level, income, employment status, ethnicity
• Personality characteristics, e.g. personal motives for volunteering
• "Life events" e.g. graduation, getting or losing a job, child rearing, relocation, etc.

Volunteer Management Structures, Policies and Practices

• Mission, vision and values statements for vol. program
• Informal "culture of volunteering" (non-official values, attitudes and practices in everyday use).
• Design and structure of volunteer program
• Design of volunteer positions
• Recruitment and selection policies and practices
• Orientation and training policies and practices
• Motivational policies and practices
• Administrative support structures and systems (e.g. reporting relationships in the organization, ICT systems used, professional development for volunteer managers).

Key Decisions Related to Volunteering

• Volunteer or not
• Choice of a particular type of work
• Choice of a particular organization
• Choice of effort level and quality of performance
• Choice of remaining or leaving

Outcomes

• Supply of volunteers
  Quantity
  Quality
• Performance of volunteers
  Quality
  Duration
• Level of satisfaction attained by volunteers

ence over it. Among the more important stakeholders for most nonprofits are funders, client groups, government regulators and legislators, partners, "competitors," suppliers and the media.

With this understanding of the framework presented in Figure 1, let us now review some of the highlights of the papers in this book showing which parts of the framework they address.

SOME HIGHLIGHTS OF THE PAPERS IN THIS BOOK

Perhaps the most common themes running throughout this book are these:

1. While the use of generally accepted "best practices" in volunteer management is desirable, there is no guarantee that they will be the main determinants of how volunteers will make their key decisions (to join, perform and remain). Other factors can be just as, and sometimes more, important.

2. Though it is tempting to believe that the implementation of "best practices" in volunteer management is just a matter of learning what they are and putting them in place, it is not as simple as that. Many forces are at work shaping which practices will be implemented and, of equal importance, which ones are most appropriate for differing circumstances. There may be an as-yet-not-fully-articulated contingency theory of volunteer management. It would attempt to articulate which structures, policies and practices should be adapted to the circumstances one is in such as the nature of the volunteer work to be done, the backgrounds of the volunteers and the characteristics of the organization and its environment.

Within each of these broad themes, however, are a number of specific insights of real value to the volunteer manager. While it is not the purpose of this chapter to summarize each of the papers, the following points illustrate their contributions to the major themes in terms of the elements of the conceptual framework in Figure 1.

Impact of Volunteer Management on Volunteer Outcomes

- Hagar and Brudney (chapter 1) show, for example, that some volunteer management practices such as careful matching, recognition programs and training are more frequently associated with high levels of volunteer retention than others.

- The value of training for volunteer managers is further reinforced by Nezhina, Brudney, and Ibrayeva (chapter 7) in their study of volunteer management in Kazakhstan.

- Rhenborg and McVey (chapter 6) show how the basic models for the organization of volunteers (centralized, decentralized, ad hoc) can produce different outcomes in Texas state volunteer programs with the centralized approach being the more effective in that system.

- Even though their paper did not deal directly with volunteer management in nonprofit organizations per se, Tschirhart and St. Claire's paper (chapter 9) contains interesting insights into how the way volunteers are managed affects their motivation. In this case, the focus was employee volunteer programs in business in which was revealed the harm that can be created by too much pressure to participate, too much, or the wrong kind, of recognition, too much publicity and not enough flexibility.

Impact of Organizational Characteristics

- In this area we learn from Hagar and Brudney (chapter 1) how the organization's size, scope and "industry" can affect the adoption of a wide range of volunteer management practices.

- Meija and Tin Hoorn (chapter 2) provide useful insights into the impact of organization type (service delivery, mutual support and campaigning) on these same practices.

- Even the paper on Time Banks by Clary (chapter 5) provides a further illustration of this point in that it represents a unique and interesting example of "mutual support" organizations and how they work.

- Similarly, Mele's (chapter 4) case study of the Sidelines organization to help women with high risk pregnancies shows us how the implementation of a new organization-wide information and communications technology completely changed the structure and operation of the volunteer management program.

- Finally, in chapter 8, Bies and Curs show us how, in Poland (but it could be elsewhere as well) the degree of formalization of the organization as a whole can affect the degree of formalization of the volunteer program within it.

Impact of the Characteristics of Volunteers

There is extensive literature on the relationship between various characteristics of volunteers and their propensity to join and remain with a nonprofit organization (see Leete, 2006 for a recent review of it). The paper by Hartenian (chapter 3), however, adds a new typology for classifying volunteers as "misfits," "missionaries" or "consultants" which could be of value to volunteer mangers in designing their programs to fit the needs of each of these different types.

Impact of the Larger Environmental Context

Finally, referring to the box labeled "Environmental context" in Figure 1, it is possible to see the primary contributions of the papers by Nezhina, Brudney and Ibrayeva (chapter 7) and Bies and Curs (chapter 8). Here we find excellent illustrations of the often overlooked contribution of national cultures on the whole phenomenon of volunteering and volunteer management. They remind us that we often take for granted the history, values, and political systems that underpin traditions of volunteering to be found in the United States and other Western countries. Also, how fragile these external conditions are; how easily that can change unless constant attention is paid to sustaining them. Indeed, there are those, like Putnam (2000), who argue that they are already under serious threat and immediate attention must be paid to them before it is too late.

A FINAL WORD: WHERE TO FROM HERE?

This volume, while making many useful new contributions to the field of volunteer management, was never intended to be the final word on the subject. While much more is known now than in the recent past, much more is yet to be discovered. For example, while there is little doubt that good volunteer management practices can have a considerable impact on the decisions of volunteers to join, perform and remain in nonprofit organizations, the exact nature and extent of this impact can vary from situation to situation. One of the pieces to this puzzle that is still missing is the effect of day-to-day interpersonal relationships between volunteers and paid staff, volunteers and volunteer managers and between volunteers themselves. While these "micro" relationships may have less impact on recruitment, they undoubtedly affect retention. Tone of voice, choice of words, body language, frequency of communication, underlying moods of stress, humor, etc., all these small elements of everyday life add up to make volunteering enjoyable and worthwhile or the opposite. Yet, to date, we lack the observational case studies that record and analyze behaviors at this level.

At the other end of the continuum, we are now more aware of how the situation in the larger organization within which a volunteer program exists can impact it through the amount and kind of support it provides. However, there is much more to be learned about the effects of the various aspects of the organization's culture. These are the nonformal, and usually unspoken, attitudes, beliefs, values and perceptions about the contribution of volunteers and how they should behave and be treated. Again, research on this topic is lacking because data of this kind are best gathered through in-depth case studies in which researchers "live" in the situation for long periods of time; not an easy methodology to apply for many researchers.

Finally, this volume has shown us that there is little doubt the environmental context of volunteering is critical. However, we need yet more studies on the impact of societal cultures such as those presented here on Poland and Kazakhstan. But more is also needed on the role of government policies, technology and, especially, changing populations demographics.

All in all, the challenges in studying and practicing volunteer management are many but the rewards are great if one continues to believe in the importance of a strong and vibrant culture of volunteering in our society.

REFERENCES

Abbott, A. (2001). *Time matters: On theory and method.* Chicago: University of Chicago Press.

Abell, P. (2004). Narrative explanation: An alternative to variable-centred explanation? *Annual Review of Sociology, 30,* 287-310.

Academie voor Lichamelijke Opvoeding [Academy for Physical Education]. (2005). *Sport, management en ondernemen [Sport, management and entrepreneurschip], Business plan.* Amsterdam: Hogeschool van Amsterdam.

Allen, N. J., & Meyer, J. P. (1990). Measurement and antecedents of affective, continuance, and normative commitment to organization. *Journal of Occupational Psychology, 63,* 1-18.

Alperson, M., & Board, T. C. (1995). *Corporate giving strategies that add business value: Research report 1126.* New York: The Conference Board.

Anderson, J., & Clary, B. (1987, July-September) Coproduction in emergency medical services. *Journal of Voluntary Action Research, 17,* 33-42.

Anderson, J. C., & Moore, L. F. (1978). The motivation to volunteer. *Journal of Voluntary Action Research, 7,* 120-129.

Anheier, H., & Salamon, L. M. (1999). Volunteering in cross-national perspective: Initial comparisons. *Law and Contemporary Problems, 62,* 43-65.

Ashforth, B. E. (1998). Epilogue: What does the concept of identity add to organization science. In D. Whetten & P. C. Godfrey (Eds.), *Identity in organizations: Building theory through conversations* (pp. 273-294). Thousand Oaks, CA: SAGE.

Ashforth, B. E., & Mael, F. (1989). Social identity theory and the organization. *Academy of Management Review, 14,* 20-39.

Association of Voluntary Service Organizations. (2003). *Legal status of volunteers: Country report Poland.* Belgium: European Volunteer Center.

Attwood, C., Singh, G., Prime, D., & Creasey, R. (2003). *Home Office Research Study 270: 2001 Home Office Citizenship Survey: People, families and communities.*

Retrieved Jan. 4, 2007, from http://www.homeoffice.gov.uk/rds/pdfs2/hors270. pdf

Austin, J. E. (1997). *Social Enterprise Series No. 2: Making business sense of community service* (Working Paper Series No. 98–019). Cambridge, MA: Harvard Business School.

Bacharach, S., Bamberger, P., & Conley, S. (1991). Work-home conflict among nurses and engineers: Mediating the impact of role stress on burnout and satisfaction at work. *Journal of Organizational Behavior, 12,* 39-53.

Barlow, J., & Hainsworth, J. (2001). Volunteerism among older people with arthritis. *Aging and Society, 21,* 203-217.

Barzelay, M. (2003). Introduction: The process dynamics of public management policy-making. *International Public Management Journal, 6*(3), 251-281.

Barzelay, M., & Gallego, R. (2006). From "new institutionalism" to "institutional processualism": Advancing knowledge about public management policy change. *Governance, 19*(4), 531-557.

Batson, C. D., Dyck, J. L., Brandt, J. R., Batson, J. G., Powell, A. L., McMaster, M. R., et al. (1988). Five studies testing two new egoistic alternatives to empathy-altruism hypothesis. *Journal of Personality and Social Psychology, 55,* 52-77.

Ben-Ner, A. (2002). The shifting boundaries of the mixed economy and the future of the nonprofit sector. *Annals of Public and Cooperative Economics, 73*(1), 5-40.

Bennett, D., & Fielding, P. (1999). *The net effect. How cyber-advocacy is changing the political landscape.* Merrifield, VA: E-Advocates Press.

Bies, A. (2003). *Nongovernmental accountability in Poland: Mandatory versus discretionary self-regulation approaches.* (Doctoral dissertation, University of Minnesota, 2003) ProQuest Digital Dissertation, AAT 3102099.

Boczoń, J., Erene, J., & Galziak, J. (1996). A new relationship between non-governmental and public sectors. In B. Synak & M. Ruzica (Eds.), *Voluntary sector in a changing society* (pp. 243-250). Indianapolis: The Indiana University Center on Philanthropy.

Boessenkool, J., & Verweel, P. (2004). 'Stop professionaliseren, red de sportvereniging' [Stop professionalizing, save the sports associations]. *Vrijwillige Inzet Onderzocht [Voluntary Effort Studied], 1*(2), 29-34.

Bograd, H. (1995). [Review of the book: The Jossey-Bass handbook of nonprofit leadership and management]. *Nonprofit and Voluntary Sector Quarterly, 24*(3), 269-271.

Bonjean, C. M., Markham, W. T., & Macken, P. O. (1994). Measuring self-expression in volunteer organizations: A theory-based questionnaire. *The Journal of Applied Behavioral Science, 30*(4), 487-515.

Boyd, B. L. (2004). Barriers to the development of volunteer leadership competencies: Why Johnnie can't lead volunteers. *Journal of Volunteer Administration, 22*(4), 17-22.

Boyle, D. (1999). *Funny money: In search of alternative cash.* London: Harper Collins.

Bozeman, B., & Bretschneider, S. (1986, November). Public management information systems: Theory and prescription. *Public Administration Review, 46,* 475-487.

Bradley, J. H., & Hebert, F. J. (1997). The effect of personality type on team performance. *Journal of Management Development, 16*(5), 337-353.

Brainard, L. A., & Brinkerhoff, J. M. (2004). Lost in cyberspace: Shedding light on the dark matter of grassroots organizations. *Nonprofit and Voluntary Sector Quarterly, Supplement, 33*(3), 32S-53S.

Brainard, L. A., & Siplon, P. D. (2000, August 31-September 2). *Cyberspace challenges to mainstream advocacy groups.* The case of healthcare activism. Paper presented at the Annual Meeting of the American Political Association, Washington, DC.

Britton, N. R. (1991). Permanent disaster volunteers: Where do they fit? *Nonprofit and Voluntary Sector Quarterly, 20*(4), 395-414.

Brown, E. (1999). The scope of volunteer activity and public service. In C. T. Clotfelter (Special Ed), *Law and contemporary problems* (pp. 16-42). Durham, NC: Duke University School of Law.

Brudney, J. L. (1990a). *Fostering volunteer programs in the public sector: Planning, initiating, and managing voluntary activities.* San Francisco, CA: Jossey-Bass.

Brudney, J. L. (1990b). Expanding the government-by-proxy construct: Volunteers in the delivery of public services. *Nonprofit and Voluntary Sector Quarterly, 19*(4), 315-328.

Brudney, J. L. (1999). The effective use of volunteers: Best practices for the public sector. *Law and Contemporary Problems, 62,* 219-255.

Brudney, J. L. (Ed.). (2005). Emerging areas of volunteering. *ARNOVA Occasional Paper Series, 1*(2). Indianapolis: Association for Research on Nonprofit Organizations and Voluntary Action.

Brudney, J. L., & Kellough, J. E. (2000). Volunteers in state government: Involvement, management and benefits. *Nonprofit and Voluntary Sector Quarterly, 29*(1), 111-130.

Brudney, J. L., & Gazley, B. (2002). Testing the conventional wisdom regarding volunteer programs: A longitudinal analysis of the Service Corps of Retired Executives and the U. S. Small Business Administration. *Nonprofit and Voluntary Sector Quarterly, 31*(4), 525-548.

Brudney, J. L., & Gazley, B. (2006). Moving ahead or falling behind? Volunteer promotion and data collection. *Nonprofit Management and Leadership, 16*(3), 259-276.

Brudney, J. L., & Meijs, L. C. P. M. (2004, November 9-11). *Creating community pay offs with winning volunteer scenarios.* Paper presented at Eurofestation, Maastricht, The Netherlands.

Brudney, J. L., & Nezhina, T. G. (2005). What is old is new again: Achieving effectiveness with volunteer programs in Kazakhstan. *Voluntas: International Journal of Voluntary and Nonprofit Organizations, 16*(3), 293-308.

Brudney, J. L., & Schmahl, S. (2001). *Volunteer administration: A survey of the profession.* A report to the Association for Volunteer Administration.

Burt, E., & Taylor, J. (2003). New technologies, embedded values, and strategic change: Evidence from the UK voluntary sector. *Nonprofit and Voluntary Sector Quarterly, 32*(1), 115-127.

Burt, E., & Taylor, J. (2004). Voluntary organizations in the UK: Repositioning within the information polity? In *challenges of public management reforms, selected conference proceedings: The eighth international research symposium on public management* (pp. 287-311). Hungary: Budapest University of Economics and Public Administration.

Bush, R. (1992). Survival of the nonprofit spirit in a for-profit world. *Nonprofit and Voluntary Sector Quarterly, 21*(4), 391-410.

Business Volunteers Unlimited. (2003). *Corporate community involvement survey, January 2003.* Cleveland, OH: Author.

Cahn, E. S. (2004). *No more throw-away people: The coproduction imperative.* Washington, DC: Essential Books.

Cahn, E. S., & J. Rowe (1995). *Time dollars: The new currency that enables Americans to turn their hidden resource—time—into personal security and community renewal.* Emmaus, PA: Family Resource Coalition of America.

Callero, P. L., Howard, J. A., & Piliavin, J. A. (1987). Helping behavior as role behavior: Disclosing social structure and history on the analysis of prosocial action. *Social Psychology Quarterly, 59,* 247-256.

Canadian Center for Philanthropy. (2004). *Employer-supported volunteering.* Toronto: Author.

Comptroller of Public Accounts. (1993). *Against the grain: High-quality low-cost government for Texas* (Vol. 2). Austin, TX: Author.

Carroll, M., & Harris, M. (1999). Voluntary action in a campaigning context: An exploratory study of Greenpeace. *Voluntary Action, 2*(1), 9-18.

Castells, M. (2000). The rise of the network society. Oxford, England: Basil Blackwell.

Chambré, S. M. (1989). Kindling points of light: Volunteering as public policy. *Nonprofit and Voluntary Sector Quarterly, 18*(3), 249-268.

Champoux, J. E. (1978). Perceptions of work and nonwork: A reexamination of the compensatory and spillover models. *Sociology of Work and Occupations, 5*(4), 402-422.

Chinman, M., & Wandersman, A. (1999). The benefit and costs of volunteering in community organizations: review and practical implications. *Nonprofit and Voluntary Sector Quarterly, 28,* 46-64.

Cihlar, C. (2004). *The state of knowledge surrounding employee volunteering in the United States.* Washington, DC: Points of Light Foundation. Retrieved Jan. 4, 2007, from http://www.pointsoflight.org/downloads/pdf/resources/research/StateOfKnowledge.pdf

Civil Society for Trust in Central and Eastern Europe. (2003). *NGO Sustainability Index.* Retrieved November 3, 2005, from http://www.ceetrust.org/poland:2003Poland/pdf

Clary, B. (1999). *Fairshares program evaluation.* Portland, ME: Muskie School of Public Service, University of Southern Maine.

Clary, E. G., & Miller, J. (1986). Socialization and situational influences on sustained altruism. *Child Development, 57,* 1358-1369.

Clary, E. G., & Orenstein, L. (1991). The amount and effectiveness of help: The relationship of motives and abilities to helping behavior. *Personality and Social Psychology Bulletin, 17*(1), 58-64.

Clary, E. G., Snyder, M., & Ridge, R. D. (1992). Volunteers' motivations: A functional strategy for the recruitment, placement, and retention of volunteers. *Nonprofit Management and Leadership, 2*, 333-350.

Clary, E. G., Snyder, M., Ridge, R. D., Copeland, J., Stukas, A. A., Haugen, J., et al. (1998). Understanding and assessing the motivations of volunteers: A functional approach. *Journal of Personality and Social Psychology, 74*(6), 1516-1530.

Clary, R. A., & Snyder, M. (1991). A functional analysis of altruism and prosocial behavior: The case of volunteerism. *Review of Personality and Social Psychology, 12*, 119-148.

Cnaan, R. A., Handy, F., & Wadsworth, M. (1996). Defining who is a volunteer. *Nonprofit and Voluntary Sector Quarterly, 25*, 364-383.

Cnaan, R., & Cascio, T. A. (1999). Performance and commitment: Issues in management of volunteers in human service organizations. *Journal of Social Service Research, 24*, 1-37.

Cnaan, R., & Goldberg-Glen, R. S. (1991). Measuring motivation to volunteer in human services. *Journal of Applied Behavioral Sciences, 27*, 269-284.

Cnaan, R., & Handy, F. (2005). Towards understanding episodic volunteering. *Vrijwillige Inzet Onderzocht [Voluntary Effort Studied], 2*(1), 28-35.

Connor, J., Kadel-Taras, S., & Vinokur-Kaplan, D. (2003). The role of nonprofit management support organizations in sustaining community collaborations. nonprofit management and leadership, 1996, *10*(2), 127-136.

Cook, L. (2002). Institutional and political legacy of the socialist welfare state. In D. S. Lane (Ed.), *The legacy of state socialism and the future of transformation.* Landham, MD: Rowman & Littlefield.

Corporate volunteer programs—a strategic resource: The link grows stronger. (1999). Washington DC: Points of Light Foundation and Allstate Foundation.

Council of Europe. (1995). Bridging the gap: The social dimension of the new democracies. The Netherlands: Parliamentary Assembly.

Covelli, L. (1985). Dominant class culture and legitimation: Female volunteer directors. *Journal of Voluntary Action Research, 14*, 24-35.

Crant, J. M., & Bateman, T. S. (2000). Charismatic leadership viewed from above: The impact of proactive personality. *Journal of Organizational Behavior, 21*, 63-75.

Cravens, J. (2000). Virtual volunteering: Online volunteers providing assistance to human service agencies. *Journal of Technology in Human Services, 17*(2/3), 119-136.

Culp, K., III. (1997). Motivating and retaining adult volunteer 4-H leaders. *Journal of Agricultural Education, 38*(2), 1-7.

Cultural Information and Research Centres Liaison in Europe (Circle Network). (2001). *Country Report Index-Poland.* Retrieved August 20, 2005, from http://www.circle-network.org/activity/newcastle2001/poland.htm

Dailey, R. C. (1986). Understanding organizational commitment of volunteers: Empirical and managerial implications. *Journal of Voluntary Action Research, 15*, 19-31.

Daniels, A. K. (1988). *Invisible careers: Women civic leaders from the volunteer world.* Chicago: University of Chicago Press.

Dekker, P. (2002). On the prospects of volunteering in civil society. *Voluntary Action, 2*(1), 31-48.

Dekker, P., & Halman, L. (2003). *The values of volunteering-cross-cultural perspectives*. New York: Kluwer Academic/Plenum.

Dewitt, J. D. (2004). *A legal handbook for nonprofit corporation volunteers* (7th ed.). Retrieved June 2, 1998, from http://www. iciclesoftware.com/VLH7/

DiMaggio, P., & Powell, W. W. (1987). The iron cage revisited: Institutional isomorphism and collective rationality in organisational fields. In C. Milofsky (Ed.), *Community organizations: Studies in resource mobilization and exchange* (pp. 77-100). New York: Oxford University Press.

Dollinger, S J., & Leong, F. T. L. (1993). Volunteer bias and the five-factor model. *Journal of Psychology, 127*(1), 29-36.

Drucker, P. (1985). The discipline of innovation. *Harvard Business Review, 63*(03), 67-72.

Drucker, P. F. (1990). *Managing the non-profit organization: Practices and principles*. New York: HarperCollins.

Dunham, R. B., Grube, J. A., & Castaneda, M. B. (1994). Organizational commitment: Utility of an integrative definition. *Journal of Applied Psychology, 79*, 370-380.

Dunleavy P., & Margetts H. (2000, September). *The advent of digital government: Public bureaucracies and the state in the Internet age*. Paper to the annual conference of the American Political Science Association, Washington.

Dunn, P. (2004). Professional corporate donation programs in Canada: An exploratory study. *Nonprofit and Voluntary Sector Quarterly, 33*, 2.

Dutton, J. E., & Pratt, M. G. (1997). Merck and Co., Inc.—from core competence to global community involvement. In N. M. Tichy, A. R. McGill, & L. St. Clair (Eds.), *Corporate global citizenship: Doing business in the public eye* (pp. 150-167). San Francisco: New Lexington Press.

Eckert, J. M., Falvo, D. R., Crimando, W., & Riggar, T. F. (1993). Training and orientation of certified ombudsperson volunteers for long-term care facilities. *Educational Gerontology, 19*(8), 743-752.

Eliasoph, N. (2003). Cultivating apathy in voluntary associations. In P. Dekker & L. Halman (Eds.), *The values of volunteering-cross-cultural perspectives* (pp. 199-212). New York: Kluwer Academic/Plenum.

Ellis, S. J. (November, 1994). The seven deadly sins of directing volunteers. *The Non Profit Times*, p. 14.

Ellis, S. J. (1996). *From the top down; the executive role in volunteer program success* (Rev. edition). Philadelphia, PA: Energize.

Enhancing business-community relations: The role of volunteers in promoting global corporate citizenship. (2001). Retrieved January 4, 2007, from http://www.worldvolunteerweb.org/fileadmin/docs/old/pdf/2004/Global_Report_EBCR.pdf

European Volunteer Center. (2005). *Voluntary action in Poland: Facts and figures*. Retrieved July 18, 2006, from http://www.cev.be/Documents/FactsFiguresPoland.pdf

Evans, P., & Wurster, T. S. (1999). Getting real about virtual commerce. *Harvard Business Review, 77*(6), 85-94.

Farmer, S. M., & Fedor, D. B. (1999). Volunteer participation and withdrawal: A psychological contract perspective on role of expectations and organizational support. *Nonprofit Management and Leadership, 9*, 349-367.

Farmer, S. M., & Fedor, D. B. (2001). Changing the focus on volunteering: An investigation of volunteers' multiple contributions to a charitable organization. *Journal of Management, 27*, 191-211.

Fayol, H. (1949). *General and industrial management* (C. Storrs, Trans.). London: Pitman. (Original work published 1916)

Fisher, J. (1993). *The road from Rio: Sustainable development and the nongovernmental movement in the third world*. Westport, CT: Jossey-Bass.

Fisher, J. C., & Cole, K. M. (1993). *Leadership and management of volunteer programs: A guide for volunteer administrators*. San Francisco: Jossey-Bass.

Forrester, S. (2003). *Kazakhstan Draft Legislation Affecting NGOs, INTRAC*. Retrieved April 25, 2003, from http://www. globalpolicy. org/ngos/state/2003/ 0610kazak. htm

Franz I., Shvetsova L., & Shamshildayeva, A. (2002). *Non-commercial sector development of Kazakhstan* (Part 1). Almaty, Kazakhstan: Institute For Development Cooperation.

Frisch, M. B., & Gerrard, M. (1981). Natural helping systems: Red Cross volunteers. *American Journal of Community Psychology, 9*, 567-579.

Frumkin, P. (2004). *On being nonprofit*. Cambridge, England: Harvard University Press.

Frysztacki, K. (1996). Voluntary sector and the development of civil society in Poland. In B. Synak & M. Ruzica (Eds.), *Voluntary sector in a changing society* (pp. 215-222). Indianapolis: The Indiana University Center on Philanthropy.

Fung, K. K. (1995, Spring-Summer). Doing well by doing good: A market for favors. *The Cato Journal, 15*. Retrieved from http://www.cato.org/pubs/journal/ cj15n1-5. html

Giddens, A. (1998). *The third way: The renewal of social democracy*. Cambridge, England: Polity Press.

Gidron, B. (1984). Predictors of retention and turnover among service volunteer workers. *Journal of Social Service Research, 8*(1), 1-16.

Gilbert, M. (1999). *The interactivity of environmental Web sites*. Retrieved February 13, 2002, from http://research.gilbert.org/siteanlyzer/archive/sa2

Gilbert, M. (2002). *Disconnected: The first nonprofit E-mail survey*. Retrieved April 13, 2002, from http://research.gilbert.org/nes/disconnected

Gonesh, A. G., Ten Hoorn, E. M., Loenen, E. J. M., van, Remmerswaal, R. E., Shimada, H., Schijndel, J. C. J., et al. (2004). *Exploration in volunteer management, program management, membership management*. Research paper Master Business-Society Management, Rotterdam School of Management, Erasmus University Rotterdam.

Government of Poland. (2003). *Law on Public Benefit Activity and Volunteerism, dated April 24, 2003*. Retrieved July 15, 2006, from http://www.usig.org/countryinfo/ laws/Poland/Poland%20PBA.pdf

Grigoryan, S. (2002). Voluneteering and volunteer management in Armenia. *The Journal of Volunteer Administration, 20*, 12.

Grossman, J. B., & Furano, K. (2002). *Making the most of volunteers*. Philadelphia: Public/Private Ventures.

Guthrie, D. (2004). *Corporate-community relations (CCR) study: 2001-2002 Survey of corporate involvement*. New York: Social Science Research Council.

Hackman, J. R., & Oldham, G. R. (1976). Motivation through the design of work: Test of a theory. *Organizational Behavior and Human Performance*, 250-279.

Hager, M. A., & Brudney, J. L. (2004). *Volunteer management practices and retention of volunteers*. Washington, DC: Urban Institute.

Hager, M. A., & Brudney, J. L. (2005). Net benefits: Weighing the challenges and benefits of volunteers. *Journal of Volunteer Administration, 23*(1), 26-31.

Hailey, J., & James, R. (2004). "Trees die from the top": International perspectives on NGO leadership development. *Voluntas: International Journal of Voluntary and Nonprofit Organizations, 15*(4), 343-353.

Hall, J. (1995, December 15). Liability Noose Deters Volunteers. *Times Higher Education Supplement, 1206*, 11.

Hall, A. (2001, November). *E-Enabling the voluntary and community sectors* [Final Report]. Glasgow: UK Government Online, Office of the E-envoy.

Hall, M., McKeown, L., & Roberts, K. (2001). *Caring Canadians, involved Canadians: Highlights from the 2000 National Survey of Giving, volunteering and participating*. Ottawa: Statistics Canada. Retrieved January 4, 2007, from http://www. givingandvolunteering.ca/pdf/n-2000-hr-ca.pdf, and http://www. statcan.ca/english/freepub/71-542-XIE/71-542-XIE2000001.pdf

Hall, P. (1999). Social capital in Britain. *British Journal of Political Science, 29*, 417-461.

Handy, C. (1988). *Understanding voluntary organizations, how to make them function effectively*. London: Penguin Books.

Handy, F., & Srinivasan, N. (2004). Valuing volunteers: An economic evaluation of the net benefits of hospital volunteers. *Nonprofit and Voluntary Sector Quarterly, 33*(1), 28-54.

Handy, F., & Srinivasan, N. (2005). The demand for volunteer labor: A study of hospital volunteers. *Nonprofit and Voluntary Sector Quarterly, 34*(4), 491-509.

Handy, F., Cnaan, R. A., Brudney, J. L., Ascoli, U., Meijs, L. C. M. P., & Ranade, S. (2000). Public perception of "who is a volunteer": An examination of the net-cost approach from a cross-cultural perspective. *Voluntas: International Journal of Voluntary and Nonprofit Organizations, 11*(1), 45-65.

Hansen J., Askarbekova D., & Yerofeeva I. (2002). *Volunteering in Kazakhstan: Key findings of a national survey*. Almaty, Kazakhstan: UN Volunteers Program. Retrieved from www.iyv2001.org

Harrison, D. A. (1995). Volunteer motivation and attendance decisions: Competitive theory testing in multiple samples from a homeless shelter. *Journal of Applied Psychology, 80*(3), 371-386.

Harrison, Y., Murray, V., &MacGregor, J. (2004). *The impact of ICT on the management of Canadian volunteer programs*. Toronto: Canadian Center for Philanthropy.

Heap, S., Ibrayeva, A., Kabdiyeva, A., Sharipova, D., & Dissenova, S. (2003). *Civil society in the republic of Kazakhstan* Almaty, Kazakhstan: International NGO Training and Research Center.

Hedley, R. (1992). Organising and managing volunteer. In R. Hedley & J. Davis Smith (Eds.), *Volunteering and society: principles and practices* (pp. 93-119). Bedford Square: London.

Helmig, B., Jegers, M., & Lapsley, I. (2004). Challenges in managing nonprofit organizations: A research overview. *Voluntas: International Journal of Voluntary and Nonprofit Organizations, 15*(2), 101-116.

Hendrix, W. H., Robbins, T., Miller, J., & Summers, T. P. (1998). Effects of procedural and distributive justice on factors predictive of turnover. *Journal of Social Behavior and Personality, 13*(4), 611-632.

Herman, M. L., & Kronstadt, J. (2003). *Ready in defense: A liability, litigation, and legal guide for nonprofits.* Washington, DC: Nonprofit Risk Management Center.

Herman, R. D. (Ed.). (1994). *The Jossey-Bass handbook of nonprofit leadership and management.* San Francisco: Jossey-Bass.

Herman, R. D. (Ed.). (2004). *The Jossey-Bass handbook of nonprofit leadership and management* (2nd Ed.). San Francisco: Jossey-Bass.

Herzog, A. R., & Morgan, J. N. (1993). Formal volunteer work among older Americans. In S. Bass, F. Caro, & Y. P. Chen (Eds.), *Achieving a productive aging society* (pp. 119-142). Westport, CT: Auburn House.

Hess, D., Rogovsky, N., & Dunfree, T. W. (2002). The next wave of corporate community involvement: Corporate social initiatives. *California Management Review, 44,* 110-125.

Higgins, J. W., & Hodgins, A. (2008). The grape escape: A FUNdraising bike tour for the Multiple Sclerosis Society. *International Journal of Nonprofit and Voluntary Sector Marketing, 13.*

Hodgkinson, V. A. (2003). Volunteering in global perspective. In P. Dekker & L. Halman (Eds.), *The values of volunteering-cross-cultural perspectives* (pp. 36-54). New York: Kluwer Academic/Plenum.

Homans, G. C. (1976). Fundamental processes of social exchange. In E. P. Hollander & R. G. Hunt (Eds.), *Current perspectives in social psychology* (4th ed., pp. 161-173). New York: Oxford University Press.

Hoogendam, A. (2000). Wat te doen als je te veel werk hebt voor te weinig mensen? [What to do when you have too much work for too few people?]. *Sport Vrijwilligerskrant [Sport Volunteer newspaper], 512,* 2-3.

Hoogendam, A. C. J., & Meijs, L. C. P. M. (1998). *Vrijwilligers in de sportvereniging: organiseren van betrokkenheid* [Volunteers in sport associations: Organizing commitment]. Utrecht, The Netherlands: NOV.

Hustinx, L. (2001). Individualism and new styles of youth volunteering: An empirical exploration. *Voluntary Action, 3*(2),47–55.

Hyde, C. (2000). Volunteerism in hostile times: An examination of feminist social movement organizations in the 1980s. *Voluntary Action, 2*(2),27-43.

Imbrogno, S. (1990). Social policy planning and social work practices in Poland. *Social Work, 35,* 302-306.

Independent Sector. (1999). *Crossing the borders: Collaboration and competition.* Working Papers. Independent Sector, Washington, DC.

Inglehart, R. (2003). Modernization and volunteering. In P. Dekker & L. Halman (Eds.), *The values of volunteering-cross-cultural perspectives* (pp. 55-70). New York: Kluwer Academic/Plenum.

Janey, J. P., Tuckwiller, J. E., & Lonnquist, L. E. (1991). Skill transferal benefits from volunteer experiences. *Nonprofit and Voluntary Sector Quarterly, 20*(1), 71-79.

Janssens, J. (2000). Steeds meer verenigingen stellen taken verplicht [More and more sport associations oblige tasks]. *Sport Vrijwilligerskrant, 512,* 3.

Jenner, J. R. (1982). Participation, leadership, and the role of voluntarism among selected women volunteers. *Journal of Voluntary Action Research, 11,* 27-38.

Johnson, M. (1998). Nonprofit organizations and the Internet. *First Monday, 4*(2). Retrieved March 2002 from http://firstmonday.org/issues/issue4_2/mjohnson

Johnson, M. (2001). *Results of the 3rd Internet survey of Australian non profit organizations.* Retrieved May 15, 2002, from www.wesleymission.org.au/pubblications/fr/survey.html

Judge, T. A., & Ilies, R. (2002a). Relationship of personality to performance motivation: A meta-analytic review. *Journal of Applied Psychology, 87*(4), 797-807.

Judge, T. A., & Ilies, R. (2002b). Personality and leadership: A qualitative and quantitative review. *Journal of Applied Psychology, 87*(4), 765-780.

Kamarck, H., & Nye, J. (2002). *Governance.com. Democracy in the information age.* Washington, DC: Brookings Institution.

Karr, L. B., & Meijs, L. C. P. M. (November, 2002). *ON MY HONOR, YOU CAN COUNT ON ME: Management strategies and organizational commitment among volunteers.* Paper presented at 31th Arnova Conference, Montreal.

Katz, D., & Kahn, R. L. (1978). *The social psychology of organizations.* New York: Wiley.

Kearns, K., Park, C., & Yankoski, L. (2005). Comparing faith-based and secular community service corporations in Pittsburgh and Allegheny County, Pennsylvania. *Nonprofit and Voluntary Sector Quarterly, 34*(2), 206-231.

Kelley, M. S., Lune, H., & Murphy, S. (2005). Doing syringe exchange: Organizational transformation and volunteer commitment. *Nonprofit and Voluntary Sector Quarterly, 34*(3), 362-386.

Kelly, K. (1998). *New rules for the new economy.* New York: Viking, Penguin Putnam.

Kemmis, D. (1990). *Community and the politics of place.* Norman: University of Oklahoma Press.

Kendall, J., Anheier, H., & Potůček, M. (2000). Ten years after: The third sector and civil society in central and eastern Europe. *Voluntas: International Journal of Voluntary and Nonprofit Organizations, 11*(2), 103-106.

Kendall, J., & Knapp, M. (1996). *The Voluntary Sector in the UK.* Manchester, England: Manchester University.

Kerlin, J. A. (2006). Social enterprise in the United States and Europe: Understanding and learning from the differences. *Voluntas: International Journal of Voluntary and Nonprofit Organizations, 17,* 247-263.

King, K. N., & Lynch, C. V. (1998). The motivation of volunteers in the nature conservancy—Ohio chapter, A nonprofit environmental organization. *The Journal of Volunteer Administration, 16*(2), 5-11.

Kirschenbaum, A., & Mano-Negrin, R. (1999). Underlying labor market dimensions of "opportunities": The case of employee turnover. *Human Relations, 52*(10), 1233-1255.

Kiser, L. L. (1984). Toward an institutional theory of citizen coproduction. *Urban Affairs Quarterly, 19*(4), 485-510.

Klein, N. A., Sondag, K. A., & Drolet, J. C. (1994). Understanding volunteer peer health educators' motivations: Applying social learning theory. *Journal of American College Health, 43*(3), 126-131.

KLON-JAWOR. (2000). *NGOs in Poland—2000 research results.* The KLON-JAWOR Association.

KLON-JAWOR. (2002). *NGOs in Poland—2002 research results.* The KLON-JAWOR Association.

KLON-JAWOR. (2004). *Podstawowe fakty o organizacjach pozarzdowych—raport z bada 2004.* The KLON-JAWOR Association.

Knoke, D., & Wood, J. R. (1981). *Organized for action: Commitment in voluntary organizations.* New Brunswick, NJ: Rutgers University Press.

Knoke, D., & Wright-Isak, C. (1982). Individual motives and organizational incentive systems. *Research in the Sociology of Organizations, 1,* 209-254.

Knokes, D. (1988). Incentives in collective action organizations. *American Sociological Review, 53,* 311-329.

Knox, T. M. (1999). The volunteer's folly and socio-economic man: Some thoughts on altruism, rationality, and community. *Journal of Socio-Economics, 28*(4), 475-493.

Konovsky, M. A., & Pugh, S. D. (1994). Citizenship behavior and social exchange. *Academy of Management Journal, 37*(3), 656-69.

Kraemer, K. L., & Danzinger, J. (1990). The impacts of computer technology on the worklife of information workers. *Social Science Computer Review, 8*(4), 592-613.

Kratcoski, P. C., & Crittenden, S. (1983). Criminal justice volunteerism: A comparison of adult and juvenile agency volunteers. *Journal of Offender Counseling, Services and Rehabilitation, 7*(2), 5-14.

Kurczewski, J., & Kurczewska, J. (2001). A self-governing society twenty years after: Democracy and the third sector in Poland. *Social Research, 68,* 937-976.

Kuti, É. (1999). Different eastern European countries at different crossroads. *Voluntas: International Journal of Voluntary and Nonprofit Organizations, 10*(1), 51-59.

La Barbera, P. A. (1992). Enterprise in religious-based organizations. *Nonprofit and Voluntary Sector Quarterly, 21*(1), 51-67.

Lange, C. (2003). German welfare organizations and the process of European integration. *Nonprofit Management & Leadership, 13*(3), 237-252.

Lawler, E. E., III. (1990). *Strategic pay: Aligning organization strategies and pay systems.* San Francisco: Jossey-Bass.

Leete, L. (2006). Work in the nonprofit sector. In W. W. Powell & R. Steinberg (Eds.), *The nonprofit sector: A research handbook* (2nd ed., pp. 159-179). New Haven, CT: Yale University Press.

Lenardo, R., Onyx, J., & Hayward-Brown, H. (2004). Volunteer and coordinator perspectives on managing women volunteers. *Nonprofit Management and Leadership, 15*(2), 205-219.

Leś, E. (1996). The role of the voluntary sector in the transformation of state welfare systems in comparative perspective: Poland, the Czech Republic and Hungary. In B. Synak & M. Ruzica (Eds.), *Voluntary sector in a changing society* (pp. 207-213). Indianapolis: The Indiana University Center on Philanthropy.

Leś, E., Nałecz, S., & Wygnański, J. (2000). *Defining the nonprofit sector: Poland.* Working papers of the Johns Hopkins Comparative Nonprofit Sector Project, No. 36. Baltimore: The Johns Hopkins Center for Civil Society Studies.

Letts, C. (2005). Nonprofit management—soup to nuts. *Nonprofit Management and Leadership, 16*(1), 109-112.

Liao-Troth, M. A. (2001). Attitude differences between paid workers and volunteers. *Nonprofit Management and Leadership, 11*(4), 423-452.

Liao-Troth, M. A. (2005). Are they here for the long haul? The effects of functional motives and personality factors on the psychological contracts of volunteers. *Nonprofit and Voluntary Sector Quarterly, 34*(4), 510-530.

Liao-Troth, M. A., & Dunn, C. P. (1999). Social constructs and human service: Managerial sensemaking of volunteer motivation. *Voluntas: International Journal of Voluntary and Nonprofit Organizations, 10*(4), 345-361.

Liao-Troth, M. A., & Griffith, T. L. (2002). Software, shareware and freeware: Multiplex commitment to an electronic social exchange system. *Journal of Organizational Behavior, 23*(5), 635-653.

Light, P. (1998). *Sustaining innovation: Creating nonprofit and government organizations that innovate naturally.* San Francisco, CA: Jossey-Bass.

Littleton, S. (2002). *Understanding Psychological Contracts in Nonprofit Organizations.* Paper presentation at the annual conference of the International Society for Third Sector Research, Cape Town, South Africa.

Locke, E. A. (1976). The nature and causes of job satisfaction. In M. D. Dunnette. (Ed.), *Handbook of Industrial and Organizational Psychology.* Chicago: Rand McNally.

Luong, P. J., & Weinthal, E. (1999). The NGO paradox: Democratic goals and non-democratic outcomes in Kazakhstan. *Europe-Asia Studies, 51*(7), 1267-1284.

Macduff, N. (2005). Societal changes and the rise of the episodic volunteer. In J. L. Brudney (Ed.), *Emerging areas of volunteering: ARNOVA Occasional Paper Series* (pp. 49-62). Indianapolis: Indiana University-Purdue University.

Maine State Commission on Public Service. (n.d.). *Volunteer liability in Maine.* Retrieved from http://www.maineservicecommission.gov/resources/mainevol.pdf

March, J. G., & Olsen J. P. (1989). *Rediscovering institutions.* New York: Free Press.

Marta, E., Guglielmetti, C., & Pozzi, M. (2006). Volunteerism during young adulthood: An Italian investigation into motivational patterns. *Voluntas: International Journal of Voluntary and Nonprofit Organizations, 17*, 221-232.

Martinez, J. M. (2003). Liability and volunteer organizations: A survey of the law. *Nonprofit Management and Leadership, 14*(2), 151-169.

McAdams, D., Tarrow, S., & Tilly, C. (2001). *Dynamics of contention*. Cambridge, England: Cambridge University Press.

McCudden, J. (2000). What makes a committed volunteer? Research into the factors affecting the retention of volunteers in Home-Start. *Voluntary Action, 2*(2), 59-75.

McCurley, S. (1995). Recruiting, developing, and managing volunteers. *Nonprofit Management and Leadership, 5*(4), 439-441.

McCurley, S., & Lynch, R. (1996). *Volunteer management: Mobilizing all the resources of the community*. Downers Grove, IL: Heritage Arts.

McCurley, S., & Lynch, R. (1994). *Essential volunteer management*. Downers Grove, IL: Heritage Arts.

McNutt, J. G., & Rowland, R., Keaney, W., & Howard, W. (2002, April 8-10). *Nonprofit on-line advocacy for children's causes: A comparison of national and sub-national patterns*. Paper presented at the Sixth International Symposium on Public Management (IRSPM VI), University of Edimburgh, Scotland.

McNutt, J., & Boland, K. M. (1999). *Electronic* advocacy by nonprofit organizations in social welfare policy. *Nonprofit and Voluntary Sector Quarterly, 28*(4), 432-451.

McNutt, J., & Boland, K. M. (2000, November 15-18). *Nonprofit advocacy in the cybercommons. A study of technologically sophisticated non-profit organizations*. Paper presented at the 29th annual meeting of the Association for Research on Nonprofit Organizations and Voluntary Action, New Orleans, LA.

Meijs L., & van der Voort, J. M. (2004). Corporate volunteering: From charity to profit-nonprofit partnerships, *Australian Journal on Volunteering, 9*, 21-32.

Meijs, L. C. P. M. (1996). Management is not always the right word. *Journal of Volunteer Administration, 14*(3), 25-31.

Meijs, L. C. P. M. (1997). *Management van vrijwilligersorganisaties* [Management of voluntary organizations] Dissertatie [Dissertation]. Utrecht, the Netherlands: NOV.

Meijs, L. C. P. M. (2004). Campaigning organisaties in verandering: Van leden management naar programmamanagement [Campaigning organizations in change: From member management to program management]. *Vrijwillige Inzet Onderzocht, 1*(1), 34-43.

Meijs, L. C. P. M., & Brudney, J. L. (2004, November 18-20). *Winning volunteer scenarios: The soul of a new machine*. Paper presented at the annual meeting of the Association for Research on Nonprofit Organizations and Voluntary Action, Los Angeles.

Meijs, L. C. P. M., & Hoogstad, E. (2001). New ways of managing volunteers: Combining membership management and program management. *Voluntary Action, 3*(3), 41-61.

Meijs, L. C. P. M., & Karr, L. B. (2004). Managing volunteers in different settings: Membership and Program Management. In R. A. Stebbins & M. Grahem (Eds.), *Volunteering as leisure/leisure as volunteering* (pp. 177-193). Oxfordshire: CABI.

Meijs, L. C. P. M., & Linden, J. van der. (1999, November 4-6). *Volunteering by young people: A student organization*. Paper presented at 28th Arnova Conference, Washinton DC.

Meijs, L. C. P. M., & Westerlaken, C. (1994). Vrijwilligersorganisaties en HRM, Talenten: beleid of misleid? [Volunteer organizations and HRM: Enthusiasm or obligation]. *Personeelbeleid 6*, 37-43.

Meijs, L. C. P. M., Handy, F., Cnaan, R. A., Brudney, J. L., Ascoli, U., Ranade, S., et al. (2003). All in the eyes of the beholder? Perceptions of volunteering across eight countries. In P. Dekker & L. Halman (Eds.), *The values of volunteering-cross-cultural perspectives* (pp. 19-34). New York: Kluwer Academic/Plenum.

Mele, V. (2005) Paradigm and practice. The innovative organization to deal with Electronic Government. In M. Khosrow-Pour (Ed.), *Practicing e-government. A global perspective* (pp. 289-309). Hershey, PA USA and London UK: OECD and Idea Group Publishing.

Miller, J. G. (1999). Cultural psychology: Implications for basic psychology. *Psychological Science, 10*, 85-91.

Miller, L. E. (1985). Understanding the motivation of volunteers: An examination of personality differences and characteristics of volunteers' paid employment. *Journal of Voluntary Action Research, 14*, 112-122.

Ministry of Agriculture and Food, Province of Ontario Canada. (1996, November). *Fact Sheet: Recruiting Volunteers*, 96-005. Retrieved MONTH DAY, YEAR, from http://www.gov.on.ca/OMAFRA/english/rural/facts/96-005.htm#intro

Mintzberg, H. (1993). *Structure in fives: Designing effective Organizations* (2nd ed.). Englewood Cliffs, NJ: Prentice Hall.

Mook, L., Richmond, B. J., & Quarter, J. (2003). Integrated social accounting for nonprofits: A case from Canada. *Voluntas: International Journal of Voluntary and Nonprofit Organizations, 14*(3), 283-297.

Monette, D. R., Sullivan, T. J, & DeJong, C. R. (1990). *Applied social research: Tool for the human services* (2nd ed.). Fort Worth, TX: Holt.

Muirhead, S. A., Bennett, C. J., Berenbeim, R. E., Kao, A., & David, V. J. (2002). *Corporate citizenship in the new century: Accountability, transparency, and global stakeholder engagement*. The Conference Board Research Report #R-1314-02-RR. New York: Conference Board.

Murnighan, J. K., Kim, J. W., & Metzger, R. A. (1993). The volunteer dilemma. *Administrative Science Quarterly, 38*, 515-538.

Murray, V., & Harrison, Y. (2005). Virtual volunteering. In J. Brudney (Ed.), Emerging areas of volunteering. Indianapolis: Association for Research on Nonprofit Organizations and Voluntary Action.

Musick, M. A. (2005). *Volunteering and monetary giving in Texas* (Investigator, Vol. 1:3). Austin, Texas: University of Texas, RGK Center for Philanthropy and Community Service.

Nathanson, I. L., & Eggleton, E. E. (1993). Motivation versus program effect on length of service: A study of four cohorts of ombudservice volunteers. *Journal of Gerontological Social Work, 19*(3/4), 95-114.

Nazarbayev, N. (1999, March 31). *Democracy is our choice/democracy is our destiny*. Speech to the Parliament and Public. Astana, Kazakhstan: Parliament of Kazakhstan.

North Cotsworld Time Bank. (n.d.). *Reaping the rewards: A brief history of the north Cotswold Time Bank.* Fairshares, Gloucester, England: Author.

Nowicki, M. (2000). Kazakhstan's nonprofit sector at a crossroad on the Great Silk Road, *Voluntas: International Journal of Voluntary and Nonprofit Organizations, 11*(3), 217-235.

O'Driscoll, M. P., Ilgen, D. R., & Hildreth, K. (1992). Time devoted to job and off-job activities, interrole conflict, and affective experiences. *Journal of Applied Psychology, 77*(3), 272-279.

Okun, M. A. (1994). The relation between motives for organizational volunteering and frequency of volunteering by elders. *Journal of Applied Gerontology, 13*(2), 115-126.

Olcott, M. B. (1998). The caspian's false promise. *Foreign Policy, 111,* 94-113.

Oliferov, S., Vinogradova, E., Birzhanova, N., & Chelidze, S. (2001). *Kazakhstan volunteers.* Almaty, Kazakhstan: Soros Volunteer House Public Foundation.

Omoto, A. M., & Snyder, M. (1995). Sustained helping without obligation: Motivation, longevity of service, and perceived attitude change among AIDS volunteers. *Journal of Personality and Social Psychology, 68*(4), 671-686.

Organ, D. W. (1988). *Organizational citizenship behavior: The good soldier syndrome.* Lexington, MA: Lexington Books.

Orlikowsky, W. (1992). The duality of technology: Rethinking the concept of technology in organizations. *Organization Science, 3*(3), 398-427.

Pargmegiani, M., & Sachdeva, T. (2000, September). *Information and public policy concerning voluntary sector use of information technologies, the internet and the World Wide Web: An international report.* Toronto: Canadian Center for Philanthropy.

Parry, E., Kelliher, C., Mills, T., & Tyson, S. (2005). Comparing HRM in the voluntary and public sectors. *Personnel Review, 34*(5), 58-602.

Paton, R., & Foot, J. (2000). Nonprofit's use of awards to improve and demonstrate performance: Valuable discipline or burdensome formalities? *Voluntas: International Journal of Voluntary and Nonprofit Organizations, 11*(4), 329-353.

Paull, M. (2000). The management of performance by volunteers: The use of performance feedback. Unpublished Master of Business Thesis, Edith Cowan University, Perth, Western Australia.

Paull, M. (2002). Reframing volunteer management. A view from the West. *Australian Journal on Volunteering, 7*(1), 21-27.

Pearce, J. L. (1993). *Volunteers: The organizational behavior of unpaid workers.* London: Routledge.

Penner, L. A., & Fritzsche, B. A. (1993). *Measuring the prosocial personality: Four construct validity studies.* Paper presented at the 101st American Psychological Association Annual Meeting, Toronto, Ontario, Canada.

Penner, L. A., & Finkelstein, M. A. (1998). Dispositional and structural determinants of volunteerism. *Journal of Personality and Social Psychology, 74*(2), 525-537.

Perry, J., & Imperial, M. (2001). A decade of service-related research: A map of the field. *Nonprofit and Voluntary Sector Quarterly, 30,* 462-479.

Peterson, D. K. (2004a). Benefits of participation in corporate volunteer programs: employees' perceptions. *Personnel Review, 33*(5-6), 615-627.

Peterson, D. K. (2004b). Recruitment strategies for encouraging participation in corporate volunteer programs. *Journal of Business Ethics, 49*(4), 371-386.

Phare Civic Dialogue Program. (1998). *Non-governmental sector in Poland.* Warsaw: Phare Civic Dialogue Programme, Cooperative Fund.

Phillips, J. M. (1998). Effects of realistic job previews on multiple organizational outcomes: A meta-analysis. *Academy of Management Journal, 41*(6), 673-690.

Phillips, M. (1982). Motivation and expectation in successful volunteerism. *Journal of Voluntary Action Research, 11,* 118-125.

Piliavin, J., & Callero, P. (1991). *Giving blood: The development of an altruistic identity.* Baltimore: Johns Hopkins University Press.

Putnam, R. (1995). Bowling alone: America's declining social capital. *Journal of Democracy, 6,* 65-78.

Putnam, R. D. (2000). *Bowling alone: The collapse and revival of American community.* New York: Simon & Schuster.

Ragin, C. C. (1987). *The comparative method.* Berkeley: University of California Press.

Regulska, J. (1999). NGOs and their vulnerabilities during the time of transition the case of Poland. *Voluntas: International Journal of Voluntary and Nonprofit Organizations, 10*(1), 61-71.

Regulska, J. (2001). NGOs and their vulnerabilities during the time of transition. In H. K. Anheier & J. Kendall (Eds.), *Third sector policy at the crossroads an international nonprofit analysis* (pp. 183-192). New York: Routledge.

Rehberg, W. (2005). Altruistic individualists: Motivations for international volunteering among young adults in Switzerland. *Voluntas: International Journal of Voluntary and Nonprofit Organizations, 16*(2), 109-122.

Rehnborg, S. J. (2005). Government volunteerism in the new millennium. In J. Brudney (Ed.), *Emerging areas of volunteering* (PAGE NUMBERS?). Indianapolis, IN: Association for Research on Nonprofit Organizations and Voluntary Action.

Rehnborg, S. J., Fallon, C. K., & Hinerfeld B. J. (2002). *Investing in volunteerism: The impact of service initiatives in selected Texas state agencies.* Austin, TX: University of Texas at Austin, RGK Center for Philanthropy and Community Service.

Reichers, A. (1985). A review and reconceptualization of organizational commitment. *Academy of Management Review, 10,* 465-476.

Riley, R. T., & Lorenzi, N. M. (1996). Behavioral Management of Computer-resistant Providers. *Behavior Health Management, 16,* 27-29.

Robinson, S. L., Kraatz, M. S., & Rousseau, D. M. (1994). Changing obligations (1994). Changing obligations and the psychological contract: A longitudinal study. *Academy of Management Journal, 37*(1), 137-152.

Rochester, C. (1999). One size does not fit all. Four models of involving volunteers in voluntary organizations. *Voluntary Action, 1*(2), 7-20.

Rochlin, S. A., & Christoffer, B. (2000). *Making the business case: Determining the value of corporate community involvement.* Retrieved January 4, 2007, from http://www

.bcccc. net/index.cfm?fuseaction=document.showDocumentByIDand DocumentID=312

Rose, R. (1997). Social capital in civic and stressful societies, *Studies in Comparative International Development, 32*(3), 84.

Rossi, P. H., & Freeman, H. E. (1989). *Evaluation: A systematic approach*. Newbury Park, CA: SAGE.

Rousseau, D. M. (1989). Psychological and implied contracts in organizations. *Employee Responsibilities and Rights Journal, 2*, 121-139.

Rousseau, D. M., & Parks, J. M. (1993). The contracts of individuals and organizations. In B. M. Staw & L. L. Cummings (Eds.), *Research in organizational behavior* (Vol. 15, pp. 1-43). Greenwich, CT: JAI Press.

Rubin, A., & Thorelli, I. M. (1984). Egoistic motives and longevity of participation by social service volunteers. *Journal of Applied Behavioral Science, 20*(3), 223-235.

Safrit, D. R., & Schmiesing, R. J. (2004). A suggested model for contemporary volunteer management: Qualitative research bridging the professional literature with best practices. *Journal of Volunteer Administration, 22*(4), 34-39.

Saidel, J. R., & Cour, S. (2003). Information technology and the voluntary sector workplace. *Nonprofit and Voluntary Sector Quarterly, 32*(1), 5-24.

Salamon, L. M. (1999). *America's nonprofit sector: A primer* (2nd ed.). New York: The Foundation Center.

Salamon, L., M., Sokolowski, S. W., & Associates. (2004). *Global civil society: Dimensions of the nonprofit sector* (Vol. 2). Bloomfield, CT: Kumarian Press.

Salamon, L. S., & Sokolowski, S. W. (2003). Institutional roots of volunteering: Toward a macro-structural theory of individual voluntary action. In P. Dekker & L. Halman (Eds.), *The values of volunteering-cross-cultural perspectives* (pp. 71-90). New York: Kluwer Academic/Plenum.

Schneider, B., & Stevenson, D. (1999). *The ambitious generation: America's teenagers, motivated but directionless*. New Haven, CT: Yale University Press.

Schwartz, E. A. (1996). *Netactivism: How citizens use the Internet*. Sebastopol, CA: Songline Studios.

Seippel, Ø. (2002). Volunteers and professionals in Norwegian sport organizations. *Voluntas: International Journal of Voluntary and Nonprofit Organizations, 13*(3), 253-270.

Social Cultural Planning Bureau. (2003a). *Ontwikkeling in Lokaal vrijwilligersbeleid* [Developments in local voluntary policy] The Hague: SCP, 70 p. Retrieved June 2, 1998, from www.scp.nl

Social Cultural Planning Bureau. (2003b). *Rapportage Sport 2003* [Report Sport 2003]. The Hague: SCP, 362 p. Retrieved June 2, 1998, from www .tijdsbesteding.nl

Sergent, M. T., & Sedlacek, W. E. (1990). Volunteer motivations across student organizations: A test of person-environment fit theory. *Journal of College Student Development, 31*, 255-261.

Sergeyenko, S. (2000). Peculiarity of internal political development in Kazakhstan during transition period. *Mysl, 15*(2), 50-70.

Shindaulletova, S. (2003). *Problems of legal regulation of volunteer activity: Review*. Almaty, Kazakhstan: Soros Volunteer House Public Foundation.

Sills, D. L. (1957). *The volunteers, means and ends in a national organization*. Glencoe, IL: The Free Press.

Simons, H. (1980). *Towards a science of the singular*. Norwich: University of East Anglia, Centre for Applied Research in Education.

Skocpol, T. (1979). *States and social revolutions*. Cambridge, England: Cambridge University Press.

Skocpol, T. (2003). *Diminished democracy: From membership to management in American civic life*. Norman, OK: University of Oklahoma Press.

Smith, D. H. (1997). The international history of grassroots associations. *International Journal of Comparative Sociology, 38*(3/4), 189-216.

Smith, D. H. (1999). The effective grassroots associations, part one. Organizational factors that produce internal impacts. *Nonprofit Management and Leadership, 9*(4), 443-456.

Smith, D. H. (2000). *Grassroots organizations*. Thousand Oaks, CA: SAGE.

Smith, J. T. (2004). What they really want: Assessing the psychological contracts of volunteers. *Journal of Volunteer Administration, 22*, 18-21.

Smith, S. R., & Lipsky, M. (1993). *Nonprofits for hire: The welfare state in the age of contracting*. Cambridge, MA: Harvard University Press.

Snellen, I. T. M., & van de Donk, W. B. H. G. J. (Eds.). (1998). *Public administration in an information age*. Amsterdam: IOS Press.

Snyder, M., & Clary, E. G., (1999). Volunteerism and the generative society. In E. de St. Aubin, D. P. McAdams, T. C. Kim (Eds.), *The generative society: Caring for future generations* (pp. 221-237). Washington, DC: American Psychological Association.

Sokolowski, S. W. (2000). The discreet charm of the nonprofit form: Service professionals and nonprofit organizations (Poland 1989-1993). *Voluntas: International Journal of Voluntary and Nonprofit Organizations, 11*(2), 141-159.

Spencer, T. (2002). The potential of the Internet for nonprofit organizations. *First Monday, 7*(2). Retrieved July 16, 2003, from http://firstmonday.org/issues/issues7_8/spencer

Stake, R. (1995). *The art of case research*. Thousand Oaks, CA: Sage.

Standley, A. P. (2001). Reinventing a large nonprofit: Lessons from four voluntary health associations. *Nonprofit Management and Leadership, 11*(3), 305-320.

Starr, F. (1991). The third sector in the second world. *World Development, 19*, 65-71.

Steinmo, S., Thelen, K., & Longstreth, F. (Eds.). (1992). *Structuring politics: Historical institutionalism in comparative analysis*. Cambridge, England: Cambridge University Press.

Stiglitz, J. E., Orszag, P. R., & Orszag, J. M. (2001). *The role of government in the digital age*. Study commissioned by Computer and Communications Industry Association.

Sundeen, R. A., & Raskoff, S. A. (2000). Ports of entry and obstacles: Teenagers' access to volunteer activities. *Nonprofit Management and Leadership, 11*(2), 179-197.

Taylor, S. (1990, April-May). Talents, tools, time. *Modern Maturity*, 79-84.

Te'eni, D., & Young, D. R. (2003). The changing role of nonprofits in the network economy. *Nonprofit and Voluntary Sector Quarterly, 32*(3), 397-414.

Technical Assistance Resource Center, Annie E. Casey Foundation and the Center for the Study of Social Policy. (2004). *Building community with time dollars*. Baltimore, MD: The Annie E. Casey Foundation.

Tellis, W. (1997). Introduction to case study. *The Qualitative Report, 3(2)*. Online serial available at: http://www. nova. edu/ssss/QR/QR3-2/tellis1/html

Texas Senate Research Center. (1993). *Texas gets a hand: Volunteerism and other contributions to selected state agencies in fiscal year 1992*. Austin, TX: Author.

Thomas, S., & Christoffer, B. (1999). *Corporate volunteerism: Essential tools for excellence in corporate community relations*. Chestnut Hill, MA: Boston College Center for Corporate Community Relations.

Thompson, A. M. III, Bono, B. A., & Rybeck, W. (1993). Work without wages: The motivation for volunteer firefighters. *American Journal of Economics and Sociology, 52*(3), 323-344.

Thompson, J. A., & Bunderson, J. S. (2003). Violations of principle: Ideological currency in the psychological contract. *Academy of Management Review, 28*(4), 571-586.

Tiehen, L. (2000). Has working more caused married women to volunteer less? Evidence from time diary data, 1965 to 1993. *Nonprofit and Voluntary Sector Quarterly, 29*(4), 505-529.

Tschirhart, M. (2005). Employee volunteer programs. In J. L. Brudney (Ed.), *Emerging areas of volunteering, ARNOVA Occasional Paper Series* (Vol. 1, No. 2, pp. 13-39). Indianapolis, IN: Association for Research on Nonprofit Organizations and Voluntary Action.

Tschirhart, M., & St. Clair, L. (2005). Corporate community service programs: Enhancing community capacity? In A. Brooks (Ed.), *Gifts of time and money: The role of charity in America's communities* (pp. 59-75). Lanham, MD: Rowman & Littlefield.

Tschirhart, M., Mesch, D. J., Perry, J. L., Miller, T. K., & Lee, G. (2001). Stipended volunteers: Their goals, experiences, satisfaction, and likelihood of future service. *Nonprofit and Voluntary Sector Quarterly, 30*(3), 422-443.

United Kingdom National Statistics. (2001). *Census*. Gloucester: Office of National Statistics.

United Nationals Development Programme. (2002). *Non-governmental organizations of Kazakhstan: Past, present, future*. Almaty, Kazakhstan: United Nations Development Programme.

United Nations Volunteers. (2001). A turning point for volunteers. In United Nations volunteers (Ed.), *Proceedings of Discussions of the UN General Assembly Debate on Government and United Nations System Support for Volunteering*. New York: United Nations Volunteers.

United States Agency for International Development. (2004). Poland. In *2004 NGO Sustainability Index* (pp. 196-203). Washington, DC: U.S. Government Printing Office.

United States Agency for International Development/Freedom House/KLON-JAWOR. (2000). *The 2000 NGO sustainability index for Central and Eastern Europe and Eurasia*. Washington, DC: USAID.

United Parcel Servuce Foundation. (2002) *A guide to investing in volunteer resources management: Improve your philanthropic portfolio*. Atlanta, GA: Author.

Urban Institute. (2004). *Volunteer management capacity in America's charities and congregations: A briefing report*. Washington, DC: Author.

United States Census Bureau. (2000). *Fact Sheet. Portland, Maine*. Washington, DC: Author.

United States International Grantmaking. (2008). *Country Codes & Laws: Poland*. Arlington, VA: Council on Foundations. Retrieved May 26, 2008, from http://www.usig.org/countryinfo/PDF/Poland.pdf

Valente, C. F., & Manchester, L. D. (1984). *Rethinking local services: Examining alternative delivery approaches* (Special Report, No. 12, pp. 56-57). Washington, DC: International City Management Association.

Van Tripj, H., Hans, C. M., & Hoyer, W. D. (1996). Why switch? Product category-level explanations for true variety-seeking behavior. *Journal of Marketing Research, 33*(3), 281-293.

Van Tulder, R. J. M. (1996). *Skill sheets*. The Hague: Delwel.

VeraWorks, Inc. (2002). *2002 fortune 500 performance on the VeraWorks quality factors for superior employee volunteer programs*. Waynesboro, PA: VeraWorks.

Vita, C. J. (1997). *Viewing nonprofits across the states*. Washington, DC: Urban Institute.

Voicu, M., & Voicu, B. (2004, November). *Promoting volunteering in Eastern Europe*. Eurofestation: European Conference and Exchange Forum about Volunteering, Maastricht, The Netherlands.

Voluntary Action-Leeds. (n.d.). Retrieved June 2, 2008, from http://www.val.org.uk

Wagner, M. (1999). Nonprofits face hurdles. *Internet Week, 732,* 79.

Walker, C., & Pharoah, C. (2000). *Making time for charity*. Kent, England: Charities Aid Foundation.

Walsum, R. van. (2001). *Parameters van Lokale Vrijwilligersorganisaties [Parameters of Local Volunteerorganizations]*. Thesis, RSM Erasmus University. 63 p.

Wandersman, A., & Alderman, J. (1993). Incentives, costs, and barriers for volunteers: A staff perspective on volunteers in one state. *Review of Public Personnel Administration, 13*(1), 67-76.

Weiser, J., & Zadek, S. (2000). Conversations with disbelievers. Retrieved January, 4, 2007, from http://www.brodyweiser.com/pdf/convdisb.pdf

Weitzman, M. S., Jalandoni, N. T., Lampkin, L. M., & Pollack, T. H. (2002). *The new nonprofit almanac and desk reference: The essential facts and figures for managers, researchers, and volunteers*. San Francisco: Jossey-Bass.

Wentland, E. J. & Smith, K. W.(1993). *Survey responses: An evaluation of their Validity*. New York: Academic.

Wild, C. (1993). *Corporate volunteer programs: Benefits to business: Report 1029* (No. 0823705013). New York: Conference Board.

Wilson, A., & Pimm, G. (1996). Tyranny of the volunteer: The care and feeding of voluntary workforces. *Management Decision, 34*(4), 24-40.

Wilson, J. (2000). Volunteering. *Annual Review of Sociology, 26,* 215-140.

Wilson, M. (1976). *The effective management of volunteer programs*. Boulder, CO: Volunteer Management Associates.

Witter, K. (2003). *Community involvement index 2003*. Chestnut Hill, MA: Center for Corporate Citizenship at Boston College.

Wittmer, D. (1991). Serving the people or serving for pay: Reward preferences among government, hybrid sector, and business managers. *Public Productivity and Management Review 14*(4), 369-83.

Wollebaek, D., & Selle, P. (2003). Generations and organizational change. In P. Dekker & L. Halman (Eds.), *The values of volunteering-cross-cultural perspectives* (pp. 55-70). New York: Kluwer Academic/Plenum.

Wright, T. A. (2003). What every manager should know: Does personality help employee motivation? *Academy of Management Executive, 17*(2), 131-133.

Wygnański, J. J. (1996). Basic statistics concerning the scope of activities of non-governmental organizations in Poland. In B. Synak & M. Ruzica (Eds.), *Voluntary sector in a changing society* (pp. 223-242). Indianapolis: The Indiana University Center on Philanthropy.

Xu, S., Haydon, L., O'Malley, M., & Bridgeforth, S. (2002). *Company sponsored volunteerism: A comparison of findings from a 1998 study, September 2002.* Newark, NJ: Prudential Financial, Global Market Research.

Yeung, A. B. (2004). The octagon model of volunteer motivation: Results of a phenomenological analysis. *Voluntas: International Journal of Voluntary and Nonprofit Organizations, 15*(1), 21-46.

Yin, R. (1993). *Applications of case study research.* Beverly Hills, CA: SAGE.

Zakour, M. J., & Gillespie, D. F. (1998). Effects of organizational type and localism on volunteerism and resource sharing during disasters. *Nonprofit and Voluntary Sector Quarterly, 27*(1), 49-65.

Zelwietro, J. (1998). The politicization of environmental organizations through the Internet. *Information Society, 14,* 45-46.

Zerabavel, I. (1991) *The fine line: Making distinctions in everyday life.* Chicago: University of Chicago Press.

Zlotnikov, S. (1997). A brief survey of the third sector development on Kazakhstan. In I. Savelyeva (Ed.), *Public associations and local government: Base and experience of interaction.* Moscow: Interlegal International Charitable Foundation for Political and Legal Research. EU-TACIS Project.

ABOUT THE AUTHORS

Angela L. Bies is an assistant professor at the Bush School of Government & Public Service at Texas A&M University, where her teaching and research focus on the nonprofit sector. Bies earned her PhD from the University of Minnesota, and her research was awarded ARNOVA's 2004 Gabriel G. Rudney Memorial Award for Outstanding Dissertation in Nonprofit and Voluntary Action Research. Bies's research focuses on accountability, capacity, advocacy, and performance in the nonprofit sector. A comparative researcher, Bies is particularly interested in the selection and implementation of management reforms in the context of emergent or changing nonprofit sectors. She has worked on research funded by the Forbes Funds and the National Science Foundation, and carried out research for the Humanitarian Affairs Division of the U.S. Department of Defense, the Minnesota Council of Nonprofits, United Way, Catholic Charities, and the Aga Khan Foundation.

Bies was previously executive director of a statewide nonprofit accountability organization in Minnesota, the Charities Review Council, director of the Minnesota Women's Center, a regional director for the American Field Service, and is a returned Peace Corps Volunteer-Kenya. She serves as a visiting faculty member at the Catholic University of Lublin, Poland, and is active in the Academy of Management's Public and Nonprofit Division and ARNOVA.

Jeffrey L. Brudney is the Albert A. Levin Chair of urban studies and public service at Cleveland State University's Maxine Goodman Levin College of Urban Affairs. Dr. Brudney has published widely in the areas of public administration, the nonprofit sector, and volunteerism. He has won several international honors and awards, including the John Grenzebach Award for Outstanding Research in Philanthropy for Education; the Herbert Kaufman Award from the American Political Science Association; and the William E. Mosher and Frederick C. Mosher Award from the journal *Public Administration Review.* In 2006, Dr. Brudney received the first-ever Association for Research on Nonprofit Organizations and Voluntary Action (ARNOVA) Award for Excellence in Teaching. He has also received the Mentor Award from the American Political Science Association for his work with minority and women graduate students and faculty. He serves on the editorial boards of several major journals in public administration and nonprofit sector studies, and is the book review editor of *Nonprofit and Voluntary Sector Quarterly.* Prior to assuming the Levin Chair, Dr. Brudney co-founded and co-directed the Institute for Nonprofit Organizations and the Master of Arts in Nonprofit Organizations degree program at the University of Georgia. He received the BA degree at the University of California-Berkeley, and the MA and PhD degrees at the University of Michigan-Ann Arbor.

Robert K. Christensen is an assistant professor in the Master of Public Administration and PhD in public policy programs at University of North Carolina Charlotte. He received JD and MPA degrees from Brigham Young University, and a PhD from the School of Public and Environmental Affairs (SPEA) at Indiana University, Bloomington.

Interested in institutional precursors of public and nonprofit performance, his research focuses on the intersection of public law, policy, and public and nonprofit administration. His work has appeared in such journals as *Administration & Society, Nonprofit Management and Leadership, Public Performance and Management Review,* and the *International Journal of Public Administration.*

He is a past recipient of the John A. Rohr fellowship and the Spencer Foundation Dissertation fellowship.

Bruce B. Clary is professor of public policy and management and senior research associate at the Edmund S. Muskie School of Public Service, University of Southern Maine. He holds a doctorate in political science from the University of Southern California. He has a specific focus on international education. Beginning in 1997, he wrote a series of successful federal grant applications to fund the Muskie Fellowship Program at the University of Southern Maine (a U.S. Department of State Program). The program is designed to bring students from the former Soviet Union to the United States for graduate study. Dr. Clary has served as coordinator since its inception. He has also worked on graduate fellowship programs with the University of Maine System in France and Bulgaria, the Soros

Foundation in Palestine, the Junior Faculty Development Program of the U.S. Department of State, and the Government of Kazakhstan (Presidential Scholarship Program).

His publications appear in a variety of journals including *Public Productivity Review and Management, Maine Journal of Health Issues, Disability Studies Quarterly, Maine Policy Review, Policy Studies Review, New England Journal of Public Policy, MIS Reports (International City Management Association), State and Local Government Review, Public Administration Review,* and *Public Enterprise.*

This book chapter is based on community currency systems. The approach, found in the Untied States, Europe and elsewhere, has the goal of fostering of volunteerism and social capital creation in communities through the earning of service credits for helping others. The research on which the chapter is based was drawn from research conducted by Dr. Clary in Maine and the United Kingdom (for which he did a program evaluation of the Fairshares Program in the late 1990s).

Stephanie A. Curs is assistant director for foreign operations at the Norman E. Borlaug Institute for International Agriculture, which is part of the Texas A&M University System. Curs has a bachelor's degree in agricultural education and development and a master's degree in public administration from the Bush School of Government and Public Service.

She previously worked as director of international programs for the World Food Logistics Organization in Washington, DC, and the Texas A&M Office of International Agriculture in Indonesia. She also served as a project specialist and intern at Texas A&M in College Station and led the efforts to develop the proposal for creation of the Borlaug Institute of International Agriculture.

Mark A. Hager is associate professor of nonprofit studies in the School of Community Resources and Development and Director of Research in the Lodestar Center for Philanthropy and Nonprofit Innovation at Arizona State University. The research for the chapter in this volume was conducted when he was senior research associate in the Center on Nonprofits and Philanthropy at the Urban Institute in Washington, DC. He was principal investigator for the federally funded study of volunteer management capacity in charities and congregations. His other voluntary action research includes studies of the scope, dimensions, administration, and financial operations of and reporting by nonprofit organizations. Hager earned his PhD in organizational sociology at the University of Minnesota with a study of the causes of nonprofit organization closure. In addition to book chapters, research reports, and professional presentations, his work on the behavior of nonprofit organizations has appeared in *Public*

Administration Review, Nonprofit and Voluntary Sector Quarterly, Public Management Review, the *Journal of Volunteer Administration, Nonprofit Quarterly,* and the *American Behavioral Scientist.*

Linda S. Hartenian is a professor of management and human resources in the College of Business at the University of Wisconsin Oshkosh. She obtained her PhD in management from the University of Kentucky in 1991 and an MS in industrial/organizational psychology from the University of Wisconsin Oshkosh in 1986. She has received the College's Innovations in Teaching Award and the Management/Human Resources Team Teaching Award (as selected by students). Hartenian's published research has included studies on ethics, research methodology, labor relations, team skills, and performance appraisal. Publications on nonprofit agency dependence on volunteers and the multidimensionality of the egoism construct are forthcoming. A "missionary-type" volunteer, her interests in animal welfare and early childhood development have spanned decades. Development of the typology presented in this chapter was supported by the College of Business and the Faculty Development Program at UW Oshkosh

Aigerim R. Ibrayeva received her MPA degree from the Kazakhstan Institute of Management, Economics, and Strategic Planning (KIMEP) in Almaty, Kazakhstan, and her MPhil degree from the Maastricht School of Management in The Netherlands. Dr. Ibrayeva works as an assistant professor and a chair of the Department of Public Administration at KIMEP in Almaty, Kazakhstan. Her teaching and research interests are in the field of organizational culture, management, and leadership in government and non-profit organizations. In 2002 Dr. Ibrayeva participated in a pioneering study to conduct the mapping of nonprofit organizations in Kazakhstan. She has also published on the development of civil society in Kazakhstan.

Matthew Liao-Troth is currently the chair of the management department, and director of the MBA program, at Western Washington University. His research focuses on the psychological contract workers have with their employers, and the human resource practices of managing a volunteer workforce. He has published his research in a variety of outlets, including *Journal of Applied Psychology,* the *Journal for Nonprofit Management,* the *Journal of Community Psychology,* the *Journal of Organizational Behavior,* the *Journal of Volunteer Administration, Mid-American Business Journal, Nonprofit Management & Leadership, Nonprofit & Volunteer Sector Quarterly,* and *Voluntas: International Journal of Voluntary and Nonprofit Organizations.*

He served on the faculty of DePaul University in Chicago and Washington University in St. Louis before Western Washington University. He also taught at the University of Arizona, San Diego State University, the University of Illinois at Chicago, and Loyola University Chicago. Outside of academia, he served as a division executive with the Boy Scouts of America for several years, and has been involved with family businesses for most of his life. He has consulted for a variety of business, nonprofit, and government organizations. He was the chair of the Public and Nonprofit Division of the Academy of Management for the 2005-2006 academic year. He received his PhD in management from The University of Arizona.

Tom McVey received a bachelor of science in speech communication at Kansas State University and a master's degree from the LBJ School of Public Affairs at the University of Texas at Austin. He is currently a doctoral candidate in the School of Communication Studies at the University of Texas at Austin where his concentration is in organizational communication. Tom is also the professional development team lead and is a senior program coordinator for the Charles A. Dana Center at the University of Texas at Austin.Tom has held a lifelong commitment to service and volunteerism. He spent 3 years working as a student coordinator for the Community Service Program at Kansas State University, provided 2 years of national service as an AmeriCorps*VISTA volunteer with Austin Groups for the Elderly and the Texas Department of Health. He also served for 7 years on the board of directors for DOVIA (Directors of Volunteers in Austin)—a nonprofit professional organization—and held the positions of treasurer, vice-president, president, and past-president. Tom also served as an instructor for three semesters teaching the Volunteer Management Academy, a course sponsored by DOVIA and Austin Community College's Department of Continuing Education. Tom has 18 years experience in program and project management and 10 years experience in volunteer management.

Lucas C. P. M. Meijs is professor of volunteering, civil society, and businesses at the Rotterdam School of Management, Erasmus University, The Netherlands. He frequently publishes on the management of volunteers, volunteering in general and corporate community involvement. He writes a bi-monthly column for Vakwerk, the national magazine on volunteering. Currently his research focusses on the future of volunteering looking at volunteering as a natural resource, the involvement of companies in corporate volunteering, the functioning of the volunteer infrastructure including volunteer centers and volunteer management in sport associations. In September 2007 he was appointed as member of the Council for

Societal Development, a national policy body on participation in The Netherlands. He serves in several boards of small mutual support (Scouting) and service delivery organizations (STRAS, mentally challenged people; Nabuur, international aid and Van Harte Resto's community restaurants). He was member of the Dutch task force on volunteering from 2001 till 2005.

Valentina Mele is an assistant professor at Università Bocconi. She teaches public and nonprofit management as well as business-government relations. She is a visiting professor at Fudan University, and at the International Organizations MBA, Université de Genève. She has worked as consultant for the Organization for Economic Cooperation and Development, the European Union, the Italian Ministry for Innovation in several projects related to information and communication technologies in public and healthcare agencies. She received her MPA at Columbia University, her PhD at Rome University and she is currently PhD candidate at the London School of Economics. The chapter is based on a 2 years research on the managerial impacts of information and communication technologies on nonprofit organizations, sponsored by Bocconi School of Management.

Victor Murray is currently adjunct professor in the School of Public Administration at the University of Victoria. From 1983 to 1995, he was director of the program in voluntary sector management in the Schulich School of Business at York University, Toronto.

Dr. Murray specializes in the study of voluntary sector organizations of all types with particular emphasis on the areas of board governance, strategic planning, inter-organizational collaboration and the assessment of organizational effectiveness. He is also an active consultant and volunteer in these areas.

As director of the Nonprofit Leadership and Management Program at York University he developed Canada's first certificate and master's level programs in that field. He is the author of many books, articles, and papers in the fields of organizational behavior and nonprofit management. His most recent publication is *The Management of Nonprofit and Charitable Organizations in Canada* (Butterworths, 2006). Currently, he is a member of the Advisory Board for the journal *Nonprofit Management and Leadership*, contributing editor for *Human Resources Management in Canada* and active in the Association for Research on Nonprofit Organizations and Voluntary Action (ARNOVA). In 2002 he was awarded ARNOVA's Distinguished Lifetime Achievement Award. In 1995 the Canadian Centre for Philanthropy awarded him the Alan Arlett medal for distinguished contributions to philanthropy research. He is at present director of the

Voluntary Sector Knowledge Network (www.vskn.ca), a Web site of the Centre for Nonprofit Management in Victoria.

Vic Murray is a Winnipegger who obtained his BA from the University of Manitoba and his graduate education from the University of Minnesota (MA) and Cornell University (PhD). He was a member of the Faculty of Commence at the University of British Columbia from 1962-66 before moving to York University. While at York he held appointments as coordinator of the organizational behavior area; chair, Department of Sociology; associate dean, chair of the university senate and member of the York Board of Governors.

Tamara G. Nezhina received her PhD degrees in public administration and policy from the University of Georgia. Currently Dr. Nezhina works as an assistant professor at the School of Public Service at DePaul University. Her teaching and research focus is on management of nonprofit organizations, volunteer management, local government, and the broader concept of civil society in the international arena. Dr. Nezhina has conducted a study of local government finance in Kazakhstan that she later presented at the conference organized by the Central Eurasian Studies Society. She also regularly presents her research on the nonprofit organizations at the ARNOVA conferences. Dr. Nezhina has published on volunteer management practices in Kazakhstan and the United State.

James L. Perry is chancellor's professor in the School of Public and Environmental Affairs (SPEA), Indiana University, Bloomington. He also holds adjunct appointments in philanthropy and political science. He has held faculty appointments at the University of California, Irvine; Chinese University of Hong Kong; University of Wisconsin, Madison; Indiana University—Purdue University Indianapolis; University of Hong Kong; and Yonsei University. He received MPA and PhD degrees from the Maxwell School of Citizenship and Public Affairs at Syracuse University.

Perry's research focuses on public service motivation, national and community service, and government reform. He is author and editor of many scholarly articles and books, among them the forthcoming *Motivation in Public Management: The Call of Public Service* (Oxford University Press, 2008), *Civic Service: What Difference Does It Make?* (Armonk, NY: M. E. Sharpe, 2004), and *Quick Hits for Educating Citizens* (Bloomington: Indiana University Press, 2006).

He is recipient of the Yoder-Heneman Award for innovative personnel research from the Society for Human Resource Management, the Charles H. Levine Award for Excellence in Public Administration, the NASPAA/ASPA Distinguished Research Award, the Paul P. Van Riper Award, and the 2008 Dwight Waldo Award. Perry is a fellow of the National Academy of Public Administration.

Sarah Jane Rehnborg is a lecturer at the LBJ School of Public Affairs and associate director for planning and development at the RGK Center for Philanthropy and Community Service, both at the University of Texas at Austin. A published author in the field, Rehnborg has served as a consultant and trainer to organizations including the Points of Light Foundation, AARP, the Corporation for National and Community Service, the Texas Commission on Volunteerism and Community Service, the Texas Department of Mental Health/Mental Retardation, the Comptroller's Office of the State of Texas and numerous local groups. As a researcher, Rehnborg lead a cross-disciplinary university team which developed a valid and reliable tool to assess programs engaging volunteers and national service participants for the Corporation for National and Community Service. She produces *The Investigator*, a periodic publication designed to encourage research in volunteerism. Currently, Rehnborg is leading an analysis of the effects of intensive service experiences on the development of Jewish identity among young Jews for the United Jewish Communities (UJC). In addition, she is developing case studies about volunteer engagement as part of a UPS-funded Volunteer Impact grant. Prior to her work at the University of Texas she led several volunteer initiatives and served as president of the International Association for Volunteer Administration. Rehnborg completed her undergraduate degree at Denison University in Granville, Ohio and earned her master's and PhD from the University of Pittsburgh.

Lynda St. Clair is associate professor of management at Bryant University in Rhode Island. She earned her doctorate in organizational behavior and human resource management from the University of Michigan in Ann Arbor. She also holds a master's degree in accounting from the University of Texas at Austin. Professor St. Clair teaches in the areas of organizational behavior, management theory, management skills, and leadership. Her research interests include competing values in organizations, community service through the work place, service learning, women's careers in higher education, metaphors of management education, and the impact of accreditation on academic quality. She is a co-author of *Becoming a Master Manager: A Competing Values Approach* [with R. E. Quinn, S. R. Faerman, M. P. Thompson, and M. R. McGrath]. She is a co-editor of *Corporate Social Responsibility: Doing Business in the Public Eye* [with N. Tichy & A. McGill] and *Pressing Problems of Modern Organizations (That Keep Us Up At Night)* [with R. E. Quinn and R. O'Neill]. She has published in *Academy of Management Journal, Consulting Psychology Journal:*

Practice and Research, Journal of Management Education, Journal for the Theory of Social Behaviour, and *Organizational Dynamics.* She is a member of Beta Gamma Sigma, Delta Sigma Pi, the Organizational Behavior Teaching Society, and has served as a representative-at-large for the Careers Division of the Academy of Management.

Esther M. Ten Hoorn studied business administration at the Rotterdam School of Management, Erasmus University Rotterdam, Master program Business-society management. Since September 2005 she is a researcher at the Department of Business-society Management of the Rotterdam School of Management, Erasmus University. Her research involves (corporate) volunteering, volunteer management and international volunteering. She was involved in several project regarding the future of volunteering in The Netherlands. Her current research project deals with international volunteerism especially linked to holidays and gap years. As of February 2008 she works as a VSO (Voluntary Service Overseas) volunteer in Nigeria for a period of 2 years assisting local communities.

Mary Tschirhart is the director of the Institute for Nonprofits at North Carolina State University and a professor in the public administration department of the University. She formerly served as the director of the Campbell Public Affairs Institute of Syracuse University and faculty member of the Maxwell School of Citizenship and Public Affairs. Before moving to Syracuse, she was a faculty member at Indiana University's School of Public and Environmental Affairs. She earned her doctorate in organizational behavior and human resource management at the University of Michigan. Professor Tschirhart teaches courses on public and nonprofit management, fund development for nonprofits, and organizational theory. Professor Tschirhart's research addresses management issues in public and nonprofit organizations. She has published on numerous topics including stakeholder management, membership dynamics, collaboration, diversity in organizations, and issues related to service and volunteer behavior. Professor Tschirhart has numerous consulting, board governance, and professional service experiences. She currently serves on the Board of the International Research Society for Public Management. She was the vice president for membership for the Association for Research on Nonprofit Organizations and Voluntary Action, chair of the nonprofit management education section of the National Association of Schools of Public Affairs and Administration, and division chair of the Public and Nonprofit Division of the Academy of Management.

Printed in the United States
125400LV00002B/143-144/P

9 781593 119249